The Wild, Wild East

The Wild,

UNUSUAL TALES OF MAINE HISTORY

Wild East

William Lemke

YANKEE BOOKS

CAMDEN, MAINE

Cover and text design by Lurelle Cheverie

Printed in the United States of America

Library of Congress Cataloging-in-Publication Data

Lemke, William.
  Wild, Wild, East.

  Includes bibliographical references.
  1. Maine--History. I. Title.
F19.5.L46 1989 974.1   89-70666
ISBN 0-912769-42-4

TO **EDGAR P. LEMKE**

with respect, gratitude and,
most of all, love.
Forever.

Contents

VACATIONLAND (TWENTIETH CENTURY)

Author's Preface

Long before there was a Wild, Wild West, Maine was the Wild, Wild East. Historians will caution that the West was never that wild—but, however briefly, it was a rough, vibrant place on the margins of civilization. So was the Downeast frontier.

Compared to more settled Massachusetts, much of Maine in the past was a vast wilderness whose ragged coast and forested interior, penetrated by great rivers, were home for all manner of un-Puritan types. Not everybody in the Province—later District—of Maine was a rogue or adventurer, but the region had its share. It seemed to attract them from the beginning—navigators like Verrazzano, pirates like Dixey Bull, Patriots on the make like Benedict Arnold. Many unusual characters were just passing through—like Davey Crockett, Kit Carson, and Wyatt Earp in their geographic setting. Well into the 19th century, Maine retained a very rough-at-the-edges quality.

This image started to change about the time the Great West was going through its wild phase. Increasingly, the migration of people, particularly the young, out of Maine to areas that offered greater economic opportunities outpaced the in-migration. The new image of Maine emerged as that of an isolated, picturesque, Yankee backwater, a good place for summer people to visit but a hard place for natives to live year-round. In a word: vacationland. The recent history of this not-so-wild Maine has brought an invasion of developers who promise to further transform the state's identity.

Whatever the future holds for Maine, this book is an attempt to preserve a vision of its past. It does not pretend to be a comprehensive history; rather it presents the most colorful incidents and characters I could find. Nor does it include some familiar stories (familiar at least to Mainers)—either because they are simply too damned familiar or because they are not historically factual. A good deal of what has passed for the truth about Maine's past turns out, upon close examination, to be local myth. The following stories are about the real Maine.

This is Maine before it became a picture-postcard L.L.Bean Disneyland. It is the Maine we have lost, warts and all.

If this book encourages a greater interest in Maine's colorful past and helps stimulate more extensive future volumes, it will have served its purpose.

I would like to acknowledge the assistance of my editors and Gloria Chamard in the preparation of this book. The encouragement of my wife Karen, the forebearance of my daughter Larissa, and the unflagging support of my parents were crucial in completing this work.

Down East
Dawn
of
America

(1524–1692)

A Gentleman in the Land of Bad People

C aptain Giovanni da Verrazzano, Renaissance gentleman explorer, was accorded no respect by the Indians he met on the Maine coast. Long before Henry Hudson showed up in the same vicinity on the *Half Moon*, the Abnakis showed Verrazzano many full Indian moons.

It was May of 1524. The Italian navigator was on the final leg of a reconnaissance of the eastern coast of North America. His voyage was underwritten by a group of Italian merchants living in Lyons and the king of France, who provided use of the recently built naval vessel *La Dauphine*. Verrazzano's mission was to explore the neglected shore from the Carolinas to Cape Breton Island in search of a passage to the Pacific that would give France access to Far Eastern markets. By the time he arrived off the granite-cragged, island-dotted Maine coast, the heavily bearded and mustachioed Giovanni was a frustrated man, in a hurry to wind up his exploration and return to France.

Somewhere off the sparkling waters of Casco Bay, probably near Small Point or Sequin Island, he took time to attempt a little trade with the natives. Verrazzano hoped to gain some examples of American commodities to whet the interest of the merchants and court he would have to face without news of a passage to the East.

Unlike other Indians Verrazzano had encountered, the Maine natives proved "of such crudity and evil manners, so barbarous, that despite all the signs we could make, we could never converse with them." When half of his crew landed, the animal-skin-clad Abnakis issued fierce yells and sprayed them with arrows before fading into the endless forest. After a couple of such unfriendly brushes, the Abnakis consented to trade with the Europeans—but under conditions which avoided direct contact. The Indians lowered items from a rocky cliff down to a French boat, taking in return "nothing but knives, fishhooks, and tools to cut with all."

The red men's behavior left little doubt they would not mind cutting the white men's throats. But the ultimate affront to the proud Verrazzano—who referred disparagingly to his own crew as "the maritime mob"—came when the unpleasant barter was concluded. As *La Dauphine* weighed anchor, the

Abnakis used "all signs of discourtesy and disdain, such as exhibiting their bare buttocks and laughing immoderately."

It was the most dramatic counterpoint to the traditional scene of peaceful, timid Indians greeting white strangers so common in the literature of early exploration. Little wonder that Verrazzano's mapmaker brother Gilarmo named the Maine coast *Terra Onde di Mala Gente* (Land of Bad People)!

There has been speculation about the cause of such behavior. The most obvious interpretation is that the Indians of Maine had suffered from relations with earlier white visitors to their shores. Perhaps European fishermen had ventured down from the Grand Banks and cheated the Indians in trade, abused their women, killed some of them, or kidnapped natives for slaves.

Or maybe the Abnakis inherently knew better than to welcome or trust the white man. In Verrazzano's case, they were smart to keep their distance. More passive Indians in the Carolinas had been rewarded for their friendliness to Verrazzano by his kidnapping of an infant from its mother. Whatever happened to that baby, history does not record. European explorers tended to view Indians as commodities to display back home along with native fruits, vegetables, minerals, and wildlife.

Verrazzano himself was a rare bird among early navigators. Of noble birth, well-educated and -connected, not a little arrogant, and possessed of undisputed maritime knowledge and ability, he was the personification of the Italian Renaissance figure. Born in 1485, probably at his noble family's ancestral palace outside Florence, he received a classical education in that most vital of Renaissance city-states. He was a contemporary of Machiavelli and Leonardo da Vinci, and, like many gifted Italian courtiers, went abroad to seek his fortune. In his case, it was to Dieppe, France, where by 1507 he was an exceptionally well-versed mariner. Sailing to Newfoundland in 1508, Verrazzano also later sailed throughout the Mediterranean. He befriended Magellan in Seville before that great navigator departed on the famous voyage that took him around South America to the Pacific, in 1517.

The French king, François I, desired to compete abroad with Spain as well as in Europe. He was therefore intrigued by Verrazzano's proposed voyage to the uncharted North American coast to search out an alternate passage to China. He provided one of Verrazzano's ships, manned by 50 sailors; *La Dauphine* was twice as big as the vessel used by Giovanni Caboto, who had claimed the North American continent for England in 1497.

Verrazzano's voyage lasted five and a half months—very good time considering the territory covered. Detractors would claim it was *too* good, that Verrazzano's published account of it was the product of his imagination. But he was too precise about many previously unrecorded landmarks to leave any doubt of his voyage's authenticity in modern historians' minds. He brought back to François I and Europe, through his *Letter* and his brother's rather crude maps, a better picture of the continent's coastline. And he was the first explorer to state flatly that North America was a vast continent barring the way westward. Of course this was exactly what the Lyons merchants did not want to hear. They were cool to financing a follow-up voyage to the same coast. François I was momentarily enthusiastic about it, but his crushing defeat in 1525 at Pavia by the Spaniards ended his interest in overseas adventure. He had enough on his hands in Europe.

According to Gilarmo Verrazzano, his brother's real aim had never been to find the elusive passage to the Orient, but instead to tap the natural resources of North America through French colonization. This sounds like revisionism induced by a dose of reality, but, if true, the navigator's concept of a New World to be developed for itself was generations ahead of what the government of France was prepared to undertake.

The impression Maine's geography made upon him was much better than that made by its inhabitants. Verrazzano could not help but be enchanted by the spectacular nature of this coast indented by numerous bays and rivers and studded by high, beautiful islands. Three of these islands he named after young princesses of Navarre at the French court. Today they are called Monhegan, Isle au Haut, and Mount Desert rather than Anne, Isabeau, and Catherine. The Maine shore reminded him of the Dalmatian coast on the Adriatic Sea. Despite the beauty of the land, Verrazzano "found nothing extraordinary except vast forests and some metaliferous hills." The European saw "no signs of cultivation," and concluded "the land appears sterile and unfit for growing fruit or grain of any kind." While Verrazzano admitted the islands often afforded "excellent harbors and channels," the mainland appeared to present no particular attraction.

When Verrazzano sighted the presence of more inhabitants, after his previous bad experience, he was not interested in establishing relations. "We had no intercourse with the people," he observed, "but we judge that they were similar in nature and usages to those we were last among."

Not far from the Daughters of Navarre on Gilarmo's map is indicated a place called *Oranbega*. It is the only Indian name on Verrazzano's map, and is of apparent Abnaki origin, meaning "place of still waters." How or why it shows up is uncertain, but slightly altered as *Norumbega* it would have a life of its own on later maps, in future narratives, and in the imagination of many Europeans. Sometimes Norumbega embraced all of what became New England. At other times it indicated a fabulous Indian village on the Penobscot River, one with friendly and *rich* Indians. Norumbega was the northern version of the legendary South American cities of gold. For generations the "Della Terra de Norumbega" would fascinate Europeans. It certainly was more attractive than Verrazzano's "Land of Bad People."

From the beginning the outsider's view of America, and Maine in particular, was a split vision, with romance pushing aside reality, and a make-believe people supplanting the original natives.

The real Land of Bad People Verrazzano encountered elsewhere.

On a later voyage to the Caribbean, the Indians of Guadalupe eagerly beckoned Verrazzano ashore. Leaving his brother and several of his crew in a small boat, Verrazzano waded ashore to accept their hospitality.

The Indians were Caribs. Cannibals. Verrazzano was quickly murdered and eaten. "To so miserable an end," a contemporary remarked, "came this valiant gentleman."

2 •

Imprisoned on a Very Small Continent

S amuel de Champlain was a careful man who probably read Verrazzano's
Letter. Verrazzano, cruising the Maine coast in the spring of 1524, had
noted that the "more elevated country" was "full of very thick
wood . . . indicative of a cold climate." As he shivered in a poorly insulated
building on Ile Sainte-Croix in the howling winter of 1604–1605, Champlain
had ample opportunity to reflect on the correctness of the earlier explorer's
observation. "Here," he wrote, "the winter lasts six months." Ironically, when
the French finally got around to seriously attempting the establishment of a
colony in the New World north of the Carolinas, they chose the worst site
possible—just before the onslaught of one of the worst winters on record.
The result was almost disaster.

Champlain was not the mastermind of this expedition that ended up on a
tiny island up the St. Croix River from Passamaquoddy Bay. That was Pierre
du Gua de Monts, a Huguenot who fought under Henri of Navarre in the Wars
of Religion which divided France in the late 1500s. When Henri grasped the
monarchy as Henri IV, he converted to Catholicism in order to win the
support of the Catholic majority. "Paris," he said with supreme cynicism, "is
worth a mass." But he took care of his Protestant friends. He issued an edict
granting religious toleration to Huguenots, and to de Monts he awarded an
annual pension and governorship of a town in the province of Saintonge.

De Monts developed an active interest in New World trade, making
several voyages to Canada. Henri IV also appointed his former comrade in
arms vice admiral and lieutenant governor over a vast region stretching from
Cape Breton Island to the 40th parallel (about where Philadelphia is located),
and granted him a monopoly of the fur trade with the Indians for a decade. It
was then up to him to mobilize private resources to bear the costs of
establishing settlements. The French treasury was a bare cupboard and the
government preferred schemes of cheap colonization. Henri's finance minister,
the Duc de Sully, was underwhelmed by de Monts' ideas. "One never draws
great riches from anything north of the 40th parallel," he wrote.

Despite Sully's sour assessment, de Monts organized a trading company
of merchants from Rouen, Saint-Malo, La Rochelle, and Saint Jean-de-Luz.
About 120 would-be colonists were recruited. They were a diverse group,

including both Protestants and Catholics. Some possessed a variety of skills, and some did not. Besides the carpenters, stonecutters, artisans, and masons, there was a decided majority who had no particular abilities. De Monts most likely made use of a clause in his contract authorizing him to take persons classified as "vagabonds, vagrants, and exiles" by force.

A few noblemen were also attracted to the venture. The most prominent among their number was Jean de Biencourt de Poutrincourt, a Catholic baron and governor of Mery-sur-Seine. He had fought against Henri in the Wars of Religion, but after the king's conversion, the Seigneur de Poutrincourt gave the monarch his whole-hearted allegiance. Henri considered the old soldier, a dashing character who could play the lute and manichord as well as wield a sword, one of his kingdom's finest gentlemen. The Seigneur was heavy with honors; his fortune, however, had been considerably lightened. His romantic ambition was to recoup his family's estate by carving a fiefdom out of the wilderness. Poutrincourt supplied the arms and soldiers to defend de Mont's colony.

Also on the expedition, which set sail from Le Havre in March 1604, was Samuel de Champlain, a junior member of the venture whose origins are as obscure as his place in history is secure. Born in a Huguenot town in Saintonge, given a common Protestant surname, and married to a Huguenot, it is likely that Champlain was initially of that faith before switching to Catholicism. Late in his life he claimed to have fought for Henri against the Catholic League, traveled to Spain, and made a two-year voyage to the West Indies. By the time he accompanied a trading expedition to New France in 1603, he was a Catholic, drawing a pension at Henri IV's court. He certainly enjoyed Henri's favor, although it cannot be proved that he was the royal geographer as his friend and early biographer, Marc Lescarbot, claimed. An accomplished mariner, excellent mapmaker, and gifted writer, Champlain was invited by de Monts to join his expedition; Henri IV encouraged him to accept and to report upon any discoveries he made.

Having dispatched three ships to the St. Lawrence to trade for furs, de Monts with two vessels arrived on the coast of Acadia* in May. He began reconnoitering for a site to colonize. His aim was to avoid the frigid winters along the St. Lawrence. After locating a fine harbor on the eastern shore of the Bay of Fundy (which Champlain named Port Royal), looking for reported copper mines, and exploring the mouth of the St. John River on Fundy's western shore, the de Monts expedition headed down the coastline to Passamaquoddy Bay.

After passing by "so many islands that we could not ascertain their number," the French went up a river they named St. Croix because of the cross-like configuration caused by its convergence with two streams. By now it was late June and, anxious to find at least a temporary site, de Monts decided to settle upon a small island in the middle of this river. Exactly why Ile Sainte-Croix was selected is explained by Champlain:

*Verrazzano had placed Acadia on the Carolina coast. Many years and maps later, its location ended up in the area roughly of present-day Nova Scotia, New Brunswick, and part of Maine. Acadia is derived from the classical Arcadia, a wooded place inhabited by happy people.

> Vessels could pass up the river only at the mercy of the cannon on this island, and we deemed the location the most advantageous, not only on account of its situation and good soil, but also on account of the intercourse which we proposed with the savages of these coasts and of the interior, as we should be in the midst of them. We hoped to pacify them in the course of time and put an end to the wars which they carry on with one another, so as to derive service from them in future, and convert them to the Christian faith. . . .

Concern for defense was reflected in the first order of business undertaken by the French—throwing up a barricade for their cannon. They immediately were attacked by hostile insects. Champlain noted that the work was made difficult because "the mosquitoes (which are little flies) annoyed us excessively." This is the first recorded description of the accursed Maine black fly. The Frenchmen's "faces were so swollen by their bites that they could scarcely see."

On the mainland, Champlain's impression was distinctly better than Verrazzano's. "The soil is the finest sort," he wrote. "If the land were cleared up, grain would flourish excellently." The construction of dwelling places, a storehouse, and chapel on Ile Sainte-Croix proceeded rapidly. The buildings were partly constructed from prefabricated material, such as windows and doors brought from France. De Monts sent the ships back to France to report this headway and pick up more provisions. Sieur de Poutrincourt, who much preferred Port Royal and received de Mont's permission to develop it later on, returned to direct the resupply effort in France.

In all, 79 souls remained in America. Gardens were planted on the island and ashore in anticipation of an autumn harvest before the onset of winter. In early September, Champlain, in a small ketch with a dozen crew and two Indian guides, began exploring further westward along the Maine shoreline.

It was a bold coast. The little party sailed "by a large number of islands, banks, reefs, and rocks, which in places extend more than four leagues out to sea." The islands were carpeted with firs and pines. The size and configuration of one island particularly struck Champlain. "It is very high, and notched in places, so that there is the appearance to one at sea as of seven or eight mountains extending along near each other," he observed. "The summit of the most of them is destitute of trees, as there are only rocks on them. The woods consist of pines, firs, and birches only. I named it Ile des Monts Deserts." Thus did one of the world's most attractive islands get its name.

The explorer traveled up a river the Indians called Pentagoet (the Penobscot), concluding that this was the river "which several pilots and historians call Norumbegue . . . I am confident that most of those who mention it have not seen it, and speak of it because they have heard persons say so, who knew no more about it than they themselves." But fabled Norumbega, the golden Indian city, was nowhere to be seen. Only a couple of empty, bark-covered cabins betrayed evidence of any human life. Legends die hard, but after Champlain's reports, belief in a city called Norumbega faded among educated Europeans. The name continued to appear on maps denoting the region around the place the Indians called Kenduskeag.

When Champlain returned to St. Croix Island, fresh food was already becoming a problem. Not much of the wheat sown ashore was available to harvest, and the soil on St. Croix turned out to be less fertile than assumed. Gardens were cultivated, but "since the island was all sandy, everything dried up almost as soon as the sun shone upon it." At low tide, the colonists dug up clams, mussels, sea urchins, and snails.

Then, on October 6, it started snowing. "Winter came upon us sooner than we expected," Champlain wrote, "and prevented us from doing many things which we had proposed." By December 3, the French huddled in their drafty dwellings, buffeted by snowstorms and winds sweeping across the river, and began to sight ice floes clogging the black waters. Increasingly isolated from the mainland, the island was taking on the aspect of a prison. Some Indians chose to encamp outside their palisades, requiring a constant guard to observe them. Failure to construct a cellar for storage meant that most of the colonists' wine froze. The well proved inadequate, forcing them to drink melted snow. As the winter, more severe than any experienced in France, dragged on, the mal de la terre took its toll. Champlain described the awful results of scurvy in rather gruesome detail:

> There were produced, in the mouths of those who had it, great pieces of superfluous and driveling flesh (causing extensive putrefaction), which got the upper hand to such an extent that scarcely anything but liquid could be taken. Their teeth became very loose, and could be pulled out with the fingers without its causing them pain. The superfluous flesh was often cut out, which caused them to eject much blood through the mouth. Afterwards, a violent pain seized their arms and legs, which remained swollen and very hard, all spotted as if with flea-bites; and they could not walk on account of the contraction of the muscles, so that they were almost without strength, and suffered intolerable pains. They experienced pain also in the loins, stomach, and bowels, had a very bad cough, and short breath. . . .

Thirty-five men died and over 20 were brought to the verge of death before the brutal winter finally ended. As late as April, Champlain recorded, the snow was piled three to four feet deep. Ah, Maine winters!

In 1606 the Paris lawyer and sometimes poet Marc Lescarbot traveled to New France with his client Poutrincourt and interviewed survivors. Lescarbot speculated on reasons for the high incidence of disease at Sainte-Croix in his classic *Histoire de la Nouvelle-France*, published in 1609. In part he blamed the diet of "cold meats, without juice, gross, and corrupted. One must then take heed of salt meats, smoky, musty, raw, and of an evil scent, likewise of dried fishes, as Newfoundland fish, and stinking rays." Drinking impure water did not, of course, help. Lescarbot added that "there is yet in New France another bad quality of the air, by reason of lakes that be thick there and the great rottenness in the woods."

The place stunk!

The main problem, however, was the site of the colony itself. "I will always be of opinion that whosoever goes into a country to possess it must not stay in the isles, there to be a prisoner," Lescarbot wrote. St. Croix was inconvenient for agriculture and lacked fresh water and sufficient wood for fuel. "But above all, there must be shelters from the hurtful winds and cold; which is hardly found in a small continent environed with water of all sides."

Despite all this, it was apparently not unrelieved grimness for everybody on the "small continent" of Ile Sainte-Croix. Christmas was officially observed for the first time in North America. Some young gentlemen entertained themselves hunting rabbits, skating on frozen ponds, even bringing down game with snowballs. They composed and circulated a handwritten periodical called the *Master William* which, according to Lescarbot, was "stuffed with all kinds of news." Perhaps the little colony may claim North America's first literary periodical. It appears those who were more active physically and mentally increased their chances of survival.

With the ending of winter, the sickness dissipated. Finally, in mid-June, the long-awaited ships from France arrived with fresh provisions, "to the great satisfaction of everyone . . . and there was not wanting, as is customary at such times, the booming of cannon nor the blaring of trumpets." De Monts sailed along the Maine coast, accompanied by Champlain acting as navigator, mapmaker, and artist, in search of a better site for colonization. Champlain was much attracted to Saco Bay, but de Monts did not share his enthusiasm. They proceeded farther south, exploring the Massachusetts shore, Champlain drawing a good sketch of the site occupied by the Pilgrims 15 years later. They then returned Downeast. At the mouth of the Kennebec, an Indian chief passed on news of the recent visit of an English vessel. He claimed its crew had killed five Indians. This was George Weymouth's *Archangel*, which had actually kidnapped some Indians. If de Monts needed further reason to retire from St. Croix, news of English competitors in the region provided it. By early August, he was directing the island's evacuation.

Taking the framework of the island's houses with them, the French sailed across the Bay of Fundy to Port Royal, where they resettled. Thus ended the first serious French colonization attempt on the Maine coast. In 1606 Champlain returned briefly to St. Croix and noticed some plants still growing in the abandoned gardens. In 1607 Lescarbot found the tiny ghost town unmolested by the Indians. In 1610 Sieur de Poutrincourt stopped by and "had prayers offered for the dead who had been buried there."

Apparently among the departed were both the Catholic priest and Protestant minister. They had quarreled on the way to America and may well have continued their feud that awful winter of 1604–1605. Now they were united forever.

• 3
_____

The Wrong Stuff at Sagadahoc?

A lmost exactly three years after the de Monts expedition reached the shores of what their king considered French territory in America, the *Gift of God* and the *Mary and John* set sail from Plymouth to plant a colony in what James I considered English territory. The chief patrons of this venture to "North Virginia" were the merchants of Plymouth; the commander of its fortress, Sir Ferdinando Gorges; and no less than the lord chief justice of England, Sir John Popham. The two vessels that weighed anchor on May 31, 1607, were captained by the chief justice's nephew, George Popham, and Raleigh Gilbert, son of the explorer Sir Humphrey Gilbert and nephew of the even more celebrated Sir Walter Raleigh. Like the earlier French effort, this English expedition had its share of famous personages and anonymous colonists. And like the French venture, it was doomed to failure on the severe Maine coast.

While making the Atlantic passage, Gilbert's *Mary and John* was detained by an unfriendly Flemish ship. Evidently George Popham either did not notice Gilbert's distress signals or simply ignored them. He kept sailing. The episode foreshadowed problems between the two men designated to govern the planned colony.

The *Mary and John* did not catch up to Popham's *Gift of God* until they met off the Maine coast in the area glowingly described in James Rosier's *True Relations*. Rosier had accompanied the Captain Weymouth who kidnapped the Maine Indians near Pemaquid. "Here," he wrote of the Muscongus Bay region, "are more good harbors for ships of all burdens than England can afford . . . [and] a land whose pleasant fertility revealeth itself to be the very garden of nature."

The Popham expedition stopped on one of these islands, where they found a cross erected by Weymouth. Their preacher delivered a sermon, undoubtedly standard Church of England fare, "giving God thanks for our happy meeting and safe arrival into the country."

After wending their way amongst the picturesque St. George Islands, the English made landfall on a bold peninsula jutting into the sea at the western entrance to Muscongus Bay. This they already knew from earlier explorations of the region to be the place called Pemaquid. Their ships anchored in a snug harbor they named Pentecost (now New Harbor), and they pushed inland, accompanied by Skidwarres, one of the Indians captured from the same area in 1605 by Weymouth. Skidwarres and two other natives had been taken into the home of Sir Ferdinando Gorges, who had plied them for information about their land. Now Skidwarres encountered Nahanda, yet another of the Weymouth Indians. He had returned to Pemaquid with another explorer, Captain Martin Pring, the previous year. A small world, indeed!

Even with this wilderness reunion, relations with the Indians on Pemaquid proved edgy. The English decided to settle elsewhere, and sailed to the mouth of the Kennebec River. Its entrance is not easily discerned by ships at sea, but Popham and Gilbert had precise instructions, since this was already considered the alternate area for a settlement. After a brief excursion up river, they decided that the best location was at the west side of its mouth. This was called Sagadahoc. It was mid-August by now, and the English were eager to establish themselves before winter set in. The spot selected, on a bluff overlooking the river, made sense from a military standpoint, but was exposed to the elements.

After yet another religious service and a long-winded recital of King James' instructions for the organization of government (Popham was to be president, Gilbert and other gentlemen his assistants), the colonists began erecting a fort and buildings. Gilbert tried again to patch up relations with the Pemaquid Indians. He sensed that trade with the natives would be vital to the colony's success. A meeting arranged in September, however, fell through, the English finding "no living creature" at the designated meeting place. The presence in an Indian canoe of brass kettles indicated earlier contact with European fishermen, but after the Weymouth episode the Indians were understandably cautious.

Gilbert next explored up the Kennebec as far as the Falls at Cushnoc (now the state capital, Augusta). His party encountered some Indians who spoke broken English. He considered them tricky and treacherous, and that was that. By September Gilbert was back at Sagadahoc, where some Indians were coaxed over by the faithful Skidwarres. There was a powwow with the colonists the next month, and apparently trade commenced.

The *Mary and John* was dispatched back to England, arriving at Plymouth in December. Sir Ferdinando Gorges immediately interviewed the ship's officers about affairs in "North Virginia." What he heard hardly pleased him. The little colony was seething with "childish factions." Apparently the qualities of its leaders contributed to the turmoil. Popham, Sir Ferdinando observed, was "an honest man, but old [54!], and of an unwieldy body, and timorously fearful to offend or contest with others that will or do oppose him." The 29-year-old Gilbert, supposedly Popham's subordinate, was "desirous of supremacy and rule," given to a "loose life, prompt to sensuality," a man with "little zeal in religions, humorous, headstrong, and of small judgment and experience." Sir Ferdinando admitted Gilbert was "valiant enough." It seems that the more energetic Gilbert was contesting the older Popham's authority.

Fort St. George was a fairly imposing structure, protected by 12 cannon, and containing a church, storehouse, and a dozen or so houses. Spanish intelligence obtained a copy of the fort's plan, which was forwarded to King Philip II in September, 1608. The Spanish agent also sent along "a report given me by a person who has been there." This statement raises the possibility of betrayal of secrets by a former colonist. Spanish anxieties about the Sagadahoc settlement would have been alleviated if they knew what Gorges was learning of its internal weaknesses.

The winter of 1607 was an especially hard one, not only on the Maine coast but throughout Europe. Yet the health of the colonists remained remarkably good. They must, however, have been getting on each other's nerves. Gorges wrote that each engaged in "disgracing the other, *even to the savages.*"* Privately despairing of their abilities, Gorges hoped to convince the king to intervene to salvage the situation. He raised the spectre of a foreign power taking advantage of any English failure. "At this instant," he warned, "the French are in hand with the natives to practice upon us."

In December the *Gift of God* was dispatched to England, carrying back about 50 colonists—and a letter written in bad Latin by President Popham to King James I. There is a distinctly unreal quality about this message. Popham makes no reference to the colony's problems, which the return of half its number had dramatized. Instead, he fawningly tells James how popular the monarch is among the natives, a questionable observation at best, and passes on the natives' assurance

> . . . that there is a sea in the opposite or western part of this province, distant not more than seven days' journey from our fort of St. George in Sagadahoc—a sea large, wide, and deep, the boundaries of which are they wholly ignorant of. This cannot be any other than the Southern Ocean, reaching to the regions of China, which unquestionably cannot be far from these regions.

Popham also promotes commercial opportunities of the colony, saying "there are in these parts shagbarks, nutmegs, and cinnamon, beside pine wood and Brazilian cochineal and ambergris . . . in the greatest abundance."

Nutmegs, cinnamon, and brazilwood! Perhaps Popham, surrounded by snowdrifts, was hallucinating. Certainly he was a very ill man. On February 5, 1608, he died, the only colonist to succumb to sickness. Gilbert became the second governor of North Virginia.

Sometime that winter the storehouse and several lodgings burned. The cause of this setback is unclear. According to one unsubstantiated story, the Indians briefly seized control of the fort and inadvertently set off a barrel of gunpowder. How could the natives have done this? Was there connivance with some colonists?

When vessels arrived from England bearing provisions (but, significantly, no new colonists) the following summer, the Sagadahoc colony superficially seemed to be doing reasonably well. Captain Davis commented that he "found all things in good forwardness, and many kinds of furs obtained from

---

*Italics mine. This is an intriguing phrase. To what extent were the Indians part of the colonists' internal squabble?

the Indians by way of trade, good store of sarsaparilla gathered, and the new pinnace all finished." Apparently the 45 remaining colonists were in good enough shape to construct the *Virginia*, the first vessel built by Englishmen in the New World.

But along with provisions came word of Justice John Popham's death. When another supply vessel arrived in September, it carried the news of Sir John Gilbert's demise. This necessitated Raleigh Gilbert's return to England, since his elder brother had left a considerable estate. With nobody able or willing to take Gilbert's place, the colony was disbanded before the onset of another Maine winter. When the unsettled settlers showed up in Plymouth two months later, Sir Ferdinando and his associates in the North Virginia Company realized "all our former hopes were frozen to death."

It was a telling phrase. The returning colonists spread the story of the country's frigidity. Gorges, in a later book, noted that the winter of 1607 was one of "unseasonable cold" in England as well, "it being the same year that our Thames was so locked up that they built their boats upon it." He was not personally impressed with the weather as the major reason for Sagadahoc's failure. Of the colonists, he comments, "Besides, they understood it to be a task too great for particular persons to undertake." In other words, they lacked the right stuff.

This interpretation has been repeated by later historians. Yet, until we learn more about the individual colonists, it must be kept in mind that our perspective, largely drawn from a "management" figure who never was on the scene, may be unfairly skewed.

However contentious, were the Sagadahoc colonists inferior to the Jamestown settlers? On a physical level, they appear to have fared much better than their fellow countrymen in "South Virginia." Gorges would later argue that a cold climate, more like England's, was actually preferable, encouraging a hardier colony.

The Indians later claimed that they had driven the English out. Was this self-serving boasting, or was there some truth in it? From the record, there seems to be an unmistakable undercurrent of hostility between the races. This may have contributed as much as the weather to the colonists' decision to leave.

This was a colony that should have succeeded. The exact reason why Jamestown's northern counterpart failed remains shrouded in a fog like that which often envelopes the Maine coast.

• 4

Showdown at St. Sauveur

T he Frenchmen," according to Sir Ferdinando Gorges, "immediately took the opportunity to settle themselves within our limits." In fact it was not until the summer of 1613—over four years after the abandonment of Sagadahoc—that a small Jesuit mission was established on Mount Desert Island, within the jurisdiction claimed by the Virginia Company.

It lasted one month.

The site was named St. Sauveur. It was located on the west bank of Somes Sound, which bisects the southern shore of the island. "This place is a beautiful hill," Father Pierre Biard wrote, "rising gently from the sea, its sides bathed by two springs; land is cleared for 20 or 25 acres and in some places is covered with grass almost as high as a man." The Jesuit noted that the colony was "in a position to command the entire coast" with a harbor "as safe as a pond."

One bright July day, this idyllic scene was shattered by the appearance of a strange vessel. Under full sail, it bore down quickly upon the French ship, aptly named *Jonas*, anchored in Biard's safe harbor. Blaring trumpets and beating drums made it abundantly clear that the intruder was not bent upon a social call. English banners fluttered in the breeze and red canvas screened the deck of the *Treasurer*, Captain Samuel Argall commanding. The sails of the French vessel had been lowered as awning and most of its sailors were ashore. A handful of men, "none of whom understood naval warfare" except the doughty Captain Charles Fleury, scrambled to prepare for the onslaught. They did not have time to even heave their anchor. "The English ship came in swifter that an arrow," Biard recalled.

The French called out to the onrushing ship to identify itself. The response was a volley of cannon and musket fire. Luckily for the French (and in this affair there was damned little luck on their side), the lowered sails of the Jonas made them difficult targets. It was, nevertheless, an unequal contest, as Biard makes clear:

> The first volley from the English was terrible, the whole ship being enveloped in fire and smoke. On our side they responded coldly, and the artillery was altogether silent. Captain Fleury cried, "Fire the cannon. Fire! But the cannoneer was not there. Now Gilbert du Thet [a Jesuit lay brother], who in all his life had never felt fear or shown himself a coward, hearing this command and seeing no one obey it, took a match and made

us speak as loudly as the enemy. Unfortunately he did not take aim; if he had, perhaps there might have been something worse then mere noise.

The English came alongside the *Jonas* and raked it with another volley. Du Thet was mortally wounded; four other men, including the Captain, were hit. The French had no choice but to surrender. As the victors climbed aboard, two frightened sailors jumped overboard and were shot dead in the water. The battle was ended.

France and England were at peace with one another in 1613, and the raid on St. Sauveur created understandable controversy. How did the French come to settle on Mount Desert Island and why did Captain Samuel Argall treat them as he did?

The key figure in this story was a woman. Antoinette de Pons, Marquise de Guercheville, was a reputed beauty who managed to escape the clutches of the always alert King Henri IV. A devout Catholic, the virtuous marquise took a special interest in missionary efforts among the Indians. Thus she became acquainted with the predicament of Father Pierre Biard. Biard was a professor of Hebrew and theology at the University of Lyons. He and Father Enmond Masse were appointed "apostles" to the struggling French colony at Port Royal by the king's confessor. But how to get there? The Jesuits had difficulty in obtaining passage on one of Sieur de Poutrincourt's ships. Two of the Huguenot stockholders refused point-blank to allow the Jesuits aboard. Alerted to their plight, the Marquise de Guercheville bought out the Protestants' shares. She and the Jesuits thus became trading partners of Poutrincourt. This combination of business with religion did not go without criticism, but it made possible the Biard-Masse mission.

For the marquise, the end justified the means. This was an attitude commonly imputed to the Jesuits. Their reputation for intrigue antagonized many Catholics, as well as Protestants. The fathers' presence was not eagerly anticipated in New France. Lescarbot could see "no need of these Docteurs sublimes who would be more usefully employed fighting heresy and vice at home." But things were changing. In 1610 Jesuit influence, already great at the French court, became greater with the assassination of Henri IV by a Catholic fanatic. A caretaker government, or regency, was established on behalf of the boy king, Louis XIII. The suspicion would long persist that somehow the Society of Jesus was involved in Henri's murder.*

It was not until early 1611 that the two Jesuits finally embarked from Dieppe on the *Grace de Dieu*. Heavy seas forced the vessel to seek safe harbor at Newport, England. By the time the French resumed their voyage 18 days later, word had filtered out about the *Grace de Dieu's* mission. London was concerned. Given Jesuit aggressiveness, did this signal the beginning of an overt threat to North Virginia? The Sagadahoc colony may have been a bust, but James I's government still considered the territory extending to the 45th parallel English.

---

*As Jesuit influence at court increased, the relative position of Huguenots in France declined, particularly when Cardinal Richelieu maneuvered them into a war and took away their military control of a number of towns. The vital Protestant role in New France was ended in 1628 when further Huguenot emigration was outlawed.

Enter Samuel Argall. He was the "ingenious, active, and forward young gentleman" who had been commissioned in 1609 to find a quicker route to the South Virginia Colony of Jamestown "to avoid all danger of a quarrel with the subjects of the king of Spain." Argall did this, and brought desperately needed provisions to struggling Jamestown as well. Virginian Gabriel Archer described Argall as "as a good mariner and a very civil gentleman." The next year, commanding Lord De La Warre's relief squadron, Argall brought new emigrants and supplies to Jamestown—just when its governor had ordered its abandonment. He subsequently traded with southern Indians for grain and sought fish as far north as Matinicus Island off the Maine coast. His charts were later used—but not acknowledged—when Captain John Smith made his famous exploration of the coast he christened "New England." Incidentally, Argall discovered the existence of the Gulf Stream on his return voyage to Virginia. On July 11, 1612, this veteran seaman was commissioned admiral of Virginia by the London-based Virginia court, and instructed to make sure the French did not encroach upon North Virginia.

After spending the fall and winter trading, fishing, and exploring off Jamestown, Argall spent the spring of 1613 making final preparations "for my fishing voyage, of which I beseeched God of his mercy to bless us." Of course Argall didn't need 14 cannon and 60 musketeers to catch sturgeon. Sir Thomas Dale, governor of Virginia, had given Argall specific orders to wipe out any French settlements he found.

Before the captain went, as one historian put it, "fishing for Frenchmen," he kidnapped the local Indian princess, Pocahontas. This episode did not reflect favorably upon Argall's reputation—but, like all his acts, it contributed to Jamestown's survival. When Pocahontas later married John Rolfe, it was Sam Argall who captained the vessel taking the newlyweds to England.

All had not been well among the French at Acadia. The unwelcome Jesuits soon alienated Poutrincourt's son, Charles de Biencourt, leader of the Port Royal colony. Biard, who extensively explored the Maine coast as far as the Kennebec River, argued with 19-year-old Biencourt over Indian policy. He also sided with Biencourt's main rival, one Robert Grave du Pont. The winter of 1611–1612 was a tense one at Port Royal. It was made more tense by the arrival of Jesuit lay brother Gilbert du Thet, the marquise de Guercheville's agent. Du Thet brought the news that the marquise had bought out de Monts' rights to development of his original grant—except Port Royal, earlier awarded by de Monts to Poutrincourt. Now Biencourt was, in effect, encircled by territory controlled by the Jesuits' benefactress. The senior Poutrincourt's agent, who had come over on the same ship, spiced things up by accusing du Thet of making remarks approving of Henri IV's murder.

After this spat subsided, Father Biard was caught sneaking aboard a departing ship and forcibly restrained from leaving Port Royal. This brought down a church interdict upon the colony. When du Thet finally managed to secure passage back to France, he informed the marquise of all this and more. She ended her partnership with Poutrincourt and dispatched Rene le Coq de La Saussaye in the *Jonas* to pick up her mistreated Jesuits and establish a separate Indian mission for them farther down the Maine coast. The preferred site was Kenduskeag on the Penobscot River. This Indian village was the physical reality of Norumbega.

Champlain thought this a most unwise move. Noting that the English had already seized a few French fishing vessels off Mount Desert Island, he warned of probable English hostility if a settlement was attempted in a region where English and French claims overlapped. He advised settlement at more distant Quebec. The marquise, however, was opposed. Father Jacques Quentin and du Thet, who now expressed a desire to end his days in New France, joined the company of soldiers, sailors, artisans, colonists, goats, and horses aboard the *Jonas*. Excluding obvious animals, there were 48 men. The queen even sent along "four of the king's tents or pavilions, and some munitions of war." Many ladies of the court chipped in to underwrite the venture. Thus the French were moving south as Samuel Argall prepared to sail north.

In May 1613 the *Jonas* reached Port Royal. Captain Charles Fleury picked up the missionaries there, and headed for the Penobscot. A heavy fog caused the ship to stop at what is now Bar Harbor; the crew argued to stay at Mount Desert; the pilot chimed in "that a ship had never gone as far as Kadesquit, and that he had no intention of becoming the discoverer of new routes." At this point local Indians, favorable to the presence of missionaries, got into the act. They used the ruse of a supposedly ailing chief requiring baptism ("He will die and go to hell") to lead Biard to a location which, true to the Indians' word, *was* better than Kenduskeag. Biard was suitably impressed, and the decision was made to locate the mission on Mount Desert Island.

True to form, the French became involved in more bickering. La Saussaye, according to Biard, "amused himself too much in cultivating the land," despite the demands of other officers that houses and fortifications should first be constructed. Meanwhile, Argall, the "admiral of Virginia" arrived in the vicinity. An Indian revealed the presence of the French by his naive description of other white men nearby. Argall swiftly attacked, using the loudly lamenting native as a guide.*

After the capture of the *Jonas*, Argall and his troops landed and searched the deserted, half-built colony. La Saussaye and the men ashore had fled into the woods, while the pilot and some of the men of the *Jonas* hid amongst the islands. The English captain located the French commander's trunks, picked their locks, and removed the commissions and royal patents. He then carefully put everything in order and relocked the trunks. When La Saussaye finally emerged the next day, the clever Argall demanded to see his authorization for the French incursion upon soil claimed by England:

> La Saussaye answered that the letters were in his trunks. These were brought, and before he unlocked them he was advised to look closely to see if they had been tampered with. . . . La Saussaye found that all was in good order, but alas, he could not find the letters! Whereupon the English captain changed his mien and his voice. Frowning in the most proper

---

*Samuel Eliot Morison, noting du Thet's death as a result of the engagement at St. Sauveur, wrote that the Jesuit thus got the death in America he desired. That is a bit harsh.

manner, 'How now,' said he, 'are you imposing on us? You give us to understand that you have a commission from your king, and you cannot produce any evidence of it. You are outlaws and pirates, every one of you, and merit death.' Then he set his soldiers to plundering, and in this the whole afternoon was consumed.

This piece of acting (based upon Biard's testimony) has contributed to the historical image of Argall as a scoundrel. Yet the Frenchmen under Argall's control were neither killed nor sold into slavery as they expected. Biard attributed this to Argall's concern about the French pilot and sailors who eluded his grasp. The Englishman, he argued, feared they would report any atrocity, possibly causing international repercussions. Whether this was the case, or whether he simply possessed human compassion, Argall allowed Father Masse and 14 companions to coast the shore in an open boat while Biard, Quentin, and 13 others were transported back to Jamestown. Governor Dale wished to hang the captives, particularly the Jesuits, but Argall interceded to prevent the executions.

Governor Dale sent Argall with a squadron of three vessels to finish what he had started at St. Sauveur. Argall took Biard along on his return down east. Biard later claimed that he refused to guide Argall to St. Croix and Port Royal, but they were located anyway. Both were found deserted, and both were razed. Later, one of those who fled Port Royal accused Biard of conspiring with the English to destroy their colony. Furthermore, it was charged that Biard was actually a *Spanish* fugitive from justice in France! The French were apparently much more inclined to fight each other than the English.

Argall was forced by a storm to cross the Atlantic, rather than return to Virginia as he intended. When he stopped in Wales for provisions, the authorities seized him as a pirate. In a final ironic twist, he had to rely upon the Jesuit captives' testimony that he was indeed an officer and a gentleman. Argall was released.

Biard and the other survivors of the incident at St. Sauveur ultimately returned to France. Interestingly, while the Jesuit was critical of the English decision to destroy St. Sauveur, he was fairly benign in his portrayal of Argall. The French government protested, and the marquise de Guercheville demanded compensation. Admiral Henri de Montmorency complained to King James of England, "But your majesty knows that for more than 80 years, the French have been in possession of it [the disputed territory], and have given to it the name of New France." But the Virginia Company and James I were not about to admit they knew any such thing. France and England were at peace, the Mount Desert colony (and, for that matter, St. Croix and Port Royal) fell within the northern boundary of the Virginia Company, and the matter was not considered sufficiently serious to break relations between the two countries. The marquise got the *Jonas* back, and had to be content with that. She sold out her interest in Acadia. Even her French contemporaries were critical of what they considered an imprudent venture.

Some historians have speculated about what the outcome might have been if St. Sauveur had been firmly established. Would the relative position of the French in America have been stronger? Of course. But it never was in the cards that the English were going to tolerate a strong new French outpost in territory they claimed. In retrospect, the shots fired at Mount Desert may be seen as the beginning of a long struggle for supremacy on the North American continent. That is the advantage of the long view. At the time, the incident was dismissed as an unfortunate skirmish on the periphery of French and English ambitions.

And Maine was where those ambitions converged.

5 •

The Pirate Dixey Bull

In the late 1620s Abraham Shurt bought Monhegan Island from some English merchants and set up a fortified trading post at nearby Pemaquid. How much business in fish, furs, grain, and assorted sundries he did—or how legitimate it was—is not altogether clear. Shurt traded with Pilgrims from Plymouth Plantation and Boston merchants from the Massachusetts Bay Colony, as well as assorted Indians, Frenchmen, and other coastal characters. He was doing well enough by the autumn of 1632 to attract the special attention of Dixey Bull.

Bull sailed into Pemaquid harbor, his ship flying the black flag of piracy. A landing party "took away from the plantation . . . as much goods and provisions as is valued to be worth five hundred pounds." They also seized "divers boats."

This was the first significant pirate raid along the New England coast. It was not without violence, although the pirates were on the receiving end. Just as the pirates "were weighing anchor, one of Mr. Short's [sic] men shot from the shore and struck the principal actor dead and the rest were filled with fear and horror." Apparently the victim of the lucky shot was not Dixey Bull.

The historical portrait that survives of Dixey is barely a sketch. In 1631, Bull showed up in Maine in the employ of Sir Ferdinando Gorges and several other associates. Gorges' party included one Seth Bull, described as a "Citizen and Skinner of London." Another Bull, apparently related, was Henry Bull of Boston, who was later kicked out of town for his support of the troublesome Anne Hutchinson. Dixey himself evidently was not on friendly terms with Massachusetts authorities, who considered him an enemy of the colony. These Bulls were a contentious lot.

Dixey, an apprentice to elder brother Seth, who became a "trader for bever," did not mind doing business with the Pilgrims, who operated trading posts on the Kennebec and Penobscot Rivers. While Bull was parlaying with some Indians near their Penobscot station, a small French vessel arrived on the scene. In apparent distress, the French requested permission to land and make repairs. Once ashore, they grabbed all the beaver skins available and seized Dixey Bull with "his shallop and goods."

When Bull was released by his captors, he swore vengeance, gathered a crew of 15 men he found along the shore, and—in a ship of unknown name— set about looking for French prey. Finding the pickings slim, Dixey started taking English vessels and became the terror of the Maine coast.

Ultimately he was bold enough to mount the attack on Pemaquid. Most of the men there were working in nearby fields when he looted the trading post, and there was slight resistance. But the potshot that killed his chief accomplice apparently cooled Dixey's ardor for more raids on similar outposts to the south.

Governor John Winthrop was notified of the raid by Captain Walter Neale of Piscataqua. The Piscataqua settlement sent out a makeshift pirate-hunting squadron of four pinnaces and shallops with about 40 men. Winthrop, after conferring with his council, agreed to dispatch his ship *The Blessing of the Bay* to join in the hunt for Bull. The Puritans took their time outfitting their force, then deferred action altogether on December 4, 1632, stating that "the extremity of the snow and frost had hindered the making ready" of *The Blessing of the Bay*. They elected to send "John Gallop with his shallop" to Piscataqua to learn what progress Neale's little armada had made. One gets the distinct impression the Puritans were less than excited about aiding the Episcopalian colonists of Maine. Gorges, a staunch royalist and established Churchman, was still promoting the development of what would be styled "the Province of Maine." Between Puritan Massachusetts and non-Puritan Maine there was bad blood from the outset.

Neale finally reached Pemaquid, but the wind and cold prevented further pursuit of Bull. The first New England naval squadron to sweep the Maine coast was a failure. Unable to catch Dixey Bull, the Piscataqua expedition stopped off at Richmond's Island on the return voyage long enough to hang a probably innocent, but available, Indian named Black Will for the murder of a merchant. If it had not been for Dixey's raid on Pemaquid, Black Will might have lived.

Meanwhile, Dixey Bull seized a vessel and tried to induce its captain to pilot his pirate crew to Virginia. This made some sense, since that colony was considered to be "a nest of rogues, whores, [and] dissolute and rooking persons." The pilot, Anthony Dicks of Plymouth, refused; three of the nervous pirates took the opportunity to desert. The description conveyed by Dicks was not one of a fearsome bond of freebooters: "They told him that they were filled with such Fear and Horror that they were afraid of the very Rattling of the Ropes."

The chastened group, according to John Winthrop, remained for a while in the region and appeared at a few settlements, where they traded peacefully and fairly. Dixie "made a law against excessive drinking," and, instead of praying, the crew amused themselves by assembling on deck to "sing a song or speak a few senseless sentences." This crowd sounds more dull than dangerous.

> They also sent a writing directed to all governors, signifying their intent not to do harm to any more of their countrymen, but to go to the southward, and to advise them not to send against them for they were resolved to sink themselves rather than be taken.

This strange letter was signed "*Fortune le garde.*" It may well have been meant to decoy any further pursuit away from the pirates' real destination.

Winthrop finally sent out Lieutenant John Mason—veteran of the Pequod War—to apprehend Dixey Bull in May of 1633. But Bull was long gone.

Where? In 1636 a London merchant, trying to get compensation for "strong watters" sold to Henry Bull, inquired into Dixey's whereabouts. He was rumored to be in England. However, according to a contemporary, "God destroyed this wretched Man,"—probably before any debts might be paid.

How? There is an unsubstantiated story that Bull was hanged at Tyburn for piracy. Still, it is not altogether clear how Dixey exited the pages of history. The records of the Skinner's Guild note on November 4, 1648, "Dixie Bull late Apprentice with Seth Bull having served the full term in his Indentures is preferred to the freedom." It would appear from this that God waited at least 16 years to punish Dixey for his piracy. In truth, he does not appear to have been much of a pirate, just a confused adventurer trying to hustle a living on the rock-bound coast.

6 •

Once Upon a Time Downeast

H igh melodrama has seldom been better illustrated than during the struggle for control of Acadia in the 17th century. The contest among battling fur traders resembled a romantic novel or television miniseries. It was a tale of passion, greed, betrayal, suffering, and (some) ultimate redemption. The cast of characters included French and English empire-builders, Pilgrims, Governor Winthrop, Louis XIV, Oliver Cromwell, an authentic Acadian heroine, and many, many more. This drama spilled over onto the Maine coast, and had repercussions that lasted for generations.

Our story starts in the ashes of Sam Argall's raid on Acadia. When Poutrincourt, back from France, viewed the charred buildings, butchered livestock, and ragged settlers of Acadia in 1614, he wisely decided to leave the whole mess to his son. Young Biencourt struggled manfully for a decade, concentrating on the fur trade rather than settlement and farming. This was to be the pattern in early Acadia, as well as adjacent Maine. Biencourt was assisted by one Charles de La Tour and his father, Claude.

When Biencourt died in 1623, he left Charles de La Tour his heir. As Charles consolidated his position on the Bay of Fundy, Claude tried to set up a trading post on Penobscot Bay at Pentagoet (now Castine). He was driven out in 1626 by Pilgrims also intent upon profits in fur.

The news of war between France and England made Charles de La Tour nervous. The French government, content to let private individuals somehow develop "New France," had never provided adequate resources for its defense. Charles dispatched his father to France with an urgent request for supplies and soldiers. He also asked for a commission officially recognizing his authority in Acadia. Louis XIII—or more accurately Cardinal Richelieu—turned the first request over to a high-powered corporation, the *Compagnie des Cent-associes*, organized to promote trade and colonization in New France. In the spring of 1628, the *Compagnie* sent out four vessels laden with provisions for Acadia.

The French fleet never reached its destination. It was intercepted by English vessels involved in the colonization scheme of Sir William Alexander. The Scot Sir William was a mediocre poet, but he was an influential courtier at King James I's court. James granted Alexander the right to establish "New Scotland" (Nova Scotia) in Acadia, which of course required ending French control. The plan was to divide New Scotland into some 150 baronies, but by 1628 Sir William had few takers. Strangely enough, one would be Claude de La Tour.

In England, now under Charles I, the captured Claude managed to ingratiate himself with Alexander. He convinced Sir William and the king that he was actually a Huguenot. Since England was then aligned with the French Protestants, this created a favorable impression. Claude also made a strong pitch regarding his knowledge of the resources and potential of New Scotland. Alexander was only too willing to grant the charming Frenchman a barony. Claude pledged his son's cooperation in this treason, and in exchange Charles was to become a baronet of New Scotland. After marrying one of the queen's maids of honor, Claude sailed to Acadia in 1629 with two English warships.

So far so good. However, Charles, whose fort at Cap Sable was the sole stronghold left in New France, did not cooperate. He swore that he "would rather have died than consent to such baseness as to betray his king."

This honorable response put Claude in the bizarre situation of mounting an attack upon his own son's fortifications. It was a battle between a father, representing one nation, and a son fighting on behalf of another; it was the only such case in colonial American history. After a two-day siege, Claude and the English were forced to withdraw. Claude de La Tour, not eager in these circumstances to return to either France or England, was grateful when his son allowed him, his wife, and their servants to settle for a house outside the fort rather than a baronial estate. Charles ordered his father not to enter the fort.

In 1631 a French raiding party looted the Pilgrims at Pentagoet of everything from beaver pelts to biscuits. This was the occasion, you may recall, that turned an English beaver-trader named Dixey Bull to piracy. The undefended outpost had been managed for awhile by a "profane young man" named Edward Ashley. In 1630 the sober Plymouth Plantation merchants removed him for "trading powder and shot with ye Indians." Ashley was a bit too colorful for Pilgrim tastes. He lived among the Indians "as a savage and went naked amongst them and used their manners. . . . "*

About this time, King Louis XIII finally granted Charles de La Tour the royal commission he desired. When a force of Alexander's Scots attacked his new fort at St. John on the Bay of Fundy, La Tour retaliated by pillaging a trading post established by the Pilgrim Isaac Allerton at Machias. La Tour also coveted the Penobscot Bay outpost, but when France got back its rights to Acadia by the 1632 Peace of Saint-Germain, the Pilgrims refused to evacuate.

Isaac de Razilly, a one-eyed French naval captain and a confirmed bachelor (his lone eye never saw a woman worth marriage), was appointed Governor of Acadia. Since the French government was still unwilling to subsidize overseas ventures, Razilly and his brother created their own colonizing corporation. La Tour was willing to share authority with Razilly, but he could not abide Razilly's cousin and lieutenant, Charles de Menou D'Aulnay. Ten years La Tour's junior, D'Aulnay was his equal in ambition.

In 1635 Razilly sent the 30-year-old D'Aulnay to forcibly remove the stubborn Pilgrims. Not taking kindly to their ejection, the Pilgrims hired the use of *The Great Hope* from their Puritan neighbors in Massachusetts. An expedition against Pentagoet was mounted, but its naval captain wasted his ammunition by firing wildly at the dug-in D'Aulnay before Miles Standish, the all-purpose Pilgrim warhorse, could land. Standish was unable to make any headway with his small force against the equally small French post.

La Tour was not pleased with D'Aulnay's increased stature, and pestered Razilly for command of Pentagoet. Razilly gave in to this demand and surprised everybody—including, no doubt, himself—by dropping dead. His brother and business partner, Claude de Launay-Rasilly (who insisted upon spelling his name with an "s") authorized D'Aulnay to represent the Razilly interests in Acadia.

Sensing he was gaining the upper hand, D'Aulnay complained to the king about the cession of Pentagoet to La Tour. Such colonial turf battles were not priority concerns in Paris. The government attempted to impose a compromise settlement. D'Aulnay was granted Pentagoet and La Tour's fort on the St. John; Port Royal, D'Aulnay's stronghold, was awarded to La Tour.

*Ashley was thus a forerunner of the more famous Baron Saint-Castin, discussed in the next chapter.

This simply complicated a bad situation. Both sides ignored the king's edict. In 1640 La Tour escalated tensions considerably by attacking some of D'Aulnay's vessels off Port Royal. La Tour lost the naval engagement and was briefly imprisoned by his rival.

It was in 1640 that La Tour gained his most passionate ally. Francoise-Marie Jacquelin accepted his offer of marriage. She was probably 38 years of age, and her origins remain obscure. D'Aulnay claimed she was the daughter of a Le Mans barber and had been a Paris "actress," but he is hardly an objective source. Most likely, La Tour's second wife (he was previously married to a Micmac Indian) came from petty nobility and was Huguenot. Whatever she did in France before 1640, it was in the New World that Jacquelin made her reputation.

In 1641 La Tour sought aid against D'Aulnay from the Puritans of Massachusetts. Several Boston merchants responded to an overture delivered by a Huguenot emissary. Like his father, Charles de La Tour was willing to use religious biases for his own ends. It is doubtful if he was really a Protestant himself, although later historians have interpreted the nature of the conflict as a mini-religious war. When, after shipping supplies to St. John, these merchants stopped off at Pemaquid, they were met by D'Aulnay. He protested their action and sent along to Governor John Winthrop a copy of a document signed by Louis XIII.

It made interesting reading. Charles de La Tour, it said, was a rebel. It was a warrant for his arrest. All his Acadian possessions were forfeited to D'Aulnay. Clearly the resourceful D'Aulnay had outmaneuvered La Tour at the French court. He warned the Massachusetts authorities that any vessel, French or English, engaged in trade with his rival would face seizure.

D'Aulnay moved quickly to consolidate his position. He bought out Razilly's brother's shares in Acadian development, extended his authority clear to Penobscot Bay, and blockaded La Tour at St. John. When a vessel with supplies and new colonists from La Rochelle arrived on the scene, it was unable to make port. La Tour and Jacquelin eluded D'Aulnay's vessels and headed for Massachusetts on the La Rochelle ship.

They entered Boston Harbor "with a fair wind, without any notice taken of them." As Governor Winthrop observed, "the Lord gave us occasion to take notice of weaknesses . . . for if La Tour had been ill-minded toward us, he had such an opportunity as we hope neither he nor any other shall ever have the like again. . . . " But La Tour had no desire to take advantage of Boston's unpreparedness that summer day in 1643. He presented documents (Jacquelin had successfully argued her husband's case in France) which appeared to revoke the King's earlier arrest warrant. Now La Tour requested aid in breaking D'Aulnay's blockade.

After only briefly checking with his council, the Puritan governor made one of his most controversial decisions. While it would not be proper to extend direct military aid to La Tour, he wrote, "we thought it not fit nor just to hinder any [person] that would be willing to be hired to aid him. . . . " Allowing the French leader to recruit volunteers and hire out five ships exposed Winthrop to furious criticism. It was not, his critics charged, the business of Massachusetts to get involved in a fight between the "idolatrous

French." It might drag Massachusetts into an unnecessary war with D'Aulnay.

Winthrop later admitted he had acted too quickly and should have first informed the Puritan elders, not to mention the general court. Yet he always maintained that his course was "warrantable and safe." The ships and seventy-odd volunteers were, he argued somewhat unconvincingly, only to conduct La Tour home, not to fight his rival. An exasperated Winthrop lamented, "is our confidence and courage all swallowed up in the fear of one D'Aulnay?" The usually astute Puritan leader burned his political fingers when he got involved in the Acadian feud.

As it turned out, the expedition was only partially successful from La Tour's standpoint. While D'Aulnay fled from St. John, the English vessels' commander refused to participate in an assault upon his fort at Port Royal. La Tour, with a mixed force of his own men and Massachusetts volunteers, landed anyway. They burned a mill, killed a few men and cattle, and looted a pile of furs. They did not dislodge D'Aulnay. Later, another English force, after trading with La Tour, raided near Pentagoet, burning down an isolated farmhouse.

All this activity prompted D'Aulnay to send his own emissary, a Capuchin friar, to clear things up with Boston. By then Winthrop had been voted out of office, in large measure due to his Acadian intervention. Colonists in Maine, who especially feared reprisal, had been vocal in their opposition. The new governor, John Endicott, negotiated a settlement which recognized D'Aulnay as the legal French ruler of Acadia.

Jacquelin again traveled to France, but this time she was not able to counter D'Aulnay's accusations against La Tour. Considered a co-traitor, she was barely able to escape to England. There, with funds secured in France, Jacquelin bought supplies and chartered a ship back to St. John.

The voyage took longer than expected. The captain, a chap named Bailey, took time off to fish on the Grand Banks. Jacquelin was forced to hide in the hold when D'Aulnay, suspecting something fishy, searched the ship off Cap Sable. Bailey then headed south to Boston. There, six months after leaving England, Madame La Tour immediately took the wayward captain to court. She sued Bailey for unnecessary delay and failure to deliver her to the agreed-upon destination. The handsome settlement Jacquelin won was sufficient to engage several ships to run D'Aulnay's renewed blockade in late 1644.

With scant hope of further aid from France, the indefatigable La Tour decided to try to extract more aid from the Bostonians. He left his wife in charge of his garrison at St. John. Several soldiers deserted and informed D'Aulnay of his adversary's absence. In mid-April of 1645, he bombarded La Tour's fort and attacked with about two hundred men. Madame La Tour repulsed D'Aulnay's repeated assaults until Easter Day. After receiving her opponent's promise to spare the survivors, she surrendered. Once in possession of the fort, D'Aulnay went back on his word. All of Jacquelin's men were executed except one who consented to serve as his comrades' hangman. The Acadian heroine was forced to watch this grisly spectacle on a scaffold with a rope around her neck. Three weeks after this degradation, she died.

The less-than-chivalrous victor was congratulated by the new king, Louis XIV, and the queen mother. D'Aulnay demanded compensation from the

Boston merchants who had traded with La Tour, but had to content himself with the award of a fancy sedan chair stolen from the Spanish viceroy in Mexico. With La Tour safely out of the way in Quebec, D'Aulnay was now confronted by his chief creditor, the French merchant Emmanuel Le Borgne. When D'Aulnay refused payment of the 300,000 *livres* Le Borgne instituted legal proceedings against the Acadian governor's estate. Despite this new irritation, D'Aulnay set about expanding his grip on Acadia. With three forts at Port Royal, St. John, and Pentagoet, he monopolized the fur trade. He also encouraged attempts at farming (a small farm was kept by D'Aulnay west of Penobscot Bay near present-day South Cushing) and shipbuilding at Pentagoet. Nevertheless, his tiny colony, numbering only about five hundred people, required trade with the English at Pemaquid and Boston to survive.

By 1650 D'Aulnay appeared to be securely established. Then, in a weird quirk of fate, his canoe capsized in the icy waters near Port Royal. By the time he was fished out, D'Aulnay was too exhausted to recover. His death left his widow, Jeanne Motin, with eight children*—and the relentless Le Borgne, who made raids on D'Aulnay's holdings.

La Tour, hearing of his rival's demise, proceeded to France where he gained an inquiry into his earlier dispute with D'Aulnay. In yet another about-face, La Tour won a royal order for his reinstatement at the St. John fort Jacquelin had lost to D'Aulnay in 1645.

Showing up at St. John with this order, the old intriguer added a marriage proposal! The practical Madame D'Aulnay accepted and, in July of 1653, became La Tour's third wife. If ever there was a marriage of convenience, this was it. Both parties were heavily in debt, and continued rivalry was in neither's interest. So they had five new children, and continued to fight off the rapacious Le Borgne, but to report that they lived happily ever after would be too simple for this saga.

Major Robert Sedgwick, a Puritan merchant commissioned by the lord protector of England to take New Netherlands from the Dutch, arrived in Boston with an expedition for that purpose. However, he was a little late. The war with the Dutch had ended. Rather than return to England empty-handed, Sedgwick decided to attack the French in Acadia. La Tour had enough trouble fending off Le Borgne and was unprepared to contend with the Puritan major. Sedgwick's 500-man force overwhelmed La Tour's garrison of 70 souls at St. John. The major plundered all the Acadian forts, including Pentagoet, and established English authority.

Hauled back to London as a prisoner, Charles de La Tour found himself in a situation similar to that of his father, Claude, decades earlier. La Tour managed to gain an audience with the mighty Oliver Cromwell. He tried to get Acadia back, arguing that France and England were at peace when Sedgwick grabbed it. But that had not prevented such things in the past, and Cromwell was unmoved. However, the lord protector did agree to recognize La Tour's rights as a baronet of "New Scotland" as his father's heir. This was the same baronetcy La Tour had spurned when his father brought news of it. But La Tour was in his sixties now, and ever the pragmatist. He pledged allegiance

---

*The D'Aulnays' four sons joined the army and were killed, while their four daughters became nuns.

to England, agreed to pay off his debt to the Boston merchants, and became a business partner of the English governor of Nova Scotia, Sir Thomas Temple.

Meanwhile, the French government granted the governorship of Acadia to D'Aulnay's old creditor and La Tour's old rival, Emmanuel Le Borgne. Le Borgne never was able to get the upper hand against Temple, but in the 1667 Treaty of Breda, Acadia (Nova Scotia) was restored to the French. Charles de La Tour did not live to see this development. However, one of his daughters by D'Aulnay's widow married the son of—you guessed it—Emmanuel Le Borgne. This set the stage for further intermarriages that confused the Acadian inheritance no end.

And what exactly *was* the western boundary of Acadia? Nobody at Breda quite seemed to know. Eventually long-contested Pentagoet was included, and territory west of Penobscot Bay as far as the St. George River.

The trials and tribulations of the competing French beaver barons retarded Acadia's development. The French government, having to contend with various wars, civil and otherwise, paid little attention to New France. When it did, it was hardly consistent. This started to change after the Treaty of Breda. While Paris was mainly concerned with the development of the St. Lawrence, Great Lakes, and Mississippi region, Acadia received more attention than it had.

The miniature civil war between D'Aulnay and La Tour, which involved the neighboring English colonists, was the prelude to a more serious chapter in New England's history. After plenty of feuding among themselves, the French would direct their future energies toward fighting the English.

7 •

The Backwoods Baron

W hen Hector d'Andigne de Grandfontaine arrived in Acadia in 1670 as its governor under restored French rule, he set up his headquarters at Pentagoet. One of the contingent of soldiers accompanying him was a young ensign, Jean-Vincent D'Abbadie de Saint-Castin. The second son of a noble family of Bearn in the Pyrenees, the 18-year-old Saint-Castin could hardly have realized he was destined to spend most of the rest of his life in this wilderness outpost.

Who *was* Saint-Castin? He was, and remains, a legendary figure. No other name conjures up such compelling—and contradictory—images as Castin's. Was he:

- The white noble who forsook his "civilized" inheritance to live among "savages" and become their leader, a noble white savage?
- A free spirit who lived as he wished in the wilderness, independent of the control of any state?
- The libertine who indulged his sexual passions with a backwoods harem?
- A cunning rogue who secretly served his nation's imperial ambitions, the sinister force behind bloody massacres along the frontier?

Like all legends, Saint-Castin was the projection of the fears and ambitions of others. He cannot be separated from the stage he acted upon. To understand the real man better, it is necessary to understand the setting which served for three decades as his habitat: Pentagoet.

Pentagoet was in the middle of disputed territory. According to Grandfontaine's instructions, Acadia stretched from Cape Breton Island to the Kennebec. But King Charles II of England granted the territory between the Kennebec and St. Croix rivers to his brother, the duke of York. Grandfontaine felt that the handful of English colonists in the region, who resented Boston's influence, would accept France's rule as long as their freedom of religion was guaranteed. A more cautious assessment was contained in a report by Jean Talon, the French intendant, to Louis XIV's chief minister, Jean Baptiste Colbert. Monsieur Talon informed Colbert in 1671 of the "princely reception" a French official had received from some English settlers. They shot off muskets and cannon in salute "and vied with one another in entertaining him."

> They showed an evident joy at the prospect of seeing Pentagoet, and the claimed territories, in the hands of the King [of France]. Whether this exterior joyfulness is an effect of the fear which they have of the French being so close, [or] of a true desire to come under the rule of His Majesty, I cannot judge."

It is safe to assume the colonists simply preferred good relations to confrontation. Indeed, there already was a pattern of commercial intercourse with the French in the area. It would continue for some time with Saint-Castin.

The young noble's earliest experience with the Maine coast and woods was as a soldier. He had come to New France in 1665 as a very young member of the crack Carignan-Salières regiment. After participating in a campaign against the hostile Iroquois, he was assigned to Pentagoet. In 1673 Grandfontaine was succeeded as governor of Acadia by Saint-Castin's old commander, Jacques de Chambly. A year later the small French fort on Penobscot Bay was overwhelmed by Dutch pirates, with the connivance of

Boston merchants. Beside looting the fort, they tortured some of its defenders, including Saint-Castin. He managed to escape and, with friendly Indians, traveled overland to Quebec, where he reported to the governor-general, Baude de Frontenac.

Exactly what passed between Frontenac and the young ensign is unknown. Did the governor-general instruct Saint-Castin to return to Pentagoet and promote an alliance with the Penobscot Indians? It is possible; Pentagoet was simply too exposed to be the residence of the governor of Acadia. Saint-Castin was already well-acquainted with the region and the Penobscot chief Madockawando.

Whatever Frontenac said, Saint-Castin made the crucial decision of his life. He returned to Pentagoet rather than returning to France to claim his inheritance. In 1674 his elder brother had followed his father to the grave. Jean-Vincent was now the third Baron Saint-Castin.

If he still represented French interests, it was not in an overt way. He came back as a civilian. Establishing a trading post nearby, he neglected the fort. He spent a good deal of time among the natives, at ease with their lifestyle. In fact, he adapted so comfortably that questions arose. The nature of Saint-Castin's sex life aroused comment. Monsieur Perrot, a later governor of Acadia, even had him arrested for his licentious behavior. Complaining to Governor-General Brisay de Denonville, Saint-Castin wrote:

> I will only say that he [Perrot] kept me under arrest ... on pretense of a little weakness I had for some women, and even told me that he had your orders to do it; but that is not what troubles him; and as I do not believe there is another man under heaven who will do meaner things through love of gain ... I see plainly what is the matter with him. He wants to be the only merchant in Acadia.

There was a persistent rumor, which spread from Pentagoet to Quebec, Boston, and beyond: The backwoods baron was a polygamist. English writers claimed Saint-Castin had a harem of 40 wives!* His alleged irregular relations led Quebec's Bishop Laval to dispatch the Jesuit missionary Father Jacques Bigot to Pentagoet to perform the Catholic rite of marriage for Saint-Castin and Madockawando's daughter, given the Christian name Mathilde. By Mathilde and perhaps others, Saint-Castin fathered an uncertain number of half-breed children.

His business activities flourished. Saint-Castin operated as a virtual free agent, trading with Indians, Englishmen, anybody. In the process he accumulated a fortune estimated at 300,000 crowns.

In 1685 the duke of York became King James II of England. Among other things, he expected Sir Edmund Andros, governor of the newly created Dominion of New England, to assert his jurisdiction over his Maine lands. In 1686 a New York judge (New York was part of the Dominion) ordered some wine stored at Pentagoet seized. He demanded that Saint-Castin apply to

---

*This may have originated from the fact that about 40 people lived and traded at Pentagoet during its heyday under Saint-Castin.

James II for a land grant and swear allegiance to the English king. Instead the baron requested a similar grant from the French court.

Governor-General Denonville had enough confidence in Saint-Castin to recommend him as the next governor of Acadia. Paris, however, awarded the post to Monsieur de Meneval. Saint-Castin, de Meneval was instructed, was to be "coerced from his vagabond life and trade with the Indians &c. and his illicit trade with the English, which he alone follows, and to be urged to pursue a line of conduct more becoming of a nobleman." Meneval broadly hinted that a man of Saint-Castin's reputed wealth should be able to rebuild the Pentagoet fort. The "vagabond" ignored this. Saint-Castin's actions at this juncture do not suggest a man dedicated to promoting his nation's interests, as much as one concerned with continuing his profitable if unorthodox existence.

But the developing political situation on both sides of the Atlantic was making lucrative neutrality difficult. In the summer of 1688, Andros embarked from Piscataqua on the frigate *Rose* and made a leisurely voyage across Casco Bay to Pemaquid. Inquiring about the state of the French fort at Pentagoet, he was informed by the Pemaquid merchants, who were very familiar with the place, that it was quite run down. After gathering up carpenters and material with which to rectify this situation (for English use), Andros sailed across Penobscot Bay to the French outpost. Saint-Castin and his retinue fled, leaving the abandoned trading station to Andros's inspection. Sir Edmund, disappointed that the baron had flown his backwoods coop, left the Catholic altar undisturbed. He carried off almost everything else. Andros left word with Madockawando that, if Saint-Castin would come over to the English side, the confiscated goods would be returned. The fort was in such bad shape that Sir Edmund did not attempt to rebuild it.

The plunder of Pentagoet aroused criticism among New Englanders, who did not particularly like Andros to begin with. After describing the governor's troops as "a crew that began to teach New England to Drab, Drink, Blaspheme, Curse, and Damm," the Boston clergyman Increase Mather pointedly asked, "What good did that Frigot do New England?" Nothing, except to rob Saint-Castin "upon which began the Bloody War." Mather was referring to the war with the French and their Indian allies which broke out in 1690, after Andros, like his master in England, was overthrown. The idea that the mistreatment of Saint-Castin set off the fighting gained considerable currency.

No doubt the baron was upset, but the attacks upon English settlements in New York, New Hampshire, and Maine resulted from Governor-General Frontenac's overall strategy. With war declared between England and France following King James II's overthrow, Frontenac's aim was to put the more populous English colonies on the defensive by devastating frontier raids. Maine was particularly vulnerable—as it always had been. The conflict called King William's War in America was unleashed by events abroad, not by the plundering of Saint-Castin's trading post. Once Andros was removed, the Bostonians immediately disavowed his raid in a message to Saint-Castin. Whether he rejected this overture is unknown, but clearly he could no longer pursue the role of free agent.

Saint-Castin participated in an attack on Casco, an English settlement near present Portland. After Fort Loyal surrendered, its defenders were apparently mistreated. Later Maine historians held the baron responsible, since his influence with his father-in-law Madockawando was supposed to be great. In fact, he was subordinate to the French commander Rene Robinau de Portneuf. Yet the baron was implicated in the minds of Massachusetts authorities.

When the ambitious but slow expedition led by Sir William Phips against Quebec failed, it was alleged that Saint-Castin's spies had tipped off Frontenac about the Massachusetts governor's preparations. The first royal governor of Massachusetts did not hesitate to hire two French deserters to either kidnap or murder Saint-Castin. The plot was foiled.

In the autumn of 1692 Phips, determined to strengthen his eastern frontier, set about building a great stone fort at Pemaquid. While he was absent from Boston supervising Fort William Henry's construction, a number of innocent folk were strung up in the witchcraft trials. Ordering an end to the trials, he hurried back to the Maine coast. His bastion there proved a costly venture, but Phips, who was born in the vicinity of Pemaquid, hoped Fort William would overawe the Indians. Recalled to England to face corruption charges, Sir William died before he could defend himself. His supposedly impregnable fort, the most imposing military structure in English North America, didn't last much longer.

Saint-Castin, with a few soldiers and a couple of hundred Indians, joined a French force under Pierre Le Moyne d'Iberville, whom Frontenac sent in 1696 to reduce Fort William Henry to rubble. The fort was commanded by Captain Pasco Chubb, a blustering bully disliked by the Indians for killing two chiefs during a prisoner exchange. Chubb talked more bravely than he fought. A two-day mortar barrage unnerved him. When Saint-Castin sent a note advising Chubb to surrender at once, Chubb's resolve had turned to jelly. D'Iberville, Saint-Castin wrote, had orders to dictate whatever terms he desired if Fort William Henry was taken by assault. And who knew what, if unrestrained, the Indians might do? This was an effective ploy. Chubb surrendered, once he was assured safe conduct to Boston.* The fort was demolished. This was Saint-Castin's last recorded military role in King William's War.

In 1698 Madockawando died. If Saint-Castin assumed the role of chief, as often claimed, it was only briefly. The next year, with the equally brief return of peace, Saint-Castin resumed his trading activity at Pentagoet. As usual, he disregarded French commercial regulations. When renewed accusations about his conduct arose, he returned to France to defend himself. He had been absent from his native land since he joined the army at 13. Saint-Castin apparently succeeded in clearing his name, and tried, at long last, to claim his Bearn inheritance. However, his sister Marie's husband, a judge, threw all kinds of obstacles in the baron's way. Around 1707 he died three thousand miles from Pentagoet.

---

*Chubb was imprisoned for his failure to adequately defend the fort. Released, he returned to his Andover, Massachusetts farm—where some Indians found and killed him.

Because he assumed legendary proportions in his own lifetime, the "real" Saint-Castin remains a most elusive character. From the historical record, he appears to have been a most intelligent and resourceful man. For many years, he was able to use to personal advantage the ambivalent nature of French-English coexistence on the frontier. It is probable he had an "understanding"with the governors-general of New France, but there is no evidence that he was some sort of malignant spirit, bent upon the destruction of the exposed English settlements. Basically, he promoted his own interest. When open war came, he, in effect, put on his French uniform again—which he just as readily shed when the King William's War was over. It is likely that he was neither as noble nor as depraved as the contending images of his legend portrayed him.

• 8

Massacre on Candlemas Day

It was snowing heavily on Sunday morning, January 24, 1692. Some of the 150 Indian braves who had spent the evening encamped at the base of Mount Agamenticus wanted to delay the planned assault upon York, Maine. But the war chiefs were impatient and the Indians, hungry after their three-week trek from points north and east, were eager to procure food as well as human victims. Scouts fanned out toward the small town on the coast, five miles distant.

This was Candlemas Day. The subject of the Reverend Shubael Dummer's sermon in not known, but it is recorded that, on the previous Sunday, the minister warned his flock to "beware of the enemy, pointing to them from the Scriptures the careless inhabitants of Laish preceding the invasion of their land by the Danites. . . . " Dummer was more prophetic than he could have imagined.

York, one of a handful of towns that hugged Maine's southern coast, presented a vulnerable target in the third year of King William's War. Its five hundred residents lived clustered in three different settlements, with only a few garrison houses for protection. Lacking a central defensive point, York could be attacked section by section. Perhaps it was the frontier community's exposed situation that drew the Abnakis, led by Madockawando.

The first York inhabitant to encounter the approaching Indians was Arthur Bragdon. He did not attend Reverend Shubael Dummer's church services. Instead, the young man, not yet 20, headed into the forest behind the town to lay his traps. He noticed a stack of Indian snowshoes leaning against a big rock. Before the young man figured out the significance of his discovery, he was grabbed by Abnaki scouts. His fate was better than that of two other woodsmen, whose heads were immediately bashed in. The Indians kept Bragdon alive for information about their target.

Dividing into two war parties, the Indians converged upon the main settlement at York Harbor, hitting the outlying settlements as they progressed. While some concentrated on the garrisons, the rest fell upon the unprotected homes. The defenders of the garrisons resisted fiercely, and successfully, but elsewhere the carnage was great. A survivor recalled:

> the Pillours of Smoke, the rageing of the merciless flames, the insultations of the heathen enemy, shooting, hacking, (not having regard to the earnest supplication of men, women or children, with sharp cryes & bitter teares in most humble manner), & dragging away others, (& none to help), is most affecting the heart.

One of the victims was the minister. Mounting his horse at his doorstep when the Indians attacked, Dummer attempted to escape. He was toppled from his horse by a pistol shot. His corpse was stripped and mutilated. In his description of the event, Cotton Mather raged, "Those bloodhounds, being sent by some Romish missionaries, had long been wishing to embrue their hands in the blood of some New England minister, and in this action they had their diabolical satisfaction." Like most contemporaries, Mather blamed Indian raids on incitement by Catholic missionaries.

The bloodletting and destruction started about 10:00 A.M. and continued until early in the afternoon. The chiefs later claimed that over a hundred English were killed, but this figure was inflated, probably to impress French authorities. Local reports placed the number at about fifty deaths. Many others were wounded. Countless livestock were slaughtered. Whatever food was not taken was systematically destroyed to increase the suffering of York's survivors. The Indians were particularly careful to extract lead from windows before firing houses. Likewise, they scooped up whatever pewter or leaden vessels they could find. Such items were valuable because they could be fashioned into bullets.

Only the inhabitants on the south side of the river that flowed through the York Harbor settlement were spared. The Indians did not dare risk crossing the water and endangering their retreat. Post riders quickly raised the alarm along the coast, and Captain John Floyd, commanding the nearest provincial troops at Portsmouth, hurried to the massacre scene. When he arrived he found almost all of the houses on the north side of the river looted and 18 burned to the frozen ground. And many captives had been seized. Their exact number remains uncertain, but at least 70 people were dragged away by the

Indians. Most were woman and children, whom the Indians preferred as hostages. About half were later ransomed at Sagadahoc; those who were unredeemed (the colonial authorities frowned upon payment of ransom, but allowed private individuals and groups to raise money) were marched through the forest to Canada.

One child initially herded among the captives was the four-year-old Jeremiah Moulton, son of tavern keeper Joseph Moulton. After killing and scalping the young boy's parents before his eyes, the Abnakis were amused by his frantic but futile attempts to escape. They ultimately let little Jeremiah Moulton get away, their laughter ringing in his ears as he headed through the snow toward his burning home.

The ordeal of the white prisoners was terrible. The Indians moved quickly to elude capture, although the depth of the snow prevented Captain Floyd from pursuit. When one mother with a three-week-old infant lagged behind, the Indians, blaming the baby for her slowness, knocked the child's brains out. They apparently did this more out of what they viewed as necessity than out of cruelty. On the other hand, one Indian delighted in dressing in the garments of the slain minister on the Sunday following the massacre. He "stalked about in the presence of the distressed captives, some of whom belonged to his church, to aggravate their feelings." *That* was cruel.

The York massacre was neither the first nor last in the brutal history of the Maine frontier. Most of the elements of horror enacted at York on Candlemas Day were the subject of grim repetition. Aside from its magnitude, this massacre was more representative than unique.

Except for this detail:

Thirty-two years after the York massacre, a New England raiding party penetrated deep into the Maine forest and inflicted a bloody blow against the Abnaki village at Norridgewock. The Indians never recovered from this attack. The leader of the white troops was Captain Jeremiah Moulton of York, Maine.

The terrified, angry child grew up to become one of the most celebrated Indian fighters of New England. Many times over he extracted vengeance for that profaned sacred day. He often justified his exploits with the old Biblical prescription: *An eye for an eye and a tooth for a tooth.*

The Wild, Wild East

(1700–1820)

9

Who Died at Norridgewock?

T he New England troops under Captain Jeremiah Moulton achieved complete surprise when they attacked the Indian village of Norridgewock on August 23, 1724. It was about three o'clock in the afternoon, and Moulton's men approached stealthily "within Pistol shot" of the town. It was a hot summer day and not an Indian was in sight. A brave eventually emerged from his wigwam and, "as he was making water, looked round him and discovered the English close upon him." The startled Indian let loose a war whoop to raise the alarm and ducked back into his wigwam to grab his rifle. The Indians shot wildly and too high while the English leveled careful, deadly volleys. It was all over in a few minutes. Among the casualties was Father Sebastien Rale.

According to a later French account by French explorer and historian Pierre Francois Xavier de Charlevoix, the elderly Jesuit was shot down beneath a cross in the center of the village. Several Indians who tried to protect their priest were killed at his side. When the English left Norridgewock the following day, the Indian survivors returned to the devastated site and viewed the corpse of Father Rale:

> They found him pierced with a thousand shots, his scalp torn off, his skull crushed by hatchets, his mouth and eyes full of mud, his leg-bone broken and all of his members mutilated in a hundred different ways. Thus was a priest treated in his mission at the foot of the cross. . . . After the neophytes had raised up and repeatedly kissed the precious remains of the father, tenderly and so justly beloved, they buried him on the very spot where, the day before, he had celebrated the holy mysteries. . . .

By this version, Rale was a martyr, who died defenseless, in the open, either trying to communicate with the English or divert attention while many Indians fled.

After the initial volleys, most of the attackers pursued the natives as they frantically attempted to cross the nearby Kennebec River. About 150 Indians made it, but many died in the water. According to the English version of Captain Johnson Harmon:

> We then returned to the Town, where we found Monsieur Rale the Jesuit, their Chief Commander, in one of the Indian houses, who had been continually firing upon a party of our Men, that were still in the Town: the said Rale having wounded one of our people, Lieut. Jacques soon stove open the door of said house, and found him loading his gun, who upon

Jacques's coming in, declared voluntarily, that he would give no quarter, nor take any; Jacques hearing that, and seeing him loading, shot him thro' the head, the said Jesuit had with him an English Boy about 14 years of age, who he had about six months in his possession, which boy, in the time of the engagement, he spitefully shot thro' the thigh, and stabbed him in the body with a sword, and so left him; but the boy not being dead, we took him with us, and thro' the care and skill of the surgeon is like to recover. . . .

Thus the same event took on a much different color. Rale was the fanatical priest who died, gun in hand, beside a mutilated prisoner. In death—as in life—the Jesuit was destined to remain a controversial figure. Who *really* died at Norridgewock?

Certainly Rale had been a marked man for a long time before 1724. The English believed Jesuit missionaries were responsible for stirring up the Indians and inciting attacks upon frontier settlements. On June 15, 1700, the General Court of Massachusetts passed an act against the very presence of Jesuits within the territory claimed by the colony. Any priest apprehended was to be thrown into prison for life. Rale, who first came to New France as a missionary in 1689, had been living among the Abnaki at Norridgewock since founding a mission there in 1694.

In 1703, France and England were again at war, and the governor of Massachusetts met with a delegation of Abnakis at Casco Bay to elicit a pledge of neutrality. Despite the anti-Jesuit law, Rale was present. He claimed to have encouraged the Indians to maintain peace, but later the Abnakis raided the town of Wells. According to the governor-general of New France, Philippe de Rigaud de Vaudreuil, Abnakis were added to the raiding party after Rale assured him they were "ready to take up the hatchet against the English whenever he (de Vaudreuil) gave them the order." The English sent 275 soldiers to Norridgewock to seize Rale in the winter of 1705. When the priest and Indians escaped, the frustrated English burned his church.

After this experience, Rale was probably frustrated himself. The French government tried, unsuccessfully, to induce his superior, Pierre de La Chasse, to have Rale recalled. He was suspected of harboring less than complete enthusiasm for the war. Yet Rale was back at his Norridgewock mission by 1710. By the Treaty of Utrecht in 1713, which ended Queen Anne's War, France again surrendered Acadia as defined by its "ancient boundaries." But exactly what those boundaries were remained unclear. The English felt they now had a right to Abnaki territory, which included Norridgewock. The Abnakis, with Rale's encouragement, refused to accept this interpretation.

The stage was set for future trouble.

During the next dozen or so years, the relative position of the English improved and Rale become increasingly nervous. The English were much closer than the French, and, while the Abnakis were devoted to the Catholic religion, they also were drawn to trade with the English.

Along with commerce came more English settlement on the lower Kennebec. The English even supplied laborers to rebuild the church at Norridgewock. Rale felt it was shoddy work and got financial assistance from France to complete the reconstruction. He was upset by the presence of a Protestant missionary, the Reverend Joseph Baxter, at Arrowsic Island. Rale called Baxter "the cleverest of the ministers of Boston," and claimed he was trying to undermine the Indians' attachment to Catholicism.

> I deemed it my duty to set myself against these first sowings of seduction. I wrote a candid letter to the minister, in which I pointed out to him that my Christians had knowledge enough to believe the truths which the Catholic Church teaches, but that they had not the skill to dispute about them . . . .

The Jesuit fired off a hundred-page memorandum in which, he later boasted, "I proved by Scripture, by tradition, and by theological argument, the truths which he had attacked by sufficiently dull jestings." Rale anticipated a comparably learned response:

> Two days after having received my letter he departed on his return to Boston, and he sent me a short reply which I was obliged to read several times in order to comprehend the sense, so obscure was the style, and the Latinity* so extraordinary. I gathered, nevertheless, by dreaming over it, that he complained that I attacked him without reason—that zeal for the salvation of souls had moved him to show the way to heaven to the savages; that for the rest my proofs were ridiculous and childish. Having dispatched to him at Boston a second letter, wherein I took up the faults of his own, he replied at the end of two years, without entering at all upon the matter in question, that I had a surly and captious spirit, such as was the mark of temperament prone to anger. Thus ended our dispute, which sent away the minister and rendered abortive the design he had formed of seducing my neophytes.

This exchange, rather pompous and silly on the surface, was revealing. Rale was worried about Catholicism's hold on the Abnakis, without which it would be difficult to restrain the Indians from falling within the growing English orbit.

Massachusetts increasingly viewed Rale as its greatest enemy on the frontier. At a 1717 conference at Arrowsic, a pro-English faction of the Indians who met with Governor Shute seemed to prevail. Rale, however, claimed to have the power to overrule any treaty agreement "his" Indians might make, and encouraged continued resistance to English claims. By 1720 the governor-general of New France was reporting to Paris that "Father Rale continues to incite the Indians of the mission at Naransouak (Norridgewock) not to allow the English to spread over their lands"—and the government of Massachusetts was offering a hundred-pound reward for Rale's arrest. At a second conference at Arrowsic, the priest packed the meeting with pro-French Indians from as far away as Canada. While the governor was prevented from making any headway, the appearance of over 250 Indians at the meeting, apparently under Jesuit direction, heightened Massachusetts' resolve to eliminate Rale. Shute reminded Vaudreuil of his colony's anti-Jesuit law, as well as a similar law passed by Parliament against any Roman Catholic priest preaching in *any*

---

*Rale was not impressed by Baxter's Latin usage.

part of the British kingdom. The governor-general pushed these protests aside and refused to recall Rale.

Massachusetts resorted to other means. In late January of 1722, an expedition commanded by Colonel Thomas Westbrook marched up the Kennebec, intent upon capturing Rale. The priest was warned by an Abnaki youth of Westbrook's imminent approach:

> I had only time to swallow the consecrated wafers, and to pack in a little box the sacred vessels, and to make my escape into the woods. The English reached the village at evening, and not having found me, they came again the next day to seek me, even to the place of our retreat. They came within gunshot when we discovered them. All that I could do was to bury myself with precipitation in the forest. But as I had not time to take my snowshoes, and as moreover there remained to me much weakness from a fall, in which some years before I had the thigh and leg broken, it was not possible for me to fly very far. The only resource that remained to me was to hide myself behind a tree. They at once ran through the various footpaths made by the savages when they went in search of wood, and they came within eight paces of the tree which covered me, for the trees were despoiled of their leaves; nevertheless, as if they had been held back by an invisible hand, they all at once retired upon their steps, and took again the route to the village.
>
> Thus, by a special protection of God I escaped their hands. . . .

Westbrook did not, however, return to Boston empty handed. While pillaging Rale's church and house, his soldiers found the literary work of the missionary's lifetime, a dictionary of the Abnaki language. (It is presently at Harvard college and has long been recognized as a major source.) They also found Rale's strongbox, which contained documents from authorities in New France—the "proof" that the New Englanders sought to portray Rale as a willing agent of French designs.

Apparently Vaudreuil realized that the Abnakis, if left to themselves, would have tolerated the eastward expansion of the English. Since France was at peace with England, New France had to rely upon the influence of missionaries like Rale in order to contain the English. Rale was cooperative, although probably more because he saw the English as a threat to his mission's existence than as a conscious agent of French policy.

In July of 1722, the Abnakis retaliated for the Norridgewock raid by attacking English settlements to the south around Merrymeeting Bay. Rale encouraged the Indians to attack the settlers' livestock rather than shed human blood. Governor Shute responded by declaring war on the Indians. For the next three years, New England expeditions were sent into the forests to fight the Abnaki. Rale was a special target. In 1723 Westbrook again tried to bag the Jesuit, but Rale again eluded his grasp. He refused the urging of the Indians to seek refuge in Canada. In October, 1723, he wrote his brother in France of the English efforts:

> They have made several attempts to surprise and capture me; they have gone so far even as to promise a thousand pounds sterling* to the one who

---

*This appears excessive, but there is no doubt the English wanted to apprehend Rale badly.

should bring them my head. You are well assured, my dear brother, that these menaces have no power to intimidate me or to abate my zeal;—too happy if I should become the victim of them, and if God shall count me worthy to be loaded with chains and to shed my blood for the salvation of my dear savages.

It was becoming very dangerous for Rale. Did he, as this letter suggests, have an urge for martyrdom? He was a man in his late sixties, afflicted by rheumatism, arthritis, and a lame leg. He had been a missionary amongst his "dear savages" since 1689, spending most of those 34 years at Norridgewock. He must have been tired.

Or did he have unlimited belief in his power to somehow stem the English tide? Repeatedly he overruled pro-English Indians by publicly browbeating them and threatening excommunication. In the summer of 1724, according to Fannie Hardy Eckstrom, a noted scholar of Indian affairs, Rale arrogantly dismissed the warning of a shaman that yet another English expedition was bearing down upon Norridgewock. Rale himself noted in a letter written on the very afternoon of the attack that he had rejected the report from Indians that some two hundred men were headed for the Abnaki village.

But I said to them, how could that be, seeing we are daily surrounding and making inroads upon them. . . . Besides, in all the war you have had with them, did you ever see them come to attack you in the spring, summer, or in the fall, when they knew you were in the woods?

Rale seemed on firm ground. The English *had* avoided summer expeditions against Norridgewock—until now. The Indians were more cautious than Rale, and decided to break camp and remove themselves up river the next day.

That, of course, was too late. Around noon on August 23, 1724, an expedition led by Captains Johnson Harmon and Jeremiah Moulton of York, Maine, drew near the village with about 160 men. Harmon, the commander-in-chief, decided to divide their force, taking his contingent to scout nearby corn fields, while Moulton headed for the village.

Moulton divided his small force into three groups, posting two of them to ambush Indians at the village's north and south gates. With only 22 men he proceeded toward the east gate, purposely leaving the west gate toward the river open. When his force was spotted, the battle developed as Moulton had planned. After the first effective English volleys and the following ambushes at the north and south gates, most of the Indians fled toward the river, where many were cut down.

At this point Rale met his death. Lieutenant Richard Jacques knew Moulton's orders: take the priest alive. "That a strong young man of 27, with a loaded gun, could not have overborne a lame old man of almost 72*, whose gun was empty, when they were together in the limits of a cabin in a town already taken seems doubtful," Eckstorm has observed. Perhaps something Rale said, in the cutting manner he could assume, provoked Jacques, a French Huguenot from Newbury, Massachusetts. A crude, violent man, who was Harmon's son-in-law and Moulton's brother-in-law, Jacques shot and

---

*Rale was actually 68 years old.

scalped the priest. Whether he acted spontaneously or had some secret instruction will never be known. Jacques assumed responsibility for his act.

The fighting was over when, near nightfall, Harmon arrived on the scene. His soldiers bivouacked in the village that evening with Moulton's men. The bodies of the dead Indians were heaped—with Rale's—in the center of the village. The English burned the village the next day as they headed back to Boston.

No Indians were present when Rale died, and the returning survivors, finding his body surrounded by those of village sachems, concluded that they had died together. This was probably the origin of the traditional French account of the priest's death. The number of attackers was inflated to over *a thousand!* The governor-general must have known this was false, but to admit that New France's most important remaining outpost in Maine had fallen to a daylight attack by a small English force may not have been what Vandreuil wanted to report. Father La Chasse, Rale's superior, did embellish the account of his old friend's death, possible trying to rekindle enthusiasm for Jesuit missions, which had been waning in France.

To the English, Rale was a menace to be eradicated. To the French, he was portrayed as a martyr. The images of both sides were predictable in the circumstances. Historian Kenneth Morrison writes that Rale has "emerged not as the determined man he was, but as a shadow of two cultural fictions."

Was Rale, in the final analysis, a man determined to protect his "dear savages"—or was he an old fanatic determined to fight an enemy he viewed as heretics? The key rests with the most contested part of Captain Jeremiah Moulton's report: the wounded captive English boy. Defenders of Rale have simply refused to accept this story. According to Thomas Hutchinson, a Massachusetts historian who interviewed Moulton, the boy was a son of William Mitchell of Scarborough. This youth, the surgeon who treated him, and the soldiers who must have seen him, had to know the truth. Captain Harmon stated under oath that Moulton's account was accurate. Unless we are to believe that they all lied to promote a negative image of the slain Jesuit, a serious question remains about Father Sebastien Rale's character. Was the mutilated boy the ultimate proof of a most angry man of God—or was he a fabrication by Moulton—a later reincarnation of another boy who was psychologically mutilated by the Abnakis in the flickering light of burning York over three decades earlier?

10

The Man Who Took the Grand Battery

At the beginning of King George's War in America, the French struck first. An expedition from Louisbourg, on Cape Breton Island, seized the nearby English port of Canso in Nova Scotia. One of the English soldiers captured in May of 1744 was Ensign John Bradstreet. Bradstreet and his companions were imprisoned at Louisbourg, reputed to be New France's most formidable bastion outside Quebec. It was supposed to defend approaches to the Saint Lawrence and serve as a base for attacks southward. Louisbourg's massive fortifications had taken nearly three decades to construct; they were similar to those designed by France's great engineer Vauban, and bristled with heavy cannon.

But Bradstreet was not overly impressed. What he saw was an isolated fortress with crumbling walls, a small garrison on the edge of mutiny, and defenses geared toward attack from the sea. Like those of 20th century Singapore, practically all of 18th century Louisbourg's cannon pointed the wrong direction—if the attack came from land. When Bradstreet was released and sent to Boston in October of 1744, he was convinced that Louisbourg could be taken by New Englanders without the support of British regulars. But when he attempted to sell his "mad scheme," Bostonians thought the Nova Scotian was a bit touched in the head.

One man was receptive: William Vaughan. Vaughan was a successful businessman with considerable political pull. He was born in Portsmouth, New Hampshire, on the opposite side of the Piscataqua River from the mighty Pepperrells of Kittery, Maine. Like the Pepperrells, the Vaughans made a fortune in fisheries. William's father, George, graduated from Harvard in 1696 and used family influence to be appointed lieutenant-governor of New Hampshire. Vaughan got into a scrape with the governor of Massachusetts, was removed from office, and died soon thereafter, leaving his eldest son, William, in charge of the family's Portsmouth enterprises. The young Vaughan also graduated from Harvard, at age 19, in 1722. His social standing placed him third in a class of 31, since rank was not determined by academic performance in those good old days, and entitled William to be addressed as "Mr." Vaughan.

Not content with managing his family's business, this aggressive gentleman established his own fishing and trading post on Matinicus Island in 1728. Then he bought large tracts of land on the Maine coast at Damariscotta. Vaughan branched out into lumbering, cutting and selling the region's valuable white pine. He thus became aligned with the friendly but controversial David Dunbar, recently appointed the "Surveyor of the King's Woods." Other speculators in Maine forestland contested Dunbar's authority, dispatching Samuel Waldo to London to argue their case. Waldo, a Boston-based merchant who was one of the great behind-the-scenes hatchet men of Massachusetts politics, soon had Dunbar's political scalp. And Vaughan had acquired a most dangerous competitor.

Vaughan was fully capable of pulling strings himself, and helped get Dunbar commissioned lieutenant governor of New Hampshire, his father's old post. By 1743 Dunbar was governor of distant Saint Helena, while Vaughan was increasingly nervous about the safety of his fishing and lumbering activities. War loomed between England and France. "The times are likely to be dangerous in such a remote place as this," the virtual baron of Damariscotta worried. He had some "70 souls, men, women, and children, that live in my houses around me, and the men usually employed in my service." With vivid memories of the impact of earlier wars, they were "in a great uproar, and say they will leave the place if some security is not procured" against anticipated Indian attacks. Vaughan was at least equally concerned about French privateers preying upon his fleets. Louisbourg was the center of French power along the coast. If this key outpost fell, the situation of William Vaughan would be improved.

Thus the jittery Vaughan was very responsive to Ensign Bradstreet's plan when he heard it in Boston. He quickly adopted the scheme as his own pet project. He traveled up and down the coast "with infinite Fatigue & Hazard," agitating for an expedition against Louisbourg. He claimed that the fortress could be taken by "1,500 raw militia, some scaling ladders, and a few armed craft of New England." If the attack was mounted immediately, in winter, even the scaling ladders were unneccessary. The militia would simply walk up to the parapets on the snowdrifts and jump over!

By December Vaughan had won enough support, particularly in Maine where he was well known, to take his plan to the governor of Massachusetts. William Shirley was not adverse to an attack on the French at Cape Breton, but he was skeptical of any expedition without British military support. Nevertheless, he presented the plan in secret to the general court. The legislators rejected it, and Shirley appeared ready to let the matter drop.

Not William Vaughan. The tireless promoter lined up a hundred fishermen and two hundred Boston merchants to petition the government on the project's behalf. Shirley's enthusiasm was revived and the crucial support of Sir William Pepperrell of Kittery was won. Attracted by the scent of potential land and loot, the conniving Samuel Waldo contributed his not inconsiderable talents. A more ambitious campaign, involving 3,000 New England troops, was finally approved by a narrow margin on February 5, 1745. A coalition of merchants, fishermen, and ambitious politicians had won approval from the general court for Bradstreet's audacious plan, as revised by William Vaughan. The original idea was not Vaughan's, but more than any individual he sold it.

The next question was momentous: Who would be commander-in-chief of the expedition? Vaughan wanted the command, but Governor Shirley was not about to let the Damariscotta man have it. He dismissed Vaughan as a "whimsical, wild projector," a bit odd considering that Shirley supported his project. The governor actually wanted to lead the expedition himself, but did not assume the command. Samuel Waldo, a former legal client of Shirley, was also interested, but the slippery speculator lacked popular appeal. Shirley settled upon the perfect political choice, the popular and very wealthy Pepperrell. Shirley never seriously considered the one applicant with any real military experience, John Bradstreet. It was a choice among merchant warriors.

The governor offered Vaughan a commission as lieutenant colonel. This was below the position of brigadier general awarded Waldo, and Vaughan spurned it, saying he preferred to accompany the expedition as a volunteer. Shirley, eager at this point to smooth Vaughan's ruffled feathers, made sure Pepperrell accepted him as member of the council of war, available for any special command. Thus William Vaughan went to Louisbourg as a most powerful volunteer.

Raising the force took a bit longer than expected, and Pepperrell's invasion force did not depart Boston harbor until early April, 1745. There was an effort made to portray the campaign as a holy war. The great evangelist George Whitefield gave it his blessing and the motto *Nil desperandum Christo duce*. The ferocious clergyman Samuel Moody of York brought along a hatchet with which to chop up Catholic idols.* Benjamin Franklin, impervious to crusades and dubious of the expedition's chances of success, estimated that since January 25 there had been 45 million English prayers offered, "which set against the prayers of a few priests in the Garrison to the Virgin Mary, give a vast balance in our favor. . . . " Franklin's satirical jab aside, it seems apparent that most of the troops raised (and fully one-third were from Maine) were more attracted by visions of plunder than by the idea of smiting the Catholic infidel one more time.

Governor Shirley was concerned about the expedition's lack of British naval support; he asked the commander of the Caribbean squadron, Commodore Peter Warren, for assistance. Warren, married to a New York heiress and ambitious to win appointment as governor of New York, was open to Shirley's request. Here was an opportunity for military success that might translate into political advancement. However, he prudently checked with the admiralty before setting sail for Nova Scotia. Meanwhile, the New England fleet sailed north to Canso without a single first-class frigate for protection. "Had even one French ship of the line intercepted," one historian has noted, "she could have blown the few small American warships out of the water, and sunk the transports at leisure." Was this Yankee luck or divine providence?

The fleet anchored off Canso, and, as the militia shook off their seasickness, they were cheered by the arrival of Commodore Warren with five warships of the Royal Navy. Now any French relief force would have to fight its way past Warren's squadron. Louisbourg was more isolated than ever.

---

*Also accompanying Pepperrell was his York County friend, Colonel Jeremiah Moulton.

The French commander, Monsieur Du Chambon, was not surprised when enemy ships appeared off Louisbourg. He had anticipated some sort of naval operation. But he was unprepared for landings of troops, preparatory to a seige. He thus hesitated when the New Englanders started disembarking on beaches to the south of his fortifications. By the time Du Chambon feebly reacted with a small sortie, he was easily beaten back.

The Yankees became more convinced than ever that God was on their side. Their spirits soared. The French command was unimaginative and timid. If Du Chambon had immediately contested the New Englanders, he could have cooled their ardor considerably. As it was, the French lost the crucial psychological edge at the outset.

Once ashore, the bouyant militia immediately set about looting and burning French homes, shooting several inhabitants. Cattle were butchered and roasted, and men broke ranks like overgrown boys to play games, sing, and celebrate. By the evening of May 11, not one of the thousands of men landed had been killed—but quite a few were dead drunk.

The following morning, the rest of Pepperrell's men landed; their only problem was the heavy surf that beat against the beaches. During the day the New Englanders got a better look at the French fortifications. Beside the walled town dominated by its citadel, there were two major positions outside Louisbourg itself. An island battery in the harbor would challenge Warren's squadron if it tried to move in closer; and on the shore, about a mile to the northwest of Louisbourg, was the grand battery. This bastion was a replica, on a smaller scale, of the main fortress, with no less than 30 heavy 42-pound cannon. The cavalier Yankees did not have a single gun of this calibre. Their plan, such as it was, was to seize the cannon from the French. Shot for the big guns was brought along in a show of spectacular overconfidence.

On the evening of May 12, General Pepperrell gave his most famous volunteer something to do. William Vaughan, with a force of 450 men, was ordered to make a night foray to "seize upon all Vessels, Men or Cattle that could be found beyond the Grand Battery." By midnight Vaughan reached the French settlement, largely abandoned, about a mile distant from the battery's big guns. Any semblance of discipline quickly dissolved as his troops ran wild, smashing or burning everything in sight. Heavy smoke drifted back over the nearby French bastion.

By 2:00 A.M., Vaughan's force had deserted him and were back at their base camp on Flat Point Cove. The Damariscotta merchant-soldier decided to spend the rest of the night about four hundred yards from the looming grand battery, reconnoitering the best location for a counter artillery position. No direct assault on the main fortifications at Louisbourg made sense until the battery was reduced, ideally with its cannon intact.

As dawn exposed the presence of Vaughan and the 13 men who constituted what was left of his command, he prepared to retreat. But something odd struck him: no smoke issued from the chimneys of the grand battery's barracks, and the flagstaff was naked.

Suspecting a French ruse, Vaughan induced a Cape Cod Indian to scout the situation, giving the red man a bottle of brandy he had apparently procured during the previous evening's pillaging. Vaughan was not known to be a drinking man, making him almost the only participant in the seige who was not. The Indian cautiously crawled up to the battery's thick masonry walls, and climbed over a parapet. Within seconds, he was frantically waving to Vaughan.

Incredibly, the grand battery was undefended!

Inside, Vaughan discovered piles of ammunition and hastily spiked cannon. A young soldier shinnied up the flagstaff and nailed his red jacket to it as an impromptu British flag. Vaughan scribbled a terse note and sent a soldier scurrying with it to Pepperrell: "May it please your Honour, to be informed yt with ye grace of God and ye courage of about 13 men I entred this place about nine a clock and am waiting for a reinforcement and flag."

While awaiting a response, Vaughan spied four boatloads of French soldiers bearing down upon the nearby beach. With eight of his men and four other New Englanders who were in the area doing some breakfast looting, he rushed out to resist the boats' landing. Despite cannonfire from Louisbourg, Vaughan's tiny force blazed away, and the French boats retreated.

Soon thereafter, troops under Brigadier General Waldo marched into the battery. The French had botched their spiking of the 42-pounders. It was not long before some were pounding away at Louisbourg.

New Englanders attributed Vaughan's success to the smoke from his night raid, claiming it had routed the French from their stronghold. In fact, the French command decided to evacuate the grand battery soon after the first English landings. Chassin de Thierry, the battery's commanding officer, informed Du Chambon that his 200 men could not hold out against a land assault. He recommended the abandonment and destruction of the battery. Etienne Verrier, the 60-year-old engineer who had spent a good part of his life building Louisbourg's fortifications, was not about to have his work blown up. He argued successfully that the battery be left intact. All ammunition should be removed and the cannon that were too big to pull out should be spiked. Du Chambon and his staff agreed, thereby compounding their strategic error. Most military analysts, then and now, believe that the bastion should not have been given up without a fight.

As it was, the French soldiers in their haste failed to remove all of the ammunition that evening. The boats Vaughan assumed were sent to recapture the fort were actually sent to remove the remaining ordnance.

He had been at the right place at the right time.

Vaughan's amazing success added to his strained relations with other senior officers, who were jealous and eager for glory themselves. His offer to lead an assault on the island battery was rebuffed. When, on May 26, the attack was finally mounted, it was bloodily repulsed.

By this time an incident had occured which undercut Vaughan's reputation. He threw himself, with his usual enthusiasm, into the task of building seige batteries. On May 19 he overloaded a 42-pound cannon in an advanced battery 220 yards from Louisbourg's west gate. The idea was to batter down the already crumbling gate. When the gun was fired, however, it blew up, knocking over another cannon, setting off kegs of gunpowder, and killing some men. This unfortunate incident was not peculiar to Vaughan. The Yankees had a tendency to knock out more of their own guns than the French ever did, due to improper use. Nevertheless, the fiasco undermined his position.

Pepperrell rejected Commodore Warren's demands for a frontal assault on the town, settling for a seige. This involved dragging a number of heavy guns into commanding positions, but avoided heavy casualties. On June 17, Du Chambon officially surrendered. It appears that he had mentally surrendered earlier. In truth, once Warren's blockade and Pepperrell's army were in place, without reinforcements Louisbourg was doomed. Vaughan's "mad scheme," even if stolen from Bradstreet, was not so mad after all. It resulted in the greatest colonial victory of the French and Indian Wars in North America.

William Vaughan wrote to a friend after Louisbourg fell, "I have lived here in great bitterness of mind, and have cheerfully done my duty at the same time, despite those who chose to fret me. . . . " Although Vaughan did not say who was undermining him, it would appear that Waldo, Warren, and perhaps Pepperrell were key culprits. He hoped to sail to London bearing the momentous news, but was denied the opportunity. Instead, Vaughan had to travel to England in an unofficial capacity. His various requests for recognition and office, perhaps the governorship of Nova Scotia, did not get a sympathetic audience from King George II or his court.

In December, 1746, the man who had done more than any other to initiate the Louisbourg campaign, and who contributed so much to its success, died of smallpox, aged 48 and a bachelor.

11 •

"F-f-fire Away!"

A pril, 1775, was a time of high excitement in Falmouth. As the American colonies teetered on the verge of warfare with the mother country, tensions between Patriots and Tories in Maine's biggest town ran high, resulting in scenes like the following between General Jedediah Preble and the Tory Sheriff William Tyng:

> . . . Gen. P. said to Mr. T. it is talked that there will be a mob. They met Mr. O. (Oxnard), T. said to O. we are going to have a mob tonight: The Gen. denied that he said so. T. contradicted him and called him an old fool, and threatened he would chastise him if he were not an old man. The Gen. threatened to cane him or knock him down if he should repeat those

> words: then T. drew his sword and threatened to run him through. Then Preble collared and shook T.; afterward T. asked pardon of the Gen. and it was granted. The populace inquired if the Gen. was satisfied, and told him he should have all the further satisfaction he desired, but he desired nothing more.

Other, more serious, episodes agitated the good folk of Falmouth. When Captain Thomas Coulson, an outspoken Tory, made clear his determination to sell mast pine to the British, despite Patriot opposition, this proved irritating. But when Coulson invited a sloop of war to assist him in thumbing his nose at the Patriots, it was considered downright aggravating. On top of this came news of the "shot heard round the world" at Lexington.

There was talk in the town of about two thousand inhabitants of seizing the *Canceaux*, a vessel sent to protect Coulson's operation. More moderate Patriot leaders squelched any such move by their Falmouth cohorts, but they could not prevent zealous sorts in the countryside from entertaining similar plans.

Foremost among these firebrands was a short, squat man with a speech impediment, Colonel Samuel Thompson of Brunswick. However physically unimpressive, Thompson was a self-made man of great zeal who had already held a number of political posts, including selectman, militia leader, and member of the provincial congress. When he set his mind upon something, he was not to be deterred. When Enoch Freeman of Falmouth attempted to dissuade the pugnacious Thompson from trying to board and capture the *Canceaux*, he failed. Freeman was afraid of the warship's captain, Henry Mowatt. Mowatt, a veteran naval officer, was not a man to trifle with.

Nevertheless, Thompson with 50 men landed at Sandy Point on Falmouth Neck, near Munjoy Hill, on the evening of May 8, 1775. They encamped, hidden from view in a stand of trees, and posted some sentinels. About 1:00 P.M. the next day, Thompson's men saw Captain Mowatt, his ship's surgeon, and a local minister land and walk up the nearby hill. The party was immediately seized.

When news of the deed became known in Falmouth, community leaders petitioned Thompson to release his prisoners. The colonel replied that war had begun with Great Britain and providence had delivered Mowatt into his hands. After receiving delegations throughout the day, Thompson marched his prisoners to a tavern, accompanied by the local militia company. Excitement grew when the *Canceaux's* sailing master threatened to bombard the town if the prisoners were not released within two hours.

Colonel Thompson, when informed of this ultimatum, replied, "F-f-fire away! F-f-fire away! Every gun you fire, I will cut off a joint."

The British officer, with the unfortunate name of Hogg, did fire two blank shots. These "frightened the women and children to such a degree that some crawled under wharves, some ran down cellar, and some out of town," according to General Preble. "Such a shrieking scene was never before presented to view here." The leading men of Falmouth, who thought Thompson had acted in a most precipitous and ungentlemanly manner, continued to press him to free his prisoners. Fearing a rescue attempt, Colonel Phinney, of

Gorham, sent for his regiment. Before the next day dawned about six hundred militia from surrounding Gorham, Scarborough, Cape Elizabeth, and Stroudwater had poured into Falmouth.

By then Thompson had agreed to parole his prisoners, under the guarantee of General Preble and Colonel Freeman. Apparently he was impressed by the argument that a blockade of the harbor by the *Canceaux's* angry Hogg would deprive Falmouth of needed food supplies.

Mowatt, however, refused to abide by the parole, claiming he had been warned that he would be shot if he set foot ashore. Thompson and the militia were upset by this turn of events, and took out their frustrations on Preble and Freeman. They were not fed all day, and their children were not allowed to speak to them. That evening the two were freed in return for provision of bread, cheeses, and rum for the soldiers.

Falmouth was under military government. Leading Tories were harrassed by disorderly militiamen. A silver cup, tankard, and gold-laced hat belonging to Sheriff Tyng were pilfered from his house. Captain Coulson's house was used as a barrack, and two of his vessels were hauled through the streets. Coulson's cellar was emptied of its liquor. One Calvin Lombard wandered inebriated down to the waterfront. There he managed to load his musket, which he fired into the hull of the *Canceaux*.

This act of violence to his ship caused Mowatt to demand that Calvin be given over to him. He also called upon the citizens of Falmouth to expel the "mob from the country" and restore Coulson's boats. Otherwise he would open fire with his cannon, considerably more lethal than Calvin's musket. Mowatt was quickly assured that the disturbances were indeed the work of country types, whom the town could not control. On May 11 Colonel Freeman, chairman of the town's committee of safety, complained, "Good God! Give us a regular government or we are undone."

"We are in confusion," Freeman wrote in another letter to his son, a member of the provincial congress. And he held Samuel Thompson responsible. His was "a very imprudent action," one that might "bring on the destruction of the Town; for we can make no defense against a Man of War, and, undoubtedly, in short time there won't be a house standing here." Did congress give Thompson orders? The lack of anybody clearly in charge was making a bad situation worse. He implored congress to "give us directions, for we are in such confusion nobody seems to be rational."

Luckily for everybody's nerves, the invaders from the countryside melted out of Falmouth by May 13. When Colonel Phinney and Thompson attempted to give orders, they responded "we have obeyed them long enough, considering what we have got by it." A few days later, Mowatt also left.

Thus ended the curious episode known as "Thompson's War," but the political fallout continued.

Falmouth's committee of correspondence attempted to get the provincial congress to censure Thompson, writing "We think Colonel Thompson's attempt was rash and injudicious, if not unjustifiable. . . . " His intervention in an already tense environment created a situation that could have caused civil war. "We are afraid that if any number of men, at any time, and in any manner, may collect together and attack anything, or any person they please, everybody may be in danger," the committee concluded.

Congress responded by sending Brunswick's loose cannon a letter, which he refused to accept, stating, "Though the congress approves of your general zeal for this country, yet it appears that your conduct . . . is by no means justifiable. . . . " Congress asked Thompson to "stay all further proceedings of this kind in the mean time." A later committee did not even bother to slap his wrist, noting simply "Thompson's conduct was friendly to his country and the cause of liberty. . . . " Thompson was made a brigadier general in 1776 and given the authority to raise troops.

Thompson continued to play an active role throughout the war. Suspected enemies of the Revolution could expect harsh treatment, however prominent their social status. He was just as vigorous with friends of the revolution. When a regiment needed for service in the 1779 Penobscot Expedition did not assemble with the dispatch Thompson required, he growled, "If they will not go I will make the country hot for them." After the Revolution, Thompson served in a variety of political posts, serving as a delegate to the Massachusetts convention that considered ratification of the Constitution.

He did not think much of the proposed new government and was typically pungent in his criticism. "It is strange that a system, which its planners say is so plain that he that runs may read it, should want so much explanation," he observed. A staunch opponent of slavery, he was not adverse to lambasting the godlike Washington: "How he has immortalized himself, but he holds those in slavery who have as good right to be free as he has. He is still for self and in my opinion his character has sunk fifty per cent."

This was the man whose political philosophy may have been summed up when he said, "We cannot have too much liberty." He had a certain homespun eloquence:

> There are some parts of the Constitution which I cannot digest; and, sir, shall we swallow a large bone for the sake of little meat? Some say, swallow the whole now and pick out the bones afterwards. But I say, let us pick off the meat and throw the bone away.

Always controversial, Thompson made many enemies. Nonplussed by their reference to his lack of education, he replied, "If I have no education perhaps I can furnish some ideas to those who have." Despite his rustic appearance, his wit was sharp and his tongue sharper. A contemporary wrote, "The brigadier was of too fiery a temperament to be either appeased or softened, but went on continually hurling his gall-bladder invective against all who failed to come up to his measure of vehement demonstrations."

Thompson's private life was not happy. His wife was insane, and one of his sons mentally retarded. His business activities—he was an innkeeper and invested in real estate—fared well, but, typically, he was involved in many disputes.

Falmouth remembered Samuel Thompson.

On October 16, 1775, Captain Mowatt returned with five armed vessels.

The following day a letter was sent ashore informing the townspeople "you have been guilty of the most unpardonable rebellion" and his instructions were "to execute a just punishment on the town of Falmouth. . . ." The "human specie" were given a short interval in which to evacuate.

The bombardment lasted for 12 hours on October 18. By nightfall most of the town was in ashes. Mowatt was acting under orders from Admiral Samuel Graves, who had undertaken a policy of terrorizing coastal rebel communities. But many in Falmouth believed Mowatt enjoyed extracting revenge for the events of the previous May. They blamed Samuel Thompson.

12 •

When Scoundrels Were Heroes

Y oung Aaron Burr and his friend Matthias Ogden showed up at Washington's camp outside besieged Boston in July of 1775, armed with a letter of introduction from the president of the Continental Congress. They were "gentlemen of reputation," John Hancock wrote, who came "not as spectators but with a view of joining the army." The American commander-in-chief had a few other things on his mind beside finding military positions for New York aristocrats. Bored and not a little disgusted with the apparent disorganization and inertia that pervaded the camp, Burr became quite sick. He shook his fever off quickly, however, when Ogden mentioned a projected campaign against Quebec, to be led by the dashing, contentious Colonel Benedict Arnold. Burr volunteered.

His friends did not think his participation was wise. Dr. James Cogswell wrote that he was "extremely sorry to hear that you are determined on the new expedition to Quebec." The campaign was bound to be "very arduous" and would "unavoidably" involve "great hardship." Noting what he judged the "delicate" constitution of the slender Burr, barely five feet, six inches tall, the doctor implored him not to go:

> I have no friend so dear to me . . . but that I am willing to sacrifice for the good of the grand—the important cause, in which we are engaged; but, to think of a friend's sacrificing himself, without any valuable end being answered by it, is painful beyond expression. *You will die; I know you will die in the undertaking: it is impossible for you to endure the fatigue. . . .*

Another friend adopted a less anxious tone when it became clear the young man was not be be dissuaded. "The enterprise is glorious," Peter Colt wrote, "and, if it succeeds, will redound to the honour of those who have planned and executed it." In a lighter vein, he added: "Don't turn Catholic for the sake of the girls."

And what exactly was the "arduous" yet "glorious" expedition? Frustrated by the stalemate in Massachusetts and worried about a British thrust from Canada that could separate New England from the other states, Washington was attracted to the idea of a preemptive strike at Quebec. This could not be mounted by sea, and instead of taking the more obvious route via Lake Champlain and Montreal, Washington favored an expedition through the Maine wilderness. It would be supplemented by a simultaneous thrust at Montreal by an army that would then move up the St. Lawrence and rendezvous with the Maine force outside Quebec. Together, these armies would assault Great Britain's key stronghold in Canada. Success would dramatically alter the course of the war.

This was the kind of bold stroke that appealed to Colonel Benedict Arnold of Connecticut. A former druggist and horse trader, familiar with Quebec, the dark-visaged, stocky Arnold had played a key role in the capture of Fort Ticonderoga. He then became involved in bickering with other patriot leaders eager for glory. It was apparently partly to rid himself of the bitching Benedict and partly in recognition of the man's great ability that Washington chose Arnold to lead the 1,100-man force. The route was from Maine's Kennebec River, across the Dead River, and to the Chaudiere River leading to the bank of the St. Lawrence River opposite Quebec. On a map made by a British officer who made the passage in 1761, the various rivers were fairly easily hooked together by portages, making it a feasible invasion route. Aronold estimated it was about 180 miles and would take 20 days to cover.

The 19-year-old Burr refused a carriage and walked the 60 miles from Cambridge to Newburyport, where the army disembarked for the Kennebec River. When a messenger from his frantic guardian arrived, Burr blustered, "How do you expect to take me back, if I should refuse to go? If you were to make any forcible attempt upon me, I would have you hung up in ten minutes."

Eleven "dirty coasters and fish boats" transported the very seasick troops to Gardinertown, on the Kennebec, where one Reuben Colburn had contracted to provide bateaux for Arnold's force. The boats were smaller than expected and poorly built of green wood.

This time Burr took a carriage to Fort Western, upriver, the last inhabited point the expedition would encounter in Maine. Contrary to local legend, Burr was not the object of an Indian princess's attentions (a story later concocted to fit Burr's amorous reputation), but he was graciously entertained by the isolated fort commander's family. He lightheartedly wrote to his sister that he was "falling on roast chickens and wallowing, if you please, in a good feather bed." Aaron continued:

> But adieu to these soft Scenes. Tomorrow I transverse the woods. You would laugh heartily to see me accoutred in my traveling Dress. . . . Over

> a pr of Boots I draw a Pr of Woolen Trousers of coarse coating. A short
> double breasted Jacket of the same. Over this comes a short coat curiously
> fringed with a belt as curious. My blanket slung over my back as that's a
> thing I never trust from me. To these add a Tomahawk, Gun, Bayonet, etc.

This outfit was made complete by a "small round Hat with a snap-up
brim," which was surmounted by "a large Fox Tail with a black Feather curl'd
up together. The Donor I suppose meant to help my Deficiency in Point of
Size."

Burr was not exactly what Arnold had in mind; the call for volunteers
stressed woodsmen experienced with bateaux. But few of the volunteers met
that specification. The closest thing to real frontiersmen were the riflemen
from Pennsylvania and Virginia. The Virginian Daniel Morgan (originally from
New Jersey) was a six-foot, 200-pound veteran of the French and Indian War;
half his teeth had been blown away by an enemy bullet, and his back was
lacerated as the result of a whipping for striking a British officer. "That is the
doing of old King George," he told soldiers, inviting them to count the scars:

> While I was in his service, upon a certain occasion, he promised me 500
> lashes. But he failed in his promise and gave me 499, so he has been owing
> me one ever since. While the drummer was laying the lashes on my back
> I heard him miscount one. I was counting after him at the time. I did not
> think it worthwhile to tell him of his mistake and let it go.

Having marched six hundred miles from Virginia to Cambridge, Morgan
and his men were hardly intimidated by the prospect of a jaunt through the
Maine wilderness. His company spearheaded the troops that headed north
from Fort Western in late September.

Then things started going wrong. The shoddily constructed bateaux,
suitable for the more placid lower Kennebec, performed poorly on the
swifter, more treacherous upper reaches of the river. Soaked and bone-tired
after making a portage at steep Skowhegan falls, Arnold's men awoke on the
morning of October 2 encased in clothing "frozen a pane of glass thick."
Winter was approaching faster than the colonel had anticipated. By the time
his army reached the site of Father Rale's grave at Norridgewock, much of its
food—dried peas, cured beef, salt codfish—was spoiled due to water seepage,
and had to be discarded. As carpenters labored to patch up the warped
bateaux, soldiers cursed Reuben Colburn. (In fairness, he had been given
little time to build the flat-bottomed vessels, and they were not as suited to
wilderness waters as the canoe.) As a steady rain pelted the expedition,
sickness spread from drinking contaminated water. "No sooner had it got
down than it was puked up," the surgeon observed.

After slogging through mud sometimes waist-deep across the 12-mile
Great Carrying Place, they reached the meandering Dead River. Progress
became torture as the soldiers struggled up a stream clogged with roots and
jagged stumps. On October 21, a hurricane-force storm toppled trees and
made camping in the forest dangerous. That night the Dead River, swollen by
the downpour, belied its name with a vengeance, rising eight to 12 feet and
flooding the various encampments. Provisions and equipment were washed
away.

Short of provisions, the men were forced to dig roots, boil leather, and eat the dogs which accompanied the expedition. Captain Henry Dearborn's pet Newfoundland, a camp favorite, was one of the sacrifices. "They ate every part of him," Dearborn recalled, "not excepting his entrails; and after finishing their meal, they collected the bones and carried them to be pounded up to make broth for another meal."

On October 25, snow began mixing with the wind and rain. Arnold refused to falter, although he admitted in a letter sent to Washington two days later, "I have been much deceived in every account of our route, which is longer and has been attended with a thousand difficulties I never apprehended."

Arnold, in advance of his army, had crossed the height of land and was in Canada when he learned that Colonel Roger Enos, who had been bringing up the rear, was retreating, with about a third of Arnold's force, back to Massachusetts. He had ordered Enos to send back those too sick to continue. Unsuspecting, Arnold had written Enos from Chaudiere Pond on October 27, "I hope soon to see you in Quebec." As word of this stunning "defection" spread, Roger Enos replaced Reuben Colburn as the main object of blue language. Dearborn's men, for example, joined in "a General Prayer that Colonel Enos and all his men might die by the way, or meet with some disaster, Equal to the cowardly, dastardly, and unfriendly spirit" they showed.

Finally, on November 2, with his depleted force on Canada's Chaudiere River, Arnold secured food from French inhabitants. The cautious Canadians did not, however, rally to the American cause as the Continental Congress had, rather foolishly, expected. By November 9, Arnold was at Point Levis, on the opposite shore of the St. Lawrence River from Quebec. Within five days he managed to cross the river and begin the city's seige. "Had I been ten days sooner," he wrote Washington, "Quebec must inevitably have fallen into our hands, as there was not a man then to oppose us." Maybe. In fact, the British had twice as large a force to defend the fort as Arnold had to attack it. He advised Washington that Quebec could be taken with a force "which in my opinion cannot in the whole be less than two thousand five hundred, although it may possibly be effected with a less number."

Arnold awaited the arrival of General Richard Montgomery, who had taken Montreal. He dispatched Aaron Burr to Montgomery with a note reading:

> DEAR SIR—This will be handed you by Mr. Burr, a volunteer in the army and son to the former president of New Jersey college. He is a young gentleman of much life and activity, and has acted with great spirit and resolution on our fatiguing march. His conduct, I make no doubt, will be a sufficient recommendation to your favor.

Burr proved to be just the type of "gentleman" Montgomery wanted on his staff; he made the young man a captain and aide-de-camp. A New York artillery captain thought Montgomery's new aide appeared "juvenile in the extreme." But he had impressed Arnold and his comrades on the long march through the Maine woods. Few regular soldiers suspected that he was a *summa cum laude* college graduate, conversant in five languages, who enjoyed the challenge of philosophical treatises.

Montgomery only had 300 men and the combined American force was far short of the 2,500 men Arnold had considered necessary. Nevertheless, with only about eight hundred men, the assault was mounted, in a swirling blizzard, on New Year's Eve. Arnold attacked the lower town from the northeast. Montgomery's thrust was from the southwest. As rockets flared, church bells clanged the alarm, and musket fire rattled in the frigid dawn, Arnold was wounded in the foot and unable to press the attack. Daniel Morgan assumed leadership, penetrated the town, and hesitated, awaiting the arrival of Montgomery.

He never came. Breaking through a series of barricades, the general, with Aaron Burr and several aides at his side, approached a cottage which seemed undefended. Montgomery said to Burr, "We shall be in the fort in two minutes. . . . " But in the next second he was killed as gunfire erupted from the cottage. Burr, miraculously unscathed, urged the men behind him to forge ahead, but another officer ordered retreat. After a futile attempt, under fire, to drag the corpse of Montgomery from the frozen field, Burr also withdrew. He had behaved with great courage, but it was too little and too late. The assault died in the frigid first day of 1776.

Many years later, Daniel Morgan was asked his opinion of Arnold and Burr. He had known them intimately during the Quebec expedition. Morgan, the man of few words who had surrendered in the streets of the lower town, was precise. Arnold, he said, was the kind of man who would cut out the heart of anybody who stood in his way. Burr would smile, speak softly and reassuringly to his adversary, and, when he dropped his guard, slit his throat. In their different ways, they were dangerous men.

After Quebec, both gained infamy as men dangerous to the Republic. Arnold betrayed his country and ended the war fighting for the British. Burr killed Alexander Hamilton in a duel and was tried for conspiracy against the government he served as vice president. The reputations of both men were blackened. If they had died in the Maine woods or at Quebec's walls, they would be remembered differently.

Dr. Cogswell had been right about the expedition's hardship, while Burr's other friend was partially correct. Even though the effort failed, it was glorious. It was a time when future scoundrels were heroes.

Bad Time at Bagaduce

P aul Revere spent part of the summer of 1779 on the Maine coast, but the experience was not a happy one. He was an officer in the expedition Massachusetts sent to Penobscot Bay to dislodge an occupying British force at Majabagaduce. Commonly called simply Bagaduce by mariners, the bootlike peninsula on the bay's eastern shore was not far from the entrance of the Penobscot River. This was where old Fort Pentagoet and Baron Saint-Castin's habitation had been built; it remained strategically important. But the history made at Bagaduce in 1779 was not of the type emphasized in most accounts of the American Revolution. Here, an unparalleled disaster befell American arms. And the silversmith-Patriot's reputation was badly tarnished.

The son of French Huguenot Apollus Rivoire, born in Boston's north end in 1734, was a man on the rise when, in July of 1779, he was directed "to take command of the Train of Artillery to be employed in the present Expedition against the Enemy now invading the Eastern Parts of the State. . . . " A skilled artisan in silver and copper, the versatile Revere was also in the engraving business, sold hardware, and made dentures "of real Use in Speaking and Eating." A hyperactive Patriot, he drew effective political cartoons and acted as a courier for Boston's committee of correspondence. His excursions throughout the countryside on rented horses was a regular feature of the prewar period, mentioned even in London newspapers before his famous April, 1775, ride. A leader of his town's working class, Revere had close ties with upscale Patriots such as Samuel Adams and John Hancock. While the fighting at Lexington raged, it was Revere who performed the prosaic but vital task of removing a trunk filled with important correspondence Hancock had left in the village.

After Lexington and Concord, Revere performed a variety of tasks for the Patriot cause. Under the supervision of Maine's Sam Thompson, he designed and printed the first issue of Continental currency. The first official seal of the rebellious colonies, as well as that of the state of Massachusetts, were his handiwork. He busied himself drawing up lists of outlawed Loyalists, prodded Patriots to action, and commanded the garrison Castle William in Boston Harbor. All this was useful but rather dull. Revere wanted a real military command. Penobscot Bay beckoned as the arena for the glory the stocky, middle-aged New Man of the Revolution sought. No doubt he anticipated that military laurels might even gain him entry into Massachusetts' social elite.

In mid-June, 1779, a British force of about seven hundred troops, under the command of Brigadier General Francis McLean, sailed down from Halifax and seized Bagaduce. On the crest of a high, wooded ridge they started to dig, with paid local help, the breastworks of Fort George. Apprised of the situation, the general court of Massachusetts acted. Without consulting Continental authorities, they raised an army, assembled a fleet, and dispatched an expedition to the Penobscot within a month. The army was placed under the command of Brigadier General Solomon Lovell, a likeable and earnest farmer who lacked military experience; his subordinate, Adjutant General Peleg Wadsworth, had been battle-tested in the Continental Army. Lieutenant Colonel Paul Revere, placed in charge of artillery, was directed "to pursue such Orders as you may from time to time receive from the said Brigadier General Lovell or other of your superior Officers, during the Continuance of the said Expedition." (Interpretation of this council order became a key point in Revere's later troubles.) The naval force, which included the three brigs of the Massachusetts Navy, one New Hampshire state vessel, three Continental Navy Vessels, 12 armed privateers, and 19 transport and provision ships, was commanded by Commodore Dudley Saltonstall, a seasoned, apparently competent captain from the Continental Navy.

All this added up to an impressive-looking armada. General McLean estimated the Yankees had over three thousand soldiers. In fact 873 men had been scraped together, well short of 1,500 the general court wanted; Wadsworth, worried about their inexperience and lack of discipline, estimated a quarter of them were old men or boys. It was not the sort of army required. Nevertheless, hundreds of the raw troops swarmed ashore on Bagaduce's northern end on July 28 in the war's biggest amphibious operation. Scrambling across rocky beaches under heavy fire from wooded bluffs, the Yankees succeeded in driving the British from the heights. They dug in about six hundred yards from the low, unfinished breastwork of Fort George. Peleg Wadsworth recalled that "the action at our landing on Bagaduce might have been called brilliant, had the event of the Enterprise been fortunate. But let military men not talk of glory who lack the success."

At the time, McLean expected a follow-up assault:

> I was in no situation to defend myself. I meant only to give them one or two guns, so as not to be called a coward, and then to have struck my colours, which I stood by some time to do, as I did not wish to throw away the lives of my men for nothing.

But if McLean did not know the weakness of his opposition, Lovell was well aware of it. To storm Fort George successfully, he needed the fleet under Saltonstall to take possession of Bagaduce harbor. From there the American warships could neutralize the fort's guns. But the commodore, confronted by three British ships under Captain Henry Mowatt, refused to attack them with his overwhelmingly superior force. Mowatt, the same Mowatt who bombarded Falmouth, was an experienced seaman who probably knew Maine waters better than most Yankee captains. He guarded the entrance to the harbor with skill and tenacity. Yet Saltonstall possessed the firepower to brush him aside. He did not possess the will. "I am not going to risk my shipping in that damned hole," he said. This attitude reflected the concern of the privateers, more interested in resuming their forays against commercial shipping than in risking damage in a naval operation.

While an exasperated Lovell spluttered "any further delay must be infamous," delay was just what Saltonstall did. He said the land force should attack Fort George and silence its guns *first*. Then he would engage Mowatt. With neither man willing to move without the other, and a coordinated assault out of the question, the result was an ineffectual seige. This bought the British time to strengthen their defenses and hope for the arrival of reinforcements. An endless succession of American war councils came to no resolution except to fritter away valuable time. The problem remained the same. Lovell and Wadsworth wanted to attack, but Saltonstall continued to hide in his shell. Revere argued that the only realistic alternative to an assault was to withdraw and assume defensive positions to the westward. Instead the seige dragged on, with no formal plan for a strategic withdrawal, until word arrived from Boston: attack without further delay.

It was too late. As the Yankees prepared to move under cover of fog on August 13, the mists lifted to reveal the approach of a British relief squadron under Commodore Sir George Collier.* That did it. The Americans hastily evacuated their positions, including the guns Revere had positioned on Bagaduce and on a harbor island, piled into their ships, and beat a panicky retreat up the Penobscot. On August 14, a few British warships set out in pursuit. "To attempt to describe this terrible day," General Lovell scribbled, "is out of my power. It would be a fit subject for some masterly hand to describe it in its true colors, to see four ships pursuing seventeen Armed vessels, nine of which were stout ships. Transports on fire, Men of War blowing up . . . and as much confusion as can be conceived." The whole fleet was captured, or destroyed by the Americans themselves. The army, what was left of it, scattered into the Maine woods along the western shore of Penobscot Bay and the Penobscot River. The Americans later listed 150 casualties; according to Dr. John Calef, a Tory who resided at Bagaduce and observed the battle, there were 474 Americans killed, wounded, or captured.

One of the casualties would be Paul Revere's reputation. He raised eyebrows by arriving back in Boston weeks before his superior officers, and reassumed command of Castle William. Soon the magnitude of the fiasco on the Maine coast filtered back to Massachusetts. As if the military humiliation were not enough, the cost of the expedition had practically drained the state treasury. The time for blame-fixing was at hand, and, on September 9, the general court appointed a special committee to investigate the disaster. Complaints against Revere's conduct were lodged by Captain Thomas Carnes, commander of marines aboard the *General Putnam*. Colonel Revere was relieved of his command of the island fort.

Revere, informed of the charges against him by the council, sent a note to that body. "I feel the highest obligations to your honors for your candor to me when the popular clamor runs so strong against me," he wrote. "Had your

---

*Ironically, Collier had argued against British occupation of Bagaduce, which he called "so infernal a place."

honors shown as little regard for my character as my enemies have done," Revere added, "life would have been unsupportable." He requested the right to "meet my accusers face to face." This was granted by the investigative committee.

Revere's initial accuser had a number of complaints, specific and general. Captain Carnes charged that Revere had disobeyed the orders of superior officers on three occasions. The first time was during the landing on Bagaduce on July 28, when General Lovell ordered Revere to take some artillery ashore. The second instance was on the day the retreat began. Major William Todd of Lovell's staff ordered Revere to remove cannon from an island in the harbor; Revere allegedly refused, saying "his orders were, to be under the command of General Lovell during the expedition to Penobscot, and that the seige was ceased, and he did not consider himself under his command." The third act of disobedience, Carnes maintained, came during the retreat toward the Penobscot River, when Revere refused General Wadsworth's order to send his vessel, the Castle William barge, to bring ashore men from a schooner threatened by pursuing enemy ships.

This was not all. Carnes also charged Revere with "neglect of duty on several occasions, unsoldierlike behavior during the whole expedition . . . which tends to cowardice. . . . " and abandonment of his men during the retreat. In his appearance before the board of inquiry, Carnes indicated Revere was often absent from his men after the landing on Bagaduce, staying aboard his transport. According to Carnes, when Revere was present, he did little:

> I hardly ever saw him in the battery to give any orders. He would be in a breastwork, one or two hundred yards distance, to see where the shots struck. If a good shot, he would say so; if a bad one, he would say so: but never to give them any instructions about the guns. He directed several pieces himself, and I said then I thought it impossible that a colonel of artillery should make such a bad shot, and know no more about artillery.

Such testimony bordered on trivial and was weakened by the fact that, on most points, it was Carnes' word against Revere's. When General Peleg Wadsworth took the stand, his testimony was far more damaging. The crucial instance was that involving Revere and his boat. After recounting the difficulty he encountered getting aid to a schooner drifting with the tide toward the enemy on the evening of August 14, Wadsworth said:

> . . . In this, I was directly opposed to Lieu.-Colonel Revere, who said that I had no right to command either him or the boat, and he gave orders to the contrary. The boat went off to the schooner and Colonel Revere was promised an arrest as soon as the army should be collected. The reason Colonel Revere gave for the boats not going off to the schooner was that he had all his private baggage at stake and asked who would thank him for losing that in an attempt to save a schooner of the state. I asked him whether he came here to take care of his baggage or to serve the state?

Under questioning, the General also indicated that Revere had been slow, to say the least, in erecting batteries. Corroborating Carnes, Wadsworth said that Revere was practically invisible during the first week ashore at Bagaduce.

"I did not see him as frequently in camp as I expected," Wadsworth mused. "That was always on my mind." He further recalled that Revere invariably opposed him in councils of war, which meant he sided with the super-cautious Saltonstall.

On October 7 the committee issued its report. Its findings exonerated Generals Lovell and Wadsworth. It concluded that, if he had been furnished more men and received proper support from the fleet, Lovell "would probably have reduced the enemy." Wadsworth was praised for conducting himself "with great activity, courage, coolness, and prudence." The regular naval commanders "behaved like brave, experienced good officers," but the committee was conspicuously silent regarding the privateers' captains. The key reason for the campaign's failure: "Want of proper spirit and energy on the part of the Commodore." As a footnote, Colonel Paul Revere was censured for misconduct.

Dudley Saltonstall, as an officer in the Continental Navy, was not subject to Massachusetts' jurisdiction. The Navy, however, had ordered a court-martial to convene in mid-September. It never met. Saltonstall was dismissed from the Navy. He retrieved his reputation slightly as the successful captain of a privateer. "The command of a Fleet did not set easy upon his shoulders, tho' he could fight a very good Battle in a single Ship," Peleg Wadsworth reminisced almost a half-century after the Bagaduce disgrace.

For Paul Revere, the committee's report was unsatisfactory. He was neither condemned nor acquitted. He was, to paraphrase a later figure involved in scandal, left twisting in the wind. Unlike the hapless Saltonstall, Revere was not blamed for the expedition's failure. But the censure left a cloud over his reputation. He demanded that the case be reopened, promising "new" evidence on his behalf. On November 11, the committee complied, hearing testimony in the lobby of the State House.

The "new" evidence Revere presented his judges was a diary he had kept from July 21, when the expedition arrived at Townsend (Boothbay), Maine, until August 19, when Revere arrived at Fort Western on the Kennebec River enroute back to Boston. Perhaps the Colonel had started this to be a record of a glorious episode in his life. A rather matter-of-fact recitation, the pages of the diary portrayed Revere as a conscientious officer who dutifully obeyed commands. In reference to the scene of the colorful exchange described by Wadsworth, Revere simply wrote, "I got most of my men together in the edge of the wood, but while my boat was getting some men from a schooner . . . I was separated from them (all but two officers and eight men) they taking into the woods." Revere then went up the river searching for his men; not finding them, he headed west through the woods himself.

Other witnesses testified in support of Revere's account of his activity during the retreat. His cousin, Philip Marrett, recalled Revere passing "the Ship Sky Rocket a little after Sundown Capt. Bush Ask'd him to come on board & Drink some grog he told him he could not stop for he was trying to collect his men."

In a lengthy letter to the committee, Revere attempted to refute the various charges. He claimed that Major Todd, who had previously served under him at Castle William, bore a personal grudge and sought to destroy him. He reminded General Ward that Todd had made allegations about his conduct to the General in the past, which he failed to substantiate, regarding misuse of rations. This man was then appointed to General Lovell's staff. "Your Honors must be sensible what a situation I was in, with such an inveterate enemy in the General's family." That Captain Carnes was likewise out to get him was intimated, although, on the record, the motive is not made clear. Revere concluded:

> That I did go up the river has been fully proved. That I came home without orders is true. Where could I have found the General or Brigadier, if it had been necessary to have gotten orders? The first went 100 miles up Penobscot River*, and the other down, and I crossed the woods to Kennebec River. My instructions from the Hon'ble Council . . . direct that I shall: "obey General Lovell, or other my superior officer . . . during the Expedition." Surely no man will say, that the Expedition was not discontinued, when all the shipping was either taken or burnt; the Artillery and Ordnance stores all destroyed. I then looked upon it that I was to do what I thought right. Accordingly, I ordered . . . my men to Boston by the shortest route. . . .

Having appealed to the committee "to determine what is more dear to me than life—my character," Revere was not pleased by its second report on November 16, 1779. It found his conduct "critizable" in his August 14 dispute with General Wadsworth "respecting the boat." The committee also found his action, in leaving the scene of the disaster without orders, "not wholly justifyable." One other junior officer, Colonel Jonathan Mitchell of Yarmouth, Maine, was also censured for his behavior during the retreat.

During the next few years, Revere repeatedly requested a full court-martial to clear his name. In January, 1780, the council refused to act, partly for fear of additional scandal being dredged up. But in March, after being bombarded by many letters and petitions from Revere, it appointed members of a court to convene in April. For reasons unknown, the court never met. Revere persevered, making a total of six different petitions to the general court. Finally, in February 1782, a court-martial was ordered and convened. Considering the years of foot-dragging that preceded it, the speed with which the court acted was remarkable. Although numerous other accusations were made against Revere by over 30 fellow officers, only the two charges upon which he was censured in 1779 were considered.

With testimony completed, the court immediately issued its report. It was approved at once by the man who had ordered the court convened, Governor John Hancock. It read:

> Colonel Revere, having closed his defence, The Court, after maturely deliberating on the whole evidence, proceeded to make up judgement.

> The Court finds the first charge against Lt. Col. Paul Revere to be supported, (to wit) his refusing to deliver a certain boat to the order of General Wadsworth when upon the retreat up Penobscot over from Majabigwaduce;

---

*General Lovell explained that he had gone up the Penobscot to negotiate with the Indians. They did not switch sides at this crucial juncture, certainly a major concern of Lovell.

but, the Court, taking into consideration the suddeness of the refusal, and more especially that the same boat was in fact employed by Lt. Col. Revere to effect the purpose ordered by the General, as appears in the General's disposition, are of the opinion, that Lt. Colonel Paul Revere be acquitted of his charge.

On the second charge, the Court considers that the whole army was in great confusion, and so scattered and dispersed, that no regular orders were or could be given, are of the opinion, that Lt. Colonel Revere, be acquitted with equal honor as the other officers in the same expedition.

So, with the Revolutionary War drawing to a close, Paul Revere was acquitted of charges stemming from his role in one of the war's worst fiascos. Many contemporaries believed the verdict reflected a desire of the authorities to close the book on the whole affair. They suspected John Hancock and his friends had repaid their political debt to their former servant.

Paul Revere's business career grew with the eclipse of his political popularity. In 1788 he opened a foundry which produced copper and brass bells and, befitting his former command, cannon. In 1801 he established a copper-rolling factory which supplied the U.S.S. *Constitution*'s copper sheathing and plated boilers for one of Robert Fulton's steam ferries. He died in 1818, a respected entrepreneur.

But he also left behind a tarnished military reputation. Perhaps understandably, he was reticent to discuss his Revolutionary past. When the historian Jeremy Belknap elicited an account of the April, 1775, ride to Lexington, Revere signed his modest recollection "A Son of Liberty." Belknap did not honor his desire for anonymity, but it was not until the 1861 publication of "The Midnight Ride of Paul Revere" in *Atlantic Monthly* that the silversmith-Patriot's fame was assured. A stirring, if rather inaccurate, poem, "The Midnight Ride" was aimed at inspiring men to join the Union Army. Paul Revere became the ultimate example of the patriot in his nation's hour of need:

Through all our history, to the last
In the hour of darkness and peril and need,
The people will waken and listen to hear
The hurrying hoof-prints of that steed,
And the midnight message of Paul Revere.

The poem made Paul Revere immortal. And its author was the grandson of General Peleg Wadsworth, who asked the real Paul Revere such a devastating question about baggage and service to the state on the retreat from Bagaduce.

14 •

Execution at Limestone Hill

A fter the Penobscot fiasco, the rest of Maine was more vulnerable than ever. The general court of Massachusetts gave the task of defending Maine to Brigadier General Peleg Wadsworth. Wadsworth was the only officer to emerge from the Bagaduce campaign with an enhanced reputation. In March, 1780, he was promised command of 600 militia and granted the power to declare martial law in Lincoln County. As he later wrote, "An Awful Power this, unless exercised with wisdom & Discretion." Within four months of his arrival at his Thomaston headquarters, Wadsworth would demonstrate just how awful his power was.

His daughter Zilpah, mother of poet Henry Wadsworth Longfellow, remembered her father as a well-proportioned man, "with a military air," who carried himself "so truly, that many thought him tall." Born in Duxbury, he entered Harvard at 17 and, four years later, having made amends for involvement in a student strike, he "received the usual honors of the Institution." With his Harvard roommate he "kept a private School in the old Town of Plymouth & fitted a number of Scholars for College & some for the Army—as I mixed the military as well as the Civil. At the end of my School I had one of the prettiest companies of Boys, perhaps that there was existing."

Peleg was an ardent Patriot. In a protest against Harvard's investment of theTory Thomas Hutchinson as governor of Massachusetts, he thundered "Show me the Man . . . in the Government of the College that is not rank Torrey, if anything. That will not cringe and bow and fawn and flatter in hopes of Some detestable Preferment, and to serve their own selfish Ends. . . . " In 1772 Wadsworth married Elizabeth Bartlett, a "lady of fine manners and womanly virtues," and they settled down in Kingston. Peleg opened a store and tried his hand at business. He also remained active in politics as captain of a minuteman company.

When the Revolution began, Wadsworth joined the army besieging Boston, first as an engineer and later as an aide de camp to General Artemas Ward. He played a key role in the fortification of Dorchester Heights, which led to the British withdrawal in 1776. The next year, he served in the Massachusetts House of Representatives; in 1778 he was made adjutant general and participated in skirmishes with the British in Rhode Island. And in 1779, as we have seen, he conducted himself honorably, if unsuccessfully, at Penobscot.

This, then, was the sort of man sent to defend Maine in the spring of 1780. He arrived at Falmouth on April 8. Finding the fort in a shambles and no soldiers in sight, he hastened up the coast (or down, in proper Maine English) to Camden. Here he found some troops, although fewer than he expected, gathering under the command of Colonel Benjamin Burton of Cushing.

The British were close and many local inhabitants, if not outright British sympathizers, were more than willing to trade with the enemy. "There is frequent and fresh Intelligence from the Enemy by means of the Intercourse kept up by many of the Inhabitants," the general noted. Without many soldiers, "I have not yet proclaim'd the Martial Law, nor does it seem expedient; til the arrival of the Troops and Boats, least the Game should be started before we are ready for the Chase."

One of the most annoying tactics of the British at Castine was their promotion of attacks by Tory privateers in vessels commonly called "shaving mills." These were large open boats manned by a half dozen or more men that roamed the indented coast, attacking shipping or launching sudden forays ashore.

Just how insecure the situation was is illustrated by the experience of Colonel Mason Wheaton. A lime sloop owned by Wheaton was grabbed by tories off Harpswell. A small schooner filled with Patriots from New Meadows gave chase and recaptured Wheaton's sloop. It was subsequently taken again by Tories, who sailed it to Castine.

Wadsworth, headquartered in Colonel Wheaton's home in Thomaston, proclaimed martial law along the Lincoln County coast (and ten miles inland) as soon as he had enough troops to exercise some military authority. He wanted to dampen loyalist activity and isolate the British at Castine. The general therefore proclaimed a line extending from Owl's Head across Penobscot Bay to the opposite mainland, beyond which no American vessel should venture. To stop Tory incursions and trading with the enemy was a tall order for a command that usually counted but a few hundred men.

Under martial law, the military had the authority to arrest any individuals of doubtful loyalty and try them by military tribunals. These tribunals could impose the death penalty. Despite the proclamation of this power, the situation did not improve appreciably. As Wadsworth recalled:

> However terror by proclamation soon began to loose effect, & small parties finding aid and encouragement from the Tories, soon began to be less cautious & the Tories really seemed to gain courage from indulgence & to be less secret in harbouring these Parties of the Enemy till at last it began to be more unsafe for a Whig than a Tory. . . .

A raiding party killed a Patriot in Broad Bay (Waldoboro), wounded his wife, and pillaged his home. This act caused Wadsworth to issue another proclamation, promising execution for the next person apprehended and convicted of aiding the enemy. That person turned out to be a dull-witted fellow named Jeremiah Braun, who lived near Damariscotta and was picked up and charged with guiding a British party into the backcountry. On August 23, Braun was tried by a court-martial convened at Wadsworth's headquarters. He was found guilty of aiding the enemy and sentenced to death by hanging.

The death sentence was not taken seriously by local inhabitants, many of whom considered Braun stupid but not malicious in his action. His sentence was viewed "as only a feint to frighten him and prevent a repetition of the crime." A number of well-known Patriots requested a pardon.

But, despite local opinion, Peleg Wadsworth was not playing games. A gallows was constructed on nearby Limestone Hill. According to local tradition, "the limb of an old pine tree was used as a substitute."

> To this, in a cart drawn by oxen . . . and in presence of the military and a few spectators, the miserable man was conducted; fainting and, as described by an eye-witness, "more dead than alive" from fear. In this situation, Mr. Coombs, who was standing near, was asked to lend his handkerchief to tie over the prisoner's eyes. Supposing it a farce, he complied; and the prisoner, to appearance already dead, was swung off to the astonishment of the spectators. . . .

Wadsworth was reportedly "greatly moved" by the deed, and was seen pacing about his room "in apparent agitation" throughout the succeeding day. Patriots were perhaps more shocked than Tories. As the local historian of Thomaston later wrote, "Many friends of the revolution regretted that such an example of severity, however necessary, should fall on such a victim." Wadsworth would always feel his harshness was proper and useful in the circumstances. "This Act of severity tho' painfull in the highest degree proved salutary," he recalled in 1828, "for there was not found another Instance of this kind, & People began to realize the sentiment that Lenity to an Enemy was cruelty to Friend. . . . "

But there is no evidence that the execution achieved the deterrent effect Wadsworth claimed. Indeed, he later found it necessary to condemn another offender, Nathaniel Palmer. Palmer was able to escape from Wadsworth's barn, where he was imprisoned awaiting execution.

Tory and British depredations continued, and martial law proved unpopular with Patriots, who often succeeded in getting the general court to overturn Wadsworth's actions. The major problem was a lack of sufficient force; lacking that, Wadsworth resorted to terror with limited results.

For many years Limestone Hill, just beyond the little town of Thomaston, had been worked for lime. Later it would become the site of the Maine State Prison.

But in 1780 it achieved another kind of fame as the site of the only military execution in Maine history.

• 15

The Further Perils of Peleg

B y January, 1781, at the age of 32, Peleg Wadsworth was again a general without an army. In August he had commanded a force of 552 men in posts stretching from Falmouth to Machias. As 1780 drew to a close, that army—hardly adequate to defend Maine to begin with—evaporated. Enlistments expired. Many men had to be discharged for lack of clothing or proper diet; for months the militia subsisted on fish from the rivers. Wadsworth was not even notified when the Falmouth garrison disbanded. Frustrated, he informed Governor Hancock that his command had dwindled to a few dozen men. Maine was open to the enemy. The general, who lived in Thomaston with his wife Elizabeth, two young children, and a Miss Fenno, a family friend, prepared to leave for Boston.

But the British at Bagaduce, learning of his vulnerability, had other plans. A raiding party of 25 men was sent. The Tory Waldo Dicke acted as pilot, of the privateer that crossed Penobscot Bay to capture Wadsworth. Landing below Thomaston on the frigid night of February 18, 1781, they quickly crossed snow-covered fields to reach their destination. Taking advantage of the hilly terrain, the raiders were upon the small house before being detected.

Hearing the crunch of snow breaking under their tread, sentinel William Boggs called, "Who comes there?" He was quickly overpowered. Contrary to instructions, the handful of militia using Wadsworth's kitchen as a guardhouse opened the door, allowing the British to fire a volley through it and rush in. Other soldiers shot out the windows of the General's bedroom, and a third group forced its way through the windows of the room Miss Fenno and the children occupied. Half-dressed, Elizabeth Wadsworth ran to Miss Fenno's room. This left only General Wadsworth not in British hands. And Peleg meant to make them pay dearly for him.

Equipped with a small arsenal of two pistols, a blunderbuss, and a fusee, Wadsworth repeatedly beat off the soldiers' attacks. When he had discharged all his weapons, he resorted to a bayonet. Finally, one of the British in the kitchen, spotted the general's white linen nightshirt in the darkness, and shot Pegleg in his left arm. Only at this point did Wadsworth surrender.

The order to cease fire was issued by the British commander, a Lieutenant Stockwell, but the soldiers in the kitchen ignored it. Unbarring and opening his door, Wadsworth asked, "My brave fellows, why do you fire after I have surrendered?"

One of the troops who rushed into the room was badly wounded. "You have taken my life," he swore, "and I will take yours." Sticking his musket barrel against Wadsworth's chest, he was about to squeeze the trigger when the gun was knocked aside by his commanding officer.

A moment later another officer arrived and illuminated the scene with a candle procured from Miss Fenno's room. The floors were bloodstained and covered with shattered glass. "Sir, you have defended yourself too well," the Englishman said. "You have done too much for one man. You must excuse haste. Shall we help you on with your clothes? You see, we are in a critical situation." He dressed hastily, his wounded arm making it impossible to wear a coat. Elizabeth Wadsworth threw a blanket over her husband's shoulders while Miss Fenno bound a handkerchief tightly about his arm to stem the loss of blood.

Then the prisoner was hustled off into the bitter cold night. The British were afraid their presence would be detected, drawing out armed patriots. As it was, the inhabitants did not hear the gunfight; the general's house was isolated from the center of town. Bleeding heavily, Peleg expressed doubt he would get far. Luckily, the coldness of the evening congealed the blood. Leaving one of their wounded at a farmhouse along the way, and releasing another poor soul captured along the way, the raiding party and its prisoners* finally reached the privateer moored offshore. The captain of that vessel, angered by the sight of some of his wounded men, berated Wadsworth for daring to fire on the king's troops. With threats he ordered the wounded man to help shove off the launch.

Calmly saying this was not possible, Peleg refused.

At this point the commander, Lieutenant Stockwell again intervened on the American officer's behalf. The prisoner was a gentleman who had made a brave defense, he said, and should be treated with all due respect. The captain's rudeness would be brought to the attention of General Campbell at Bagaduce. And that was that.

Driven by an icy north wind, the privateer bore the suffering Wadsworth across the bay. Meanwhile, back in Thomaston, Mrs. Wadsworth and Miss Fenno had to contend with hordes of gawking neighbors, who crowded into the devastated house. "Here they did nothing but gaze about with an idle curiosity, or make useless, numerous, and very troublesome inquiries. Scarcely anything could be more wearisome, or more provoking," one chronicler observed.

Incredibly, General Wadsworth's son Charles, aged five, had slept through the whole attack. Wadsworth, however, did not know this. He had seen his baby daughter, also named Elizabeth, before leaving but was worried that his little boy was not in sight. Had he been killed? Troubled by such thoughts, Peleg arrived at Bagaduce at the end of what must have been for him a very long day.

He did not get an especially friendly reception from the inhabitants. Many of the spectators who crowded the shore were Loyalists, including a number

---

*Accounts of Wadsworth's capture mention another American soldier, also wounded and taken prisoner. What became of this man is not made clear.

of refugees from other parts of the country. Indeed, there were plans to make eastern Maine a haven for displaced supporters of Great Britain, to be called "New Ireland," with its capital at Bagaduce. Thus a chorus of jeers and epithets greeted the arrival of the man who had done his best to thwart the loyalist cause. Wadsworth was relieved to be placed under guard by British soldiers in Fort George.

The irony of ending up in the fort he had, in the summer of 1779, tried so hard to take by force could not have escaped Peleg Wadsworth. General Campbell and his staff treated him as a fellow professional. The British general was the very model of civility, making sure Wadsworth's wound was treated by a surgeon, inviting the American to breakfast, letting him walk about the fort's parade ground, and providing him with books to pass the time. He even made the captain of the privateer apologize for his behavior.

Yet Peleg remained a prisoner. Letters were dispatched, under a flag of truce, to Camden, and there sent to his wife and Governor Hancock. He was relieved to learn that his family, including little Charles, was safe and sound. "I am extremely afflicted at the idea of your situation," he had written his wife. "The windows dashed, the Doors broken, the House torn to pieces and Blood and Slaughter around. . . . " Like the survivor of an accident, he must have relived the scene endlessly. About two months after his capture, Mrs. Wadsworth and the redoubtable Miss Fenno were allowed to visit Bagaduce.

They were escorted by Major Benjamin Burton, who had been under Wadsworth's command at Camden. A native of Cushing, Burton had, during a visit to Boston in 1773, joined the gang of Patriots tossing British tea in the harbor. When the Revolutionary War began, he served as an officer in the Continental Army for several years before, serving for nine months under Wadsworth. Discharged just a few days before the general's capture, he was eager to see his old chief. Whether or not they had the opportunity to discuss an escape during the ladies' visit is unrecorded. Wadsworth was hoping that a prisoner exchange could be worked out.

Miss Fenno, making use of an officer's attraction for her, learned that the British had no intention of allowing such a trade. Instead, they meant to transfer the general to Halifax or New York. When, after a ten-day sojourn, the women were about to depart, Miss Fenno whispered, "General Wadsworth, take care of yourself."

He got her meaning. A few days later, Peleg was told a parole was out of the question. General Campbell, apparently reflecting new orders, became markedly cooler toward Wadsworth. From the servants who still attended him, he learned that he was to be sent to England, "as a rebel of too much consequence to be safely trusted with his liberty."

In mid-April Wadsworth acquired a roommate: Major Burton. After accompanying Mrs. Wadsworth and Miss Fenno to Boston, he had been apprehended by the enemy on his return off Monhegan. Burton learned, from what he overheard from his captors, that the British commander was awaiting the return of a privateer, which would transport them to London. If any further proof were required, the preemptory refusal of the British to consider a proposal for Wadsworth's exchange from Governor Hancock was final confirmation of what the future held.

Reunited they immediately began plotting their escape. Wadsworth had developed a good idea of the fort's layout. It was a more formidable structure than the one he had confronted from the outside in 1779. Now it had higher walls, a ditch with *chevaux-de-frise* and guardhouses. Wadsworth and Burton hatched a plan which required that they first make a hole in the ceiling they could climb through. They would then exit the building through the space between the roof and ceiling joists, passing over the adjacent officers' rooms, and lower themselves into an entryway by using blankets. Then they would proceed to the walls, make their way to the north bastion, climb over the parapet, and jump into the ditch, being careful not to impale themseves on the pointed pickets of the *chevaux-de-frise*. Once out of the fort, they would proceed to a nearby cove that bordered the narrow neck of land connecting Bagaduce peninsula to the mainland of Penobscot Bay's eastern shore. Proceeding north toward the Penobscot River, the two men would cross it and head westward to freedom.

For a dollar, the prisoners managed to obtain a gimlet from their barber. It is said that this fellow, named Barnabas Cunningham, had no suspicion that the gimlet "was intended for anything more than amusement."

The American prisoners set about amusing themselves the way prisoners usually do with such an instrument. They bored holes in the ceiling board. This kind of activity required keeping a very close watch on the sentries who paced back and forth before their door, which had a window they could peer through. They could thus bore in snatches of only a few seconds at a time. For the shorter Wadsworth, this was a problem; the six-and-a-half-foot tall Burton ended up doing most of the furtive drilling. Wadsworth swept the telltale shavings into their fireplace.

After three weeks a rectangular series of holes were bored. The interstices were cut with a penknife, leaving the corners intact to hold the board in place. The work was disguised by stuffing a paste made from chewed bread into the perforations. The prisoners anxiously waited for an evening of sufficiently bad weather to cover the noise of removing the board and crawling above the ceiling. A week passed without an opportunity. Time was running out. The privateer might arrive any day.

Another problem developed: Butter, inadvertently mixed in the bread paste, melted in the summer heat, discoloring the wall about the drilled board. Fortunately, their captors were not particulary observant.

On the evening of June 18, a violent thunderstorm was followed by torrential rain. Snuffing their candle, Wadsworth and Burton pretended to retire, but were almost instantly up and clothed. In the darkness Burton expended an hour cutting the corners of the ceiling board with his penknife. Once it was removed, he clambered through the opening. It was not easy. There was considerable noise, masked by the beating of the rain, which also muffled the cackling of roosting birds Burton disturbed as he proceeded over the joists.

The shorter Wadsworth, further hampered by his weak left arm, barely managed to make it through the hole. By the time he succeeded, he was unable to find his companion. The entry door was ajar and, guessing that

Burton had already left, the general passed through it. In the rain and pitch blackness he picked his way about the walls to the north bastion.

Suddenly the sergeant of the guard boomed, "Relief; turn out."

Wadsworth heard a scrambling noise nearby. He thought it was Burton. The rain, however, kept the sentinels in the guard houses oblivious to the sound. Wadsworth himself swung over the parapet and avoided being tripped over by the approaching relief. He used his blanket to lower himself into the *chevaux-de-frise*. Once he was certain the soldiers had gone around the wall and out the fort's gate to relieve the sentinels, Peleg crept out of the ditch. He sneaked past the guard into an open field.

Crossing the open space, Wadsworth encountered a maze of rocks, stumps, and brush, which he stumbled through in the drenching rain and darkness, ultimately reaching a spot where he and Burton had agreed to rendezvous if separated. But the major failed to materialize. Wadsworth made his way to the cove. It was low tide and he was able to wade about a mile to the opposite shore. Here he briefly followed a road; then he was back in the woods.

By dawn he had reached the eastern bank of the Penobscot River. The rain had ended and Wadsworth could hear reveille sounding from Fort George. Soon his absence would be noted. He continued to wade along the water's edge, making sure no tracks would be left for the British bloodhounds. Neither did he wish to be spotted by local inhabitants; he was well aware of the Loyalist sentiment on this side of the river.

The sun helped dry his clothes. Locating a canoe, the general was wondering whether its owner was nearby and friendly when another figure approached. It was Benjamin Burton.

After greeting his friend, Wadsworth learned his story. Burton had assumed the general was unable to negotiate the hole in their cell's ceiling. He proceeded on alone and was surprised at the wall by the sergeant's cry. Believing he had been discovered, he leaped over the parapet, falling upon a *cheval-de-frise* containing four, rather than six, sets of pickets. This was lucky: otherwise, Burton would have landed upon some of their points and been killed. Like Wadsworth, he had hugged the shore, wading through bone-cold water choked with slippery seaweed.

The British dispatched a barge filled with troops to search for the escapees. Eluding it, Wadsworth and Burton paddled to the western shore. Unwilling to risk contact with anyone, they fled into the woods. The next day, after stopping briefly in Canaan (Lincolnville), the men again headed into the thick forest, aiming for the headwaters of the St. George River. Burton's pocket compass proved invaluable. They ate scraps of food they had saved while imprisoned and stuffed in their pockets. Wadsworth, much less used to wilderness travel, lagged behind, but Burton did not leave the weakened general. The forest was sweltering by day, but nights were frigid.

By the end of the third day, they reached the Upper Settlement (Warren) on the St. George River. Encountering friendly Patriots, Wadsworth was taken to an inn not far from the house where he had been captured in February.

As anticipated, the British sent out a party to recapture them. Burton, heading for his Cushing home, would have been taken if he had not been protected by an armed guard. He only spent one night in his fortlike stone house. The next day he was off to Boston. Unable to fill a vacancy in the Continental Army, he joined the Navy. In October, 1781, the ship he served on was captured by the British off Ireland, where he was imprisoned until the following February. Removed to confinement in England, he was released and made the long journey home by way of France. Arriving in New London, Connecticut, with eight shillings in his pocket, he was back in Maine by the end of May. He settled down to farming, was a lieutenant-colonel in the militia, and held various local offices. He later became a deacon of the Warren Baptist Church.

The perils of Peleg ended earlier. In the summer of 1781 he returned to his family in Massachusetts. But Maine drew him back in 1784, and he built Portland's first brick house. Active for many years in Maine business and politics, he finally retired to a mansion in "the mountains of Hiram." His daughter Zilpah became mistress of the brick house in Portland; her husband was one Stephen Longfellow, and one of their children was named Henry Wadsworth. He always was a bit in awe of his grandfather.

16 •

Sam Ely vs. the Hideous Monster

T his is the story of the feud between Henry Knox and Sam Ely—and its abrupt, strange conclusion. Major General Henry Knox was a very big man, shaped like the mortars he commanded during the Revolution. He had a penchant for doing things on the grand scale. When he and his family assumed official residence at the imposing mansion he had built in Thomaston in 1795, he invited everybody in the area to a mansion-warming reception. "We had a small company on the Fourth of July of upwards of five hundred people!" he enthused in a letter to a friend. Most of the folks who partook of the general's hospitality that summer day were curious to see the man whose presence many considered a boon to the economic development of Downeast.

But not everybody was of like mind. Sam Ely of Ducktrap (now Lincolnville) urged resistence to the man he called the "Unmasked Nabob" and "a Hideous

Monster." As opposition to Knox mounted, there was talk of assassinating the general and burning his house, *Montpelier*.

Neither man was born in Maine, but both were drawn to Massachusetts' frontier district after the war. By that time, Maine was experiencing a minor land boom. Knox and Ely represented opposite extremes. Knox's ambition was to build an empire, while Ely, with a different vision of the future, meant to thwart him. They did not come to Maine to fight, but it was inevitable that they would be antagonists. They were two very different products of the Revolution.

Henry Knox, a humble bookseller in Boston at the outset of the Revolution, had risen—through a combination of personality, innate ability, and sheer opportunism—to a position of power in the new Republic. A close friend of George Washington, a man not noted for easy intimacy, Knox served as the Virginian's right-hand man throughout the Revolution. Later, he was Washington's first secretary of war. His huge size, which only increased as he grew older, imparted a hog-like image, complete with low forehead, massive jowls, beady eyes, and understandably bowed legs. By the time he came to Maine, the general weighed well over three hundred pounds. Knox's obesity was compensated for by a quick wit and a bluff, good-natured personality. Well-read and skilled at polite conversation, Knox could shine in upper-class salons, while his expansive, down-to-earth approach, sprinkled with colorful profanity, made him equally formidable in dealing with ordinary people. Despite his appearance, Knox was intellectually agile, perhaps even slippery.

After spending most of his adult life on the government payroll, Knox sought to build a fortune for himself and his brood. Friendly with big-time speculators like William Duer, who ended up in debtor's prison, and Senator William Bingham of Pennsylvania, reputedly the richest man in America, the general likewise gambled in land speculation. Beginning in 1785, he utilized his influence with the Massachusetts legislature to gain recognition of his rights to control of the old Waldo patent in Maine. Building upon the quarter interest he had through his wife (the daughter of Thomas Flucker, a royal official of Massachusetts who married old Samuel Waldo's daughter), Knox, by a series of tricky legal maneuvers, gained control over most of the patent from the other Waldo heirs. The land stretched from Waldoboro to the site of Bangor (or most of present-day Knox and Waldo counties). He hoped to attract more settlers to the region and develop its many resources, including lumbering, lime production, livestock-raising, and agriculture. Apparently he intended to emulate the lifestyle of the Virginia gentry and Philadelphia aristocracy he had long associated with. The pretentious, two-storied, 19-room *Montpelier* reflected this. Knox did nothing in a small way. It is recorded that he employed up to 103 workmen on his various projects.

No doubt he was a character. The booming voice that issued commands to troops crossing the Delaware River to attack Trenton now echoed down Thomaston's sparsely settled streets. Dressed wholly in black, including a silk handkerchief to cover a mangled left hand (which Knox continually wound and unwound while conversing),* and armed with a walking cane,

---

* Knox had lost two fingers as the result of a prewar hunting accident.

Knox was always an imposing figure. Anecdotes about the general soon proliferated. One involved a "very rough, uncouth man" from New Canaan (Northport), who traveled to Thomaston to settle title to his holdings with Knox. "My name is Calef," he informed Knox. "Allen Calef, some call it Calph, but it isn't. It's Calef." The general facetiously replied, "Calef, Calph, calf, it isn't calf the son of a cow is it?" "No," the fellow punned back, "but I've know many an ox that was." This response so tickled the proprietor that he wined and dined Mr. Calef. Another story is more revealing:

> One of his townsmen was liable to a peculiar convulsive affection of his jaws, which frequently, especially when a little excited, would set his mouth wide open in the midst of a conversation with no power to close it again or speak for some time. On one occasion in his eagerness to get a hearing on some business matters with Knox, this affection manifested itself with extraordinary pertinancy. The General, witnessing the phenomenon, and growing impatient of its continuance, at length put an end to it by thrusting the head of his cane into the man's mouth, begging his pardon, and adding, "I thought I must *shut up your mouth*, in some way;—if I couldn't with money."

If such antics endeared him to the local folk, it was another story with Lady Knox (who was almost as fat as the general). She made no secret of her dislike of frontier life. On one occasion, while the general was absent, she leveled a small cemetery because its presence on *Montpelier's* grounds displeased her. This indiscretion so upset Knox, that he reputedly pulled hair from his head. The transition from salon to backcountry was not possible for the granddaughter of Samuel Waldo. The reports of Knox's bickering with Lucy—whom he still loved dearly, and by whom he had twelve children— actually enhanced his own standing. This is reflected in a local story about Knox's response when some townsmen, intending to scare the general while he was skating on the St. George River one winter evening, accosted him garbed in sheets. Knox called out, "Who are you and what do you want? If you are angels you won't hurt me; if you are men, I never feared the face of man yet; and if you are devils come right home with me, I married your sister."

But all was not good-natured accommodation with Knox's Maine venture. His difficulties stemmed partly from his tendency to bite off more financially than he could chew. He was always teetering on the edge of bankruptcy, and this did little to reassure settlers. Then there was another problem and, like everything about Knox, it was a big one. Many of those who settled on the lands of the old Waldo patent during and after the Revolution were "squatters." Assuming that the Waldos and the Fluckers, all Tories with the exception of Lucy Knox, had forfeited their title, and also anticipating that, at worst, they might have to "quiet" their right to settle at nominal fees (as was the case on state land), these people simply settled without claim to the land. This was not a new practice in Maine, where land titles had long been hopelessly confused. Many of the more recent "squatters" were Revolutionary War veterans. Now along came Knox with every intention of enforcing his authority as the new proprietor. After some initial ambiguity in the wording of the 1785 resolve of the general court, Knox made it clear, again through a friendly legislature, that he would not "quiet" the rights to most of his land.

This spelled trouble. The "squatters," poorer citizens, were apprehensive about their future and distrusted Knox. Discontented but unused to political organization, they required a leader. This is where Samuel Ely enters the picture.

He was already infamous with the more respectable throughout New England before he headed Downeast. Samuel Ely was ten years Knox's senior, born in Connecticut in 1740. A Yale graduate with his sights set on the ministry, he served his first parish in Somers, Connecticut. A strong minority was soon advertising its willingness to hire "some candidate that we never heard to preach in the meeting-house in place of Mr. Ely." It was not until 1770 that Sam managed to get properly ordained. Soon thereafter he was dismissed from his Somers pulpit. It is likely that his trouble came not so much from an inability to preach as from *what* he preached. A statement by Yale president and fellow clergyman Timothy Dwight indicates this: "He possessed the spirit and so far as his slender abilities would permit, the arts, of a demagogue, in an unusual degree. . . . Wherever he went, he industriously awakened the jealousy of the humble and ignorant against all men of superior reputation, as haughty, insolent, and oppressive." The rest of Ely's life was, according to Dwight, "nothing but guilt and infamy."

Strong words, but Sam never evoked a neutral response. From Connecticut he migrated to the backcountry of Massachusetts and Vermont. He popped up at the Battle of Bennington as a volunteer acting independent of any authority. He collected so much booty that he was court-martialed. He was released, the court figuring what he got he won. Ely soon became involved in the agitation of western Massachusetts farmers against the Boston government. The yeomen thought they were oppressed by the new political elite. This was in 1782. Ely became so prominent in disturbances that the whole affair was later called "Ely's Rebellion." The itinerant parson was given to hot rhetoric. Once, inciting a crowd against the Northampton County government, he shouted, "Come on, my brave boys, we'll go to the woodpile and get clubs enough and knock their Grey Wiggs off and send them out of the World in an Instant." For this sort of talk he was jailed by the state supreme court in Springfield, but a mob assembled and promptly released him.

The old Patriot Joseph Hawley was worried by these goings-on: "We are not certain, who, besides the Devil, sprang Ely first. But we are not at loss who Ventilates the flame, for the fire is now become such a flame as I cannot describe. . . . " Hawley suspected the influence of British gold. But while Ely was telling the plain people they had been betrayed by the leaders of the Revolution—that even King George's rule was preferable—his radicalism was homegrown. As one historian wrote, the Revolution was not simply over home rule, but who would rule at home. Mixing evangelical religion with democratic politics, Ely spoke for the little people. Taking his message across the border, he was soon charged with being a "pernicious and seditious man," and banished from Vermont for 18 months.

Back in Massachusetts, he was imprisoned to serve out his earlier conviction. He petitioned the general court for relief, writing, "Venerable gentlemen I am alive and that is all as I am full of Boils and Putrefyed Sores all over my Body and they make me stinck alive Beside having some of my feet froze which makes it Difficult to walk. . . . " If this was not graphic enough, he added in a postscript, "Sir I am so raw that I have not been able to ware any Breeches for above a month." A special resolve of the legislature released Ely upon his promise to cease seditious activity.

Returning to Vermont in 1783, Samuel Ely was a phantom for the rest of the decade. Although later accused of participation in Shays' Rebellion, an uprising of western Massachusetts farmers, there is no proof of his involvement. He is next heard from in Alna, Maine, in 1790. New England's busiest radical was not quiet long. No picture of Ely or prose description remains. From all that we know of him, the image of a lean and hungry fellow emerges. None of the great Knox's humor is recorded, but plenty of passionate intensity.

Well before Henry Knox resigned as secretary of war and moved to his Thomaston estate, relations with poorer settlers on what were now his lands had deteriorated. The general court, ironically, was petitioned to investigate the validity of Knox's title and powers. A petition from residents of Ducktrap and New Canaan complained "we find our difficulties to be such as is not equalled in any part of the Eastern Country (except in your Honrs. Patent). . . . " Legislators from Thomaston and Waldoboro warned Knox, through an intermediary, that "a *revolution* would *certainly* take place" if the general did not change his tactics. The petitions, however, were rejected. In the upper house, now known as the senate, two petitions were burned to show the legislators' revulsion at insinuations against a fellow gentleman's character. This was the state of affairs when Parson Ely moved to Ducktrap, already a center of resistance to Knox.

What Knox feared was a replay of the kind of rebellion that had previously occurred in Massachusetts. His friend General David Cobb of Gouldsboro, one of Washington's wartime aides and now William Bingham's chief land agent in Maine, had confronted a mob while serving as a judge in Taunton. "I will hold this court if I hold it in blood," he had said. "I will sit as judge, or I will die as a general." Now Cobb feared the development of a similar confrontation in Maine.

Sam Ely soon criticized George Ulmer, Ducktrap's most well-to-do settler. Not coincidentally, he was a major supporter of Knox. In February, 1793, Ulmer responded by beating Ely and challenging him to a duel. In April, Ulmer's mill dam on the Ducktrap River was torn down in apparent retaliation. And in June, Ulmer arrested Sam for performing a couple of illegal marriage ceremonies. In July, one of the General's land surveyors reported a threat from Micajah Drinkwater:

> On our Tour we had the pleasure of seeing the famous Drinkwater, one of the GREAT SAMUEL ELY's disciples, who among others are going to Prevent our Surveying the Sea shore by Ducktrap etc, Knock us on the head, Break our Instruments, Moor us in Owls head Bay, with a Variety of other Corporal Punishments which are to be inflicted upon us if we attempt to Survey as before-mentioned and they even carry their threats so far as to say that Even General Knox himself will share the same fate if he attempts to take an active part in Enterprise.

In September, Ely was fined for assaulting one of Knox's rare supporters on Islesboro "with a large stick."

Sam Ely did more than threaten or inflict violence. In October, 1793, he wrote a lengthy petition to the general court. Aside from legal questions about Knox's title to the Waldo patent and administration of the land, there was, for Ely, the overriding question of whether *anybody* should be granted so much land:

> 1st Query what ought to entitle General Knox to a grant of a tract of Land superior in extent to any Lord in Europe or America, has he done more for his Country than hundreds of us, no verily—

> 2d Query whether it would not be just as to make a grant to every faithful Soldiers, or thirty miles square as to Knox and others— Yes—

> 3d Query, whether reason and Justice does not forbid such large grants in a free Republic as tending to militate against its safety and future prosperity—

The Parson carried this document, signed by over 150 neighbors, to Boston. There, in June, 1794, he lobbied the general court. The assembly voted in favor of an investigation of the situation on Knox's lands, but the general's allies in the senate stalled any action.

In 1795 Knox and other proprietors undertook surveys of the Maine backcountry, where their claims overlapped. Settlers suspected a coordinated assault on their property rights. Acts of intimidation against surveyors mounted. When, in November, Jonathan Jones of Balltown (now Jefferson and Whitefield) aided a party of harrassed surveyors, two of Jones's barns were burned. At a meeting in Ducktrap, of which Ely was assumed to be the moving force, a couple of hundred men vowed to drive out Knox and his agents. In February, 1796, one of Knox's employees wrote the general, who was spending the winter in Boston, about the plot to pay *Montpelier* a "Jones visit." Knox was urged to make concessions, but Knox was in no mood to compromise.

Instead, he informed Governor Samuel Adams of the disturbances. "I have no doubt," he wrote, "they are fomented by one Samuel Ely, a person said to be obnoxious to the laws on account of his atrocious conduct in the insurrection of 1786 in the western parts of this commonwealth."* Acting quickly, Adams passed this along to the legislature, reminding the lawmakers that Ely had violated the terms of his 1783 bond.

Old Sam remained active in "Insurrection Business," traveling throughout the backcountry, addressing various plantation meetings, calling for the passage of resolves upholding settlers' rights against Knox's machinations. He claimed he had diligently searched Knox's public records—and no valid claim existed. In addition, the busy Ely distributed copies of a pamphlet with the compelling, if wordy, title *The Unmasked Nabob of Hancock County: or, the Scales Dropt from the Eyes of the People*. It was supposed to be "Knox's Last

---

* Knox thus promoted the idea Ely was involved in Shays' Rebellion. It is an understandable mistake.

Will and Testament," and included a clause reading "I will to have my patent descend in the line of Waldo, Flucker, and my heirs forever, expecting the several rising sets of heirs, as proprietors, will call every thirty or fifty years upon the people to pay for their lands." And so on.

In mid-March, Ely's old adversary George Ulmer was commissioned juctice of the peace. He was empowered to execute an order for the parson's arrest from the general court. Ulmer also had a proclamation from Governor Adams denouncing Ely. At this point Ely disappeared from sight.

He reportedly resurfaced in Ducktrap in September, 1796. It was said that he got friends to petition the general court for release from his bond. (It was also later reported that the Parson conspired with 80-odd cohorts to execute more violent resistance.) It was even said that Ely went to Boston to personally seek a pardon. Another pamphlet appeared: *The Deformity of a Hideous Monster, discovered in the Province of Maine, by a man in the Woods, looking after Liberty. Printed near Liberty Tree, for the good of the Commonwealth.* He still had a way with words. "Let me have a high scaffold that all may see a martyr die for the common cause of the people," he wrote. The parson was in a mood for martyrdom.

On January 30, 1797, the general court received a document entitled *Last Petition of an innocent Man a plaintive worm, involved in one Continual Round of Distress, Miseries and Torture or a Man persecuted in the Bowels of a Free Republic By a systematic Junto of Luxurious Sons, Patentee Land Jobbers and Voluptuous Joles* (jowls). Ely unleashed yet another denunciation of Knox's manipulations and the danger he saw of too much property in the hands of too few men. He denied the charges made against him. Again there was a special note of persecution:

> Knox and his party . . . Say that his opposers must be crushed or he will lose his Patent and I am the Man . . . Knox and his agents have said repeatedly that if I{t} were not for my Pen and Dam Tounge, he could make all the settlers pay for their lands at his own Price meaning in other words he could cheat them as he pleased.

The petition was dismissed, and Samuel Ely was never heard from again. There is simply no existing record of what happened to him. Later stories emerged that he died in his native Connecticut or drowned in Ducktrap. His wife, Temperance, remained in Islesboro, and in 1803, General Knox conveyed title to Ely's small lot on Saturday Point in Ducktrap to Temperance. It cost $87.50.

Did Sam Ely go "undercover" as he apparently did in the 1780s? It is odd that there is no record of his death. What is clear is that, with his abrupt disappearance, organized resistence to Knox collapsed. The claims disputes were mostly settled; Knox's property rights in the valuable "wild" lands beyond the coast were secured. He had prevailed.

But the general did not live long to savor his victory. In 1806 he died as the result of a chicken bone lodged in his esophagus. And, despite all his energy and ambition, he died deeply in debt to numerous creditors. His impoverished heirs lived for a while in the dilapidated *Montpelier*, which was torn down to make way for a railroad in 1871.

Nobody knew—or was saying—what had happened to Sam Ely, but the ruin of the house of Knox was in plain view. Some attributed that to Ely's curse.

• 17

The Secret of the Sea Fight Far Away

D uring the War of 1812, Captain Lemuel Moody was the keeper of the Portland Observatory atop Munjoy Hill. Early on September 15, 1813, he had the best view in town of the naval encounter 40 miles distant. With the aid of an English telescope, Captain Moody could see the U.S.S. *Enterprise* approach another ship beyond Seguin lighthouse. At 8:30 A.M. a puff of smoke issued from the strange vessel, followed by an answering puff from the *Enterprise*. The challenge to combat had been made and accepted. Moody shared this information with the expectant crowd gathered at the base of the brown-shingled observatory. Although it was Sunday, the Yankees responded with a lusty cheer.

The *Enterprise* headed out to sea. To the untrained eye the 12-gun American warship seemed to be fleeing from its adversary. In fact, the *Enterprise* was seeking open water upon which to maneuver from advantagous position. Also, the American commander, Lieutenant William Burrows, wanted to gauge his British opponent's seaworthiness. "I shall outsail her," he informed his crew. "Then outshoot her!"

This is precisely what happened—but not immediately. Hours of maneuvering were followed by hours of no action whatever as the two warships lay becalmed nine miles west of whalebacked Monhegan Island. The crowd on Munjoy Hill melted away in the autumn afternoon, believing that no battle would be fought.

But at 3:00 P.M. the wind came up and the two vessels closed. Soon both were enveloped in smoke. For 45 minutes the battle raged. It was a desperate, silent affair that Captain Moody watched with a handful of others he allowed up on the observatory's tower. Henry Wadsworth Longfellow, then seven years old, would later recall hearing the noise of the "sea fight far away" rolling across Casco Bay "In My Youth," but this was a case of poetic license. The pounding of the cannon could not be heard 40 miles away.

The battle off Monhegan was one of the most decisive American victories of the War of 1812. Just how decisive became apparent to Portlanders the next day, when the *Enterprise* returned to Union wharf with the captured 16-gun H.M.S. *Boxer*. Broken masts, shot-away rigging, and a hull pockmarked with holes bore grim testimony to the superiority of Yankee gunnery. According to one observer "there was no place on one side of the *Boxer* where he could not reach two shot holes at the same time by extending his arms." It was a wonder that the men who had constantly worked her pumps since the fatal encounter were able to keep the British ship afloat until it made Portland. In a war that was generally disastrous for American arms, this victory was something to celebrate.

But patriotic reaction was tempered by compelling evidence of loss. Both commanders were carried ashore enshrouded in their nation's flags. The *Boxer's* Lieutenant Samuel Blyth, 29, had died instantly when the fight began, nearly cut in two by an American cannonball. Lieutenant Burrows of the *Enterprise*, although painfully wounded by a British sniper soon afterward, refused to be carried below deck until the *Boxer* had surrendered. He died eight hours later. The two young antagonists, both ambitious for glory, were buried side by side in Portland's Eastern Cemetery. The only other American fatality, Lieutenant Kervin Waters, would linger on for two years before finally succumbing at age 18. The wounded numbered 12 Americans and 17 Englishmen. How many British died is unknown, since their dead were tossed overboard, but probably 25 men perished.

This was considerable carnage and drama for a town which, a generation before, had survived a naval bombardment without a single casualty. The impact of the event was heightened by a solemn funeral pageant for the fallen captains. Thus absorbed, the citizens of Portland were unaware of the background of political intrigue. And, because it involved the reputation of Maine's most prominent politician, it would be a long time before this part of the *Boxer-Enterprise* story became known.

In the summer of 1813, the secretary of the navy had dispatched the *Enterprise* to Portland "for the protection of the coast in the neighborhood." When Lieutenant Burrows assumed command in August, the British brig *Boxer* was an established nuisance in Maine waters. Earlier that month, it had captured a schooner off the mouth of the Sheepscot River. Then, in September, a fisherman arrived in Portland with word that a British warship had fired upon a Swedish-registered vessel, the *Margaretta*, as it entered the Kennebec River. Burrow assumed this was the *Boxer* and, with local assistance, sallied forth despite contrary winds and tide.

The hostile intruder was indeed the *Boxer*. But it had no intention of seizing the *Margaretta*. Many years later—in 1873—merchant Charles Tappan explained:

> At the commencement of our war with Great Britain in 1813, the United States had few if any factories in the manufacture of woolen cloths and blankets, and the soldiers were clad in British cloths and slept under

British blankets. It was understood no captures would be made of British goods owned by citizens of the United States, and many American merchants imported, via Halifax and St. John, N.B., their usual stock of goods. In 1813 I went with others in the "Swedish" brig *Margaretta* to St. John, N.B., and filled her with British goods, intending to take them to Bath, Maine, and enter them regularly and pay the lawful duties thereon. All we had to fear was American privateers; and we hired Capt. Blyth, of H.B.M. Brig *Boxer*, to convoy us to the mouth of the Kennebec River, for which service we gave him a bill of exchange on London for £ 100. We sailed in company, and in a thick fog, off Quoddy Head, the *Boxer* took us in tow. It was agreed that when we were about to enter the mouth of the river two or three guns should be fired over us, to have the appearance of trying to stop us, should any idle folks be looking on. . . .

The shots fired and reported to Lieutenant Burrows, alerting him of the *Boxer*'s presence, were simply part of a charade to cover a smuggling operation involving Bath merchants. News of the subsequent battle and capture of the *Boxer* must have instilled emotions other than patriotic pride in these gentlemen. "Our bill of exchange we thought might in some way cause us trouble," Tappan remembered, "and we employed Esquire K. to take 500 specie dollars on board the captured ship and exchange them for the paper, which was found in Captain Blyth's breeches pocket."

Whether the mysterious "Esquire K." was William King of Bath or, more likely, an intermediary, it was vital for King to have the incriminating note removed from Lieutenant Blyth's corpse. A prominent merchant and politician, half brother of the Federalist leader Rufus King, and friend of President James Madison, General King had been placed in charge of the military defense of the District of Maine and had issued stern orders to his subordinates to punish anyone trading with the enemy.

Which was exactly what William King was doing, as the note in the dead captain's pocket proved. Having violated federal trade regulations before the war, he was not about to let the complication of war with Great Britain get in the way of profit and his family's comfort. He traded with the British for a lot more than blankets. On another occasion, an American privateer stopped one of his vessels in the West Indies, clearly engaged in illicit trade. When the privateer's captain threatened to seize the ship, the captain of King's vessel responded:

> . . . His answer was, that his ship belongs to *General William King*, that no person dared to seize her, if he did Mr. *Madison* was a friend of Mr. King and would order her release. . . . He then threatened me with the power and standing of his owner. I knew General W. King to be what is called a good Democrat and friendly to the executive. I considered such a seizure at this time would be made a handle by the enemies of the administration and I released him. . . .

Captain Joshua Barney concluded that the episode involving King's vessel was typical, writing "I found out that the Revenue was defrauded by the eastern men without ceremony." At least, in the case of the *Margaretta*, a Massachusetts-built brig King had a half interest in, there was minimal ceremony of placing her under Swedish colors. This was easily arranged through one Peleg Tallman, a business associate who happened to be appointed Swedish vice consul for the District of Maine.

According to local Bath tradition, General King did draw the line when a rather cheeky British commander announced his intention of sailing up the Kennebec to have supper with him. The Englishman probably knew more about King's business activities than his neighbors did. When the commander attempted his social call, King replied he "could take supper in Hell." That was good copy.

In 1814 the British again seized control of eastern Maine. After easily scattering jumpy Maine militia in the fog at Hampden, they marched up to Bangor, which they occupied for 31 hours. The redcoats than reestablished a base at Castine. General King was ordered to assemble a force to eject them. This was not an easy task, given the lack of support shown by the beleaguered Madison administration and its political opposition in Boston. King was still trying to put something together when he learned that peace had been negotiated between the United States and Great Britain.

Mainers felt let down by Massachusetts during the war, and relations between Maine and Boston remained strained. King emerged as the leader of the movement in favor of separation from the Bay State. In 1820 he became the first governor of the new State of Maine. A big man with piercing eyes framed by bushy brows, his look "was the personification of dignity." Admirers thought King had more natural ability than his more polished half-brother Rufus, the last Federalist candidate for president. William, the Democrat, was considered a master politician but was handicapped by his educational limitations. "Had he only been blessed with a finished education, he would have been one of the first men in the United States; for he had the skill of Talleyrand, but much more virtue."

There was the matter of his smuggling. In 1824 two of King's former protégés, with whom he had fallen out over patronage disputes, published a pamphlet charging King and his friend Mark Langdon Hill* with illegal trade with the British before and during the War of 1812. The old general counterattacked with his own pamphlet belittling the motives and credibility of his accusers—already in disrepute for *their* smuggling activity! His success in this strategy drew attention away from the fact he never really disproved their allegations, which were documented. He lied when he intimated he was unaware that his ships were trading with the enemy. In reality, King was very closely directing their voyages.

The best that can be said for the man is that he was simply doing what many other merchants of both parties were doing. His hometown of Bath was second only to Eastport in the volume of illicit business it conducted. Indeed, for the old upper crust and new elite King represented, smuggling was an old tradition. The War of 1812 was supposedly fought over America's right to freedom of the seas. In a perverse way, the *Boxer* was simply helping merchants like King continue that freedom when the *Enterprise* showed up.

A statue of William King now represents Maine in our nation's capitol.

---

*Hill was wealthier than King, who later lost his fortune. He was a very influential figure; his critics composed a popular rhyme: "Twixt Hill and Hell there's but one letter."

State o' Maine

(Nineteenth Century)

18

Portland's Whorehouse Riots

O n November 11, 1825, the Portland *Eastern Argus* reported yet another riot, the third in a little more than a year. "If these affairs are suffered to go on at this rate," the paper editorialized, "Portland will soon receive and *deserve* the name of mob-town."

The violence originated a year earlier in outrage directed against "a nest of little, mean, filthy boxes of that description commonly called houses of ill-fame, tenanted by the most loathsome and vicious of the human species, and made a common resort for drunken sailors and the lowest off-scouring of society." Prostitution dens in downtown Portland aroused criticism from neighbors and, reportedly, even the buildings' owners wished to have them torn down.

The matter was not, however, dealt with in a legal manner. Instead:

> A company of laboring people, truck men, boys &c. understanding the feelings of the owners and the wishes of the neighbors, assembled in the evening, turned out the tenants and tore the buildings to the ground, while some hundreds of citizens stood looking on and sanctioning the whole proceeding by their presence and their silence.

The mob "grew over zealous in the good work" and headed off to other sections of town, destroying similar property. The success of this undertaking and the virtual inaction of authorities, according to the *Argus*, was an example "left to work its effect upon the minds of lower classes of people, the idle, the mischievous, and the vicious. . . . It was a kind of sport that had peculiar attractions for idle roaring boys and raw Irishmen. . . . "

In the spring of 1825, about 2 o'clock on the morning of May 17, another mob assembled. By this time the ladies of ill repute had relocated. The crowd knocked down several of their new abodes. A sizeable house on Crabtree's Wharf was impervious to attempts to haul it down, so the mob set the building afire. The respectable folk of Portland were awakened "in the dead of night by the ringing of bells and the cry of fire."

This was considered a bit much. A committee appointed at a special town meeting investigated the affair. Several individuals were arrested and tried for disturbing the peace. One black man, unable to post bond, was jailed for several months until the court of common pleas convened. Ultimately, all of the accused were discharged, but the authorities hoped that their actions would deter further riots.

Meanwhile, prostitutes established new quarters yet again. There was a third, more violent confrontation. A mob attacked a two-story dwelling on Fore Street occupied by a black barber named Gray. Gray had already been convicted once of running a whorehouse. He had appealed to the state supreme court, which upheld his conviction. This was a few days before the attack on his house.

> But the mob chose to render more speedy justice than the laws would do and accordingly on Saturday night they threw a few rocks into Gray's house, broke the windows, &c. But either from want of sufficient forces or from meeting more resistance that they expected, they desisted till Monday evening, when they resumed their attack with increased force. . . .

Gray, armed to the teeth and accompanied by his family and some others, was ready. So were his adversaries. The result was a regular shootout.

> . . . In the course of the assault, the mob fired guns into the house, and guns were fired from the house upon the mob. Which fired first we are not informed. One man in the street, an Englishman by the name of Joseph Fuller, was killed almost instantly and six or eight others were wounded, some severely. After this the crowd soon dispersed. We examined the house on Tuesday morning, and found the windows mostly stove in, rocks scattered about the floors, and lead shot in the plastering opposite the windows.

Thus ended the Portland Whorehouse Riots. The outbreaks were not unique to the Maine city. In the same year—1825—mob of rioters in Boston tore down houses of prostitution. Police who attempted to intervene were beaten up. The city marshal suffered the indignity of having "the contents of a feather-bed poured uon his head. . . . When a riot hit Salem soon after Portland, the *Eastern Argus* sighed, "Misery loves company." Nobody really tried to stop the Portland riots.

If nothing else, the outbreaks demonstrated the existence of underlying class, ethnic, and racial divisions in the seaport community. The elite initially encouraged mob action by the city's poor—and denounced their activity when things got out of hand.

And the whores set up business again.

19

The Missing Governor

G overnor Enoch Lincoln is missing.

Lincoln was the third governor of Maine. In 1829 he became, at 41, the first governor to die in office. He was buried on the grounds of the new state capitol, whose site in Augusta he had been instrumental in selecting. In 1842 the state erected a special tomb for Lincoln and other state officials. It was called the "State Burying Ground," but few availed themselves of the tomb, which was surmounted by an obelisk-shaped monument on a knoll overlooking the Kennebec River.

Recently it was learned that even Governor Lincoln was no longer utilizing the tomb. To the justified embarrassment of state authorities who supervise such matters, the remains of Lincoln and his cohorts are missing. Nobody knows where they have gone. It is a bizarre twist in the story of an uncommon public man, now largely forgotten. Like his corpse, Enoch Lincoln's memory deserves recovery.

He came from a family of governors. His father Levi Lincoln, Jefferson's attorney-general, was lieutenant governor of Massachusetts and succeeded to the top post when James Sullivan (of Maine) died in 1808. Later, in 1825, Enoch's older brother Levi Lincoln, Jr., was also elected governor of the Bay State. Enoch, slight and delicate in appearance but of a feisty temperament, entered Harvard as a sophomore in 1806, but was expelled the next year for undefined misbehavior. After studying law at his native Worcester, he was admitted to the bar and practiced briefly in Salem.

In 1812, he moved to rural Fryeburg in the District of Maine. At that time a social center of western Maine, Fryeburg was a relatively old town, near the site of a famous battle of the 18th century Indian Wars. The romantic Lincoln enjoyed walking through the woods and studying Indian lore. The society of Fryeburg was quite contentious during the five years that Lincoln practiced law there. According to what Judge Otis Russell Johnson called "a well founded tradition," Enoch challenged another Fryeburg lawyer to a duel, asking a judge to carry the message demanding satisfaction. "But the particulars of the remarkable episode are not known," Johnson observed, "and may well remain in oblivion." They have so far.

Yet Lincoln was very attached to the small town in the mountains. In 1816 a book of poetry entitled *The Village* was anonymously published. We now know that Lincoln was its author and that it was based upon Fryeburg. In a dedication "To The People," the unnamed author confided: "The following work, composed in a village adjacent to the White Hills, is offered to you, although not without hope, yet with fear and trembling. The name of the Author is concealed, because it is too humble to add weight to his claims, and his pride is too cautious to hazard the mortification of pointed neglect."

In fact, the slender volume *has* been neglected. A copy presented to the Portland Public Library still has uncut pages; no attempt has yet been made to separate them and read the hidden poetry. Lincoln's book was the first book-length epic poem written in Maine, and its subject matter was wide-ranging, expressing opinions advanced for the time. Even adult minds might be agitated—if they read it.

It starts off celebrating the natural setting.

> Range upon range, sublimely piled on high
> You lofty mountains prop the incumbent sky.

But Lincoln soon moves to a description of the native Indians. He criticizes the red men's savage warfare ("His eye's first joy the slaughter of the fight") and describes in gruesome detail the torture Indians inflicted upon one another. But Lincoln also, through the words of an angered dead sachem, rebukes the white man for his treatment of the Indian:

> For you, my bad spirits, who hover around
> Blast your lives with each curse, and with plagues taint the air
> May famine, disease and contention abound,
> Till our lands you restore and own wrongs you repair.

After rendering poetic homage to Maine's "tall, straight pines," he pays tribute to his favorite tree ("Yet not the maple feel the woodman's stroke"). Abruptly, he moves to another social theme:

> Fair maple! let thy leaves my brow surround,
> And laurel wreath I trample on the ground,
> The suffering Negro in West Indian isles,
> Soothed at thy name, amid his sorrow smiles
> Hope's cheering rays dispel his gloomy care,
> And tinge with dawning light his deep despair.
> Do not our soil and frosty clime insure
> Sweets as salubrious, exquisite and pure,
> As those which burning suns, or humid air
> With swarming insects filled, and slaves prepare?
> They do!—Our blest New England's fruitful soil
> Requires no culture by a servile toil:
> No master's torturing lash offends the ear,
> No slave is now, nor ever shall be, here.

Lincoln moved into a passionate condemnation of slavery—in the present and past. He warned of civil war as a consequence. In his appendix, the poet expressed belief in the black's "natural inferiority of intellect." "But they are men," he wrote, "and no plea of private advantage or public policy can justify their enslavement, or palliate the enormities committed in stealing them from their native country, subduing them to obedience, and working them as if they were beasts in human shape. . . . "

Lincoln also denounced the cruelty of shooting songbirds, advocated temperance, criticized the denial of higher education to women ("The Christian tyrant's Turkish doctrine this. . . . "), and warned of what he saw as the dangers of political party spirit. He spoofed politicians who:

> Decry the statesman, puff the stupid knave,
> Support the traitor, stigmatize the brave,
> Call wisdom folly, Honor's self defame,
> Discolor truth and everything misname,
> And why? Forsooth a rival to disgrace,
> To win a salary or steal a place. . . .

Although the lyrical style is adequate and the images sometimes moving, nobody would find this great poetry. Yet in scope and in the advanced sentiments expressed—for 1816—it was a worthy work. Certainly it was not the sort of endeavor associated with the typical politician.

For the secret poet was a public man. He became aligned with the popular Democrat Albion Parris of Paris, and moved to that town in 1817. Supposedly the citizens of Paris offered him a seat in Congress if only he would stay among them. Yet Lincoln missed Fryeburg, describing Paris as "a place which will never be home to me." In 1818 he was elected to fill out the term of Albion Parris, who had accepted a federal judgeship. Reelected several times, he was nominated by his party once again to succeed Albion Parris—this time as governor—in 1826. Lincoln won without any real opposition and became, at age 38, chief executive of Maine. He was reelected twice, and his tenure was free of controversy. His views were enlightened. Lincoln was, as one admirer wrote, "the advocate of as entire freedom of thought and action as human society can endure."

Although he was a successful public figure, admired for the elegance and polish of his state papers, Enoch Lincoln's real interests were historical and literary. For many years he had conducted research and collected manuscripts about Maine's Indians. He had started writing notes about their languages. The governor, who resided in Portland, then the site of the state capital, purchased a home in Scarborough. There, after his term ended, he intended to live as a gentleman farmer and write a book about the Indians. He even thought of writing a history of Maine.

But this was not to be. One of the accomplishments of Lincoln's administration was the decision to relocate the capital in more central Augusta. In July, 1829, he was present at the laying of the cornerstone of the new capitol building. Indeed, he stood on it to address the crowd. Later, in October, he was invited to speak at the opening of the Cony Female Academy in Augusta. By this time he was depressed by the recent death of his mother and physically weak. Yet the education of young women was close to the bachelor governor's heart. He felt it his duty to accept the invitation. When he arrived in Augusta, "he mentioned two or three times that he had come to die there," and barely managed to give his address. Lincoln immediately went to the home of General Cony, the state's adjutant general and an old friend. When he talked of impending death, the general, unaware of the seriousness of Lincoln's condition, said, "Well, well, governor, we can give you a good tomb here." When his health rapidly deteriorated, Lincoln said to the general's wife with a faint smile, "Well, madam, I believe I shall have to accept your husband's invitation."

He was feisty to the end. Once, during a bout of delirium, the governor insisted he must get up. Cony's son told him he must lie down. "Must, there is no such word for me," Lincoln said. "I will not be controlled, sir."

"But," the young man said, "I entreat you, I beg of you to lie down."

"Oh," Lincoln responded, "that is another affair; that is talking rationally." On October 8, 1829, near the end of his 41st year, the governor died.

When I recently visited the "State Burying Ground" where Governor Lincoln was interred, it was almost obliterated from general view by surrounding birches, pines, and his favorite maple. The trees are numbered. The state still knows where *they* are.

Cigarette butts are scattered about. An animal hole is at the tomb's front and the vault door has a crack in it big enough to extend a hand through.

It does not matter. Enoch Lincoln—that free spirit—is gone. A ghoulish photograph taken in 1903, when the tomb was opened, shows a battered skeleton on the floor. Are these Lincoln's remains, already on their way out?

Nobody seems to know. But we should care. Enoch Lincoln was a different kind of governor. He loved poetry more than power.

20 •

"They Must Thirst Mightily for My Blood"

In April, 1838, the remains of Representative Jonathan Cilley, killed three months earlier in a duel that shocked the nation, were returned to Maine. His friends did not wait for the boat carrying his body to land, but advanced into the water of Rockland Harbor and took the coffin on their shoulders. Once ashore, they continued to carry the body to the "martyred" Cilley's Thomaston home.

Cilley had fallen in a duel with another congressman, William Graves of Kentucky, outside Washington, D.C. , on Feb. 24, 1838. He was accorded a state funeral in the Capitol rotunda, attended by President Martin Van Buren, the Cabinet, and Congress.

The fatal encounter, the most infamous since Aaron Burr gunned down Alexander Hamilton in 1804, provoked widespread condemnation and a call for an investigation of "the late murder." The seconds preferred to call it "this unfortunate affair of honor."

The controversy had hardly abated when Cilley was finally buried in Thomaston. Among those who eulogized him on April 19 was William Farley, a former political rival, who described Cilley as "a warm partisan. Of an ardent temperament. Burning for distinction . . . it was impossible that he should not have had his enemies as well as friends."

Jonathan Cilley was the epitome of the new breed of professional politicians who appealed to the "common man" ("common women" couldn't vote) during the Jacksonian era. Born in New Hampshire in 1802, the grandson of a Revolutionary War general and brother of a hero of the War of 1812, Cilley studied at Bowdoin College. Noted for his political enthusiasm as well as his scholarship, he graduated near the top of the famous Class of 1825.

The 38 Boys of Bowdoin who composed the Class of 1825 were a most remarkable group. There was Henry Wadsworth Longfellow, who became America's most beloved poet, and Nathaniel Hawthorne, the nation's most famous novelist. John Stevens Cabot Abbott became a leading author of children's literature, while cleryman George Barrell Cheever's *Deacon Gile's Distillery* landed him in jail for libel, but hardly deterred his crusading soul. James Ware Bradbury become a U.S. senator; Samuel Page Benson and Cullen Sawtelle were elected to Congress. Horatio Bridge was key figure in the mid-19th century U.S. Navy—and biographer of his friend Hawthorne. Others graduates were prominent lawyers, doctors, clergymen, teachers, and businessmen. But none of the famous class achieved the tragic notoriety of Cilley, who was remembered by a contemporary as "a warm-hearted fellow—but always seeming as if he wore a mask."

Cilley went straight from the Bowdoin pines to coastal Thomaston to clerk in the law office of Judge John Ruggles, a powerful figure in the Maine Democratic Party. Soon the rising Cilley had established his own practice, married the daughter of a prominent merchant, and become editor of the local newspaper. Noted for his folksy oratory and political skills, Cilley was elected to the state legislature in 1831.

He won a bitter libel suit and broke with Ruggles, setting off an equally bitter feud within Democratic ranks. By 1835 Cilley was nevertheless elected speaker of the Maine House of Representatives. He soon moved up, winning a seat in Congress in 1836.

His obvious zest for political warfare impressed—and disturbed—former Bowdoin classmate Nathaniel Hawthorne, who found his old friend "a daring fellow, as well as a sly one," whose "harsher traits" had become more pronounced since college days.

In the late 1830s, Washington was a political war zone. The Democratic administration, burdened with an economic depression, faced growing Whig opposition. In this overheated partisan atmosphere, violent rhetoric often was accompanied by real violence. The Dueling Code was taken seriously by Southerners, who often taunted less warlike Northern members with veiled and open threats.

Cilley immediately made clear his disdain for Southern intimidation tactics, demonstrating almost an eagerness to tangle with Southern fire-eaters. One of this type was Henry Wise, the high-strung Whig representative from Virginia. On February 12, 1838. Wise presented a motion to create a committee of inquiry to investigate a charge of corruption made in the New York *Courier and Enquirer* against an unnamed member of Congress.* The *Enquirer's* editor, Colonel James Watson Webb, had demanded congressional action. Cilley objected. No investigation, he said should be undertaken upon an unspecified charge in the press.

Cilley also said he understood the editor involved was the same one who had once opposed the National Bank "and afterward was said to have received $52,000 from the same institution and gave it his hearty support." He doubted this individual's charges "were entitled to much credit in an American Congress."

Wise seemed much more interested in portraying Cilley as protecting an unnamed fellow Democrat—maybe, he intimated, even protecting himself. Cilley stood his ground and the Virginian took his seat with a loud aside, "But what is the use of bandying words with a man who won't hold himself accountable for his words?" His meaning was clear.

The situation grew more ominous when Editor Webb showed up in Washington on February 21. Webb practiced an intensely personal type of journalism. The former soldier, whose dueling habits ended his military career, was said to have beaten up rival newspaper editors in the streets. A big man and a bully, Webb was a Northerner who subscribed to the Code of Honor. In the capital to attend a lavish dinner for Big Whigs hosted by Daniel Webster, the colonel prevailed upon William Graves, and obscure Whig congressman from Kentucky, to deliver a note to Jonathan Cilley.

The note Graves handed Cilley on Webb's behalf demanded "the explanation which the character of your remarks renders necessary." The two young congressmen, on friendly terms to this point, stood in a secluded corner of the house. Cilley returned the note to Graves, saying he was not accountable to a journalist for words spoken on the floor. He emphasized that he meant no disrespect toward Graves.

Initially, Graves seemed satisfied, but he had second thoughts after discussing the matter with members of his state's delegation, notably Henry Clay. Clay drafted a note for Graves asking Cilley to state that he did not base his refusal "upon any personal objection to Colonel Webb as a gentleman."

Cilley refused to accept Graves's right to interrogate him.

On the morning of February 23, Wise arrived at Cilley's boarding house, carrying a note from Graves requesting "that satisfaction which is recognized among gentlemen." Wise's appearance as Graves's second contributed to Cilley's belief that there was a conspiracy of his enemies to destroy his "reputation as a public man."

He accepted the challenge, even though he considered its pretext "absurd." Why? It was a question many of his friends would ask. "He avoided his

---

*Ironically, Senator Ruggles identified himself as the target of the charge. A special inquiry by fellow senators exonerated him.

colleagues," Representative Fairfield lamented, "and took advice from more belligerent characters."

Cilley maintained that his honor and that of New England dictated his course: "I see into the whole affair. . . . It is an attempt to browbeat us. They think that as I am from the East I will tamely submit." He realized sentiment in Maine was against dueling, but said "I am sure that my people will be better pleased if I stand the test than disgrace myself by humiliating concessions."

As the challenged party, Cilley decided the weapons and procedure. He informed Graves via his own second, General George Jones of the Wisconsin Territory, that he would fight with rifles at 80 yards on February 24, at noon. "I expect the Kentuckian would prefer pistols." Cilley explained to Jones, "therefore I demand rifles that I may be on an equality."

Wise complained that the terms were "barbarous," but Senator Clay admonished Graves that no Kentuckian could back down from a contest with rifles. There was some difficulty procuring a gun for Graves. The duel was postponed until three o'clock that Sunday afternoon.

Mrs. Graves dispatched the marshal of the District of Columbia to stop the affair, and Colonel Webb, believing he should fight Cilley, charged about the capital looking for the Maine congressman, loudly proclaiming his intention to "shoot him on the spot." But neither the marshal nor Webb knew where the impending duel was to occur.

Meanwhile, the Graves and Cilly parties met at the Anacostia Bridge and proceeded toward Marlboro, Maryland, until they found a suitable snow-covered field. Cilley was accompanied by Jones, Representative Bynum (Democrat, North Carolina), Representative Duncan (Democrat, Ohio, and surgeon), and Colonel Shamburg of the Dragoons. With Graves were Wise, Senator Crittenden (Whig, Kentucky), Representative Menifee (Whig, Kentucky), and a Dr. Folz. Two other Kentucky congressmen showed up, making a total of ten congressmen present.

Wise drew the choice of positions, giving Graves the advantage of a wooded backdrop while Cilley's position was in the open, facing into a steady wind.

Jones called out the prescribed words: "Gentlemen, are you ready?" Nobody answered in the negative. He then cried: "Fire! One, two, three, four." No shot could be fired after "four."

On the first exchange of fire, Cilley discharged his rifle into the ground. Whether this was deliberate or resulted in the touchiness of the gun's hair trigger is unclear. Both sides interpreted it differently. What was clear was that Graves took careful aim and meant to hit Cilley. He missed.

Jones argued that Cilley had rendered satisfaction to Graves and that the duel should be concluded. But the Kentuckian, through Wise, insisted that Cilley concede James Watson Webb was a gentleman and man of honor. This was exactly what Cilley would never say, and a second exchange of fire ensued.

The roles were reversed: Graves accidentally fired into the ground, while Cilley drew a bead on the Kentuckian, barely missing him. Graves excitedly told Wise, "I must have one more shot." With Cilley refusing concessions, the duel was, incredibly, allowed by the seconds to proceed. As the guns were again loaded, Wise said to Jones, "If this matter is not terminated on this shot, and is not settled, I will propose to shorten the distance."

"They must thirst mightily for my blood," Cilley remarked to Representative Bynum.

These were his last words. Cilley's ball missed Graves by a few inches, but Graves's lead hit Cilley right in the stomach. He toppled over, his rifle breaking off at its breech as it hit the frozen ground. Blood stained the snow red.

"How is your friend?" asked Wise.

"My friend is dead, sir," Jones answered.

Dead at 35, the only New Englander and only incumbent congressman to fall in a duel, Jonathan Cilley left behind a wife and three small children, one a newborn daughter he never saw.

In the aftermath, a house investigation called for Graves's expulsion and the censure of Wise and Jones. Amidst partisan bickering, no action was taken. Congress eventually passed an anti-dueling law, restricting the practice in the District of Columbia. Democrats charged, and many contemporaries believed that Cilley was the victim of a plot hatched by his adversaries to shut the promising young politician up.

Yet many also agreed with the words of William Farley at the Thomaston meeting house: "Highly as I esteemed Mr. Cilley, deeply as I lament his loss, I cannot justify him in the course he took in accepting the offered challenge. It was a fatal, an unjustifiable error."

21 •

When the Chickadee Screamed

N ever in Maine's history was the state motto "Dirigo"—"I lead"—more appropriate than it was in 1839. On her own initiative, and without Federal sanction, Maine became the only state in the Union to take military action against a foreign power. Her aggressiveness almost led to a third war between the United States and Great Britain. If the eagle did not exactly scream in the "Aroostook War," the chickadee did.

The dispute was about land, lots of it, in the Aroostook region. At stake was valuable timberland and, to Mainers, their honor. Ever since the 1783

Treaty of Paris between the United States and Great Britain, the precise location of the boundary line between Maine and the Province of New Brunswick remained unresolved. A compromise settlement proposed by the King of the Netherlands in 1831 was rejected by Maine, which considered all of the disputed territory rightfully hers. Many in Maine felt that Washington's enthusiasm for pressing the issue with Great Britain was underwhelming.

In the Aroostook region, tensions along the disputed frontier accelerated. In 1837 a state census agent, sent to Madawaska to distribute to its residents (considered Maine citizens) their share of the federal surplus, was arrested and imprisoned in Fredericton. Without bothering to investigate, the British lieutenant governor of New Brunswick assumed the agent was attempting to bribe the inhabitants to support Maine claims to the territory. The prisoner was later released, but conditions worsened that winter with reports of increased numbers of Canadian loggers encroaching upon the valuable timberlands of the Aroostook.

A special agent, George Buckmore, was commissioned by Maine and Massachusetts (which still administered the northern forest lands within her former district) to explore the area in December and ascertain exactly what the situation was. He was to report his findings to the succeeding Maine legislative session.

On January 23, 1839, newly inaugurated Governor John Fairfield revealed Buckmore's report to a secret session of the legislature. The weather outside the capitol was cold and blustery, but Fairfield's message was sufficient to warm the blood of the assembled senators and representatives. "A large number of men, many of them, I am informed, from the British Provinces are trespassing very extensively upon the lands belonging to this State," Fairfield announced. These intruders "not only refuse to desist, but defy the power of this Government to prevent their cutting timber to any extent they please." The land agent estimated $100,000 of timber would be removed that winter. "These facts . . . present a case in which not merely the property, but the character of the State, is clearly involved," the governor concluded.

He planned to act—with the legislature's approval, of course. If Washington would not move, Maine would go ahead and redeem her own character. Fairfield intended to send the land agent with a posse to disperse the Canadian camps. The legislature passed the necessary resolution and appropriated $10,000 to execute the mission. Land Agent Rufus McIntire of Parsonfield, a lawyer who had served four terms in Congress, was nearly 70 but game. He thought little of the British and less of "Blue Nose" Canadians. Like many citizens of Maine and the rest of the nation, Old Rufus still considered Great Britain America's greatest enemy.

McIntire was thus eager to fight. Accompanied by the burly sheriff of Penobscot County, Major Hastings Strickland, and a large posse, he proceeded north during the first week of February. After rousting out a number of Canadians along the way, the posse encamped at the mouth of the Little Madawaska River. McIntire displayed more zeal than caution: during the night of February 12, he and two others were surprised and seized by armed men. They were taken to Fredericton by sled and jailed.

Strickland eluded capture and hurried from Madawaska to Augusta as quickly as relays of horses would transport him. Fairfield received the electrifying news in the early morning hours and promptly dealt with "the extraordinary emergency." Reinforcing the posse in the Aroostook, he requested more men and money—a lot more—from the legislature. "If there ever was a time when the spirit of independence and self-respect should assert itself," he said, "that time is the present." A draft of 10,343 militia was speedily voted and $800,000 was appropriated for the protection of public lands.

Meanwhile, New Brunswick's warden, McIntire's equivalent, was grabbed by Maine authorities and transported to Bangor. "Just look at the contrast," a newspaper correspondent shrilled from Houlton. "The British Land Agent was brought here in a coach with four horses, a prisoner, carried to the Bangor House, and invited to one of the best rooms in the House, and received the best of fare, while our Agent was dragged on a horse sled to Fredericton and incarcerated within the walls of a prison. Should not such treatment cause the blood of every American to boil with indignation?"

Indeed! Mainers responded to the call to arms with enthusiasm bordering on mania. "We experience no difficulty in procuring men to go on this service against the trespassers," Fairfield noted. "On the contrary, it is hard work to keep them back."

Nor was New Brunswick exactly placid. Governor Harvey called upon Fairfield to withdraw the Maine force gathering in the disputed area. Rather ominously he observed "it is proper that I should acquaint your Excellency that I have directed a strong force of Her Majesty's troops to be in readiness to support Her Majesty's authority and protect Her Majesty's subjects in the disputed territory in the event of this request not being immediately complied with." Harvey also issued a proclamation that was regarded in Maine as a virtual declaration of war. Five hundred British regulars arrived in Madawaska from Quebec with eight cannon; within a short time thereafter a regiment of 800 troops was reported disembarking at Halifax. More were rumored on the way.

Fairfield responded by ordering about 4,000 of the state soldiers into the Aroostook. For him the hour of decision was at hand. "Now is the time to strike a blow for our rights," he wrote his anxious wife (who had not accompanied him to Augusta, either). "If we let this golden opportunity pass without improvement, we shall deserve to lose our territory and win the contempt of the world."

On February 26, the governor mounted his horse "and acted the Commander-in-Chief," reviewing a contingent of 600 soldiers in Augusta before a huge crowd. "The windows of all the houses were full, tops of houses covered, trees full of boys, and the streets crowded with men." Fairfield delivered a short address to his troops "designed to infuse into them a little spirit and military ardor." "And perhaps before this moment," the governor cried, "your soil has not only been polluted by the invader's footsteps, but the blood of our citizens may have been shed. . . . " This was "responded to by the shouts and claps of the whole multitude."

Maine was swept up in a giddy war euphoria. For the moment, politics took a back seat. (Cynics might say it was in the driver's seat, as Democrats and Whigs jostled each other to issue statements of war readiness.) A Whig newspaper editorialized, "A holier spirit than that of party should now animate the people." An instant anthem called the "Maine Battle Song," notable more for its spirit than its grammar, included the following stanza:

> We'll lick the red coats any how
> And drive them from our border;
> The loggers are awake—and all
> Await the Gin'ral's order;
> Britannia shall not rule the Maine,
> Nor shall she rule the water;
> They've sung that song full long enough,
> Much longer than they oughter.

Belatedly, the Van Buren administration realized all the fuss on the Maine frontier was serious. Maine's action was bringing the country to the brink of war with Great Britain. Congress authorized the president to raise 50,000 federal troops for Maine's support. Ten million dollars was appropriated to cover the cost of any conflict. Fairfield's friend, Senator Buchanan, thundered, "Should Maine act in accordance with the spirit of these resolutions, then if war should come, it will find the country unanimous." All this activity and bombast impressed British observers, but the administration was nervous.

General Winfield Scott, who had hastened back to Washington from frontier duty elsewhere, recalled, "Every branch of the Government felt alarmed at the imminent hazard of a formidable war—but little having been done in a twenty-four years' peace to meet such exigency." Scott, a hero of the War of 1812, was the administration's chief diplomatic troubleshooter. President Van Buren dispatched the general at once to Maine. According to his *Memoirs*, Scott said to Van Buren, "Mr. President, if you want *war*, I need only look on in silence. The Maine people will make it for you fast and hot enough. I know them; but if *peace* be your wish, I can give no assurance of success. The difficulties in its way will be formidable."

The President replied: "Peace with honor."

Arriving in Maine, Scott found the state in a fever pitch of combativeness. New Brunswick was likewise belligerent. He realized that the best hope for peace was to have both parties back off for a time "and to remit the whole question in issue to the two paramount Governments at Washington and London, from which it had been improperly wrested by the impatience of Maine at the dilatoriness of American diplomacy."

Accomplishment of this task was made more difficult by publication of a joint memo signed by Secretary of State John Forsyth and British envoy H. S. Fox. It advised Mainers to withdraw from the disputed area without any reciprocal obligation by the British. This only added fuel to the fire. Referring to himself in the third person, the general later wrote, "This bungle Scott had first to adjust between Democratic authorities—State and Federal—he himself being a Whig!"

Scott had a low opinion of the Democratic majority in the Maine legislature, but he worked hard to gain Fairfield's confidence. The governor did not want war; he wanted Maine's rights upheld. "I hope I shall be able to take a course which shall preserve our honor and yet not unnecessarily provoke hostilities," Fairfield wrote in early March. Establishing a working relationship with Fairfield, Scott also cultivated—with the governor's knowledge—his long-standing friendship with Sir John Harvey. It so happened that, during the War of 1812, Scott had saved Harvey's life on one occasion. Another time he recovered and returned to Harvey personal property, including a miniature portrait of Harvey's bride-to-be.

Harvey, anxious to avoid responsibility for war, was receptive to Scott's overtures. The Maine and New Brunswick governors had already released their mutual land agent prisoners. The sticking point was Harvey's insistence upon the withdrawal of Maine's armed forces. Now Scott invited Harvey to declare, in effect, that it was not his intention, with renewed London-Washington negotiations expected, "to seek to take possession of that territory, or to seek, by military force, to expel therefrom the armed civil posse or the troops of Maine." He was certain Fairfield would follow suit by declaring his peaceful intentions, removing state military forces, and leaving only the land agent and a small civil posse "to protect the timber recently out, and to prevent further depredations." In fact, Fairfield had already agreed to such a deal; no copy of Scott's note was provided to the governor for two months. If the legislature requested official papers, Fairfield could disclaim knowledge of the proposition.

Thus the "Aroostook War" ended with a flurry of deft political maneuvers. Maine, for the time being, was left in control of the Aroostook territory. Except for some bloody noses incurred in a Houlton barroom brawl (British and American soldiers drank together) and a Fort Fairfield farmer killed by a ricocheting bullet during a celebration of peace, it was a bloodless conflict. One soldier died of measles, although it was rumored he died of boredom. Maine's winter soldiers marched back to the warmth of their homes after six frosty weeks of truly cold war. Although the "Aroostook War" was treated in retrospect as some kind of enormous Yankee joke, it had been a close thing. Whatever John Fairfield's opposition to personal "affairs of honor," it was another matter when he believed Maine's honor was at stake.

If Mainers were proud of their show of force in 1839, they felt betrayed by the ultimate result of international negotiation of the dispute.

Negotiations between Britain's Alexander Baring, Lord Ashburton, a speculator in Maine lands, and Secretary of State Daniel Webster resulted in a "compromise" settlement that gave Maine considerably less acres than if she had accepted the 1831 award arbitrated by the Dutch king. Ashburton and Webster had a few drinks and, as gentlemen who couldn't care less about Maine's exact northern frontier, spent much of their effort trying to "sell" the settlement to Maine's commissioners. Exactly how they came to accept the deal is still not clear; Governor Fairfield renounced responsibility and let the legislature, grudgingly, approve the Webster-Ashburton Treaty. The Tyler administration in Washington utilized a secret fund and the services of the slippery Congressman F.O.J. "Fog" Smith of Portland to create a favorable press in Maine for the treaty. Many Mainers thought they had been had—and available evidence indicates they were right. But the fires of '39 were only embers by 1842. Generations of Mainers had a bone of contention to continually chew upon.

The "Aroostook War" was over. Or was it? According to Henry David Thoreau, who spent some time in the north woods of Maine, the *real* Aroostook War was the war lumbermen—American or Canadian—were waging against Maine's timber resources. *That* war continued.

• 22

The Nativists Were Restless

T he mid-19th century in America was a time of considerable anxiety, created by the impact of rapid economic and social change. One reaction was the rise of anti-"foreigner" sentiment and agitation, or *Nativism*. Nativism usually found expression in hostility toward recent Catholic immigrants. Politically, it was reflected in the emergence of the American Party. Its adherents were commonly called "Know-Nothings" because, fearing all manner of conspiracies, they often feigned ignorance when asked questions about their political beliefs. (Some critics might consider them just plain ignorant and the name most appropriate.) By 1854 Nativism and Know-Nothingism were rampant. In Maine, two ugly examples occured in Bath and Ellsworth.

Bath authorities did not expect trouble on the evening of July 6. Mayor Bernard C. Bailey, along with other upright citizens, was listening to one Dr. Boynton lecture on geology. Meanwhile, a crowd in the square in front of the custom house was being harangued—for the second day in a row—by a Know-Nothing agitator. The meeting was interrupted by a hack with drawn curtains headed down Front Street toward the railway station. The crowd cleared a lane for the carriage. When, however, the hack turned around and tried to return through the crowd, tempers flared. Its activity was interpreted as a deliberate attempt to disrupt the meeting.

In the ensuing commotion, somebody shouted "To the old South!" This sent the mob swarming up South Hill like angry hornets. The object of their atte··tions was a church rented by Bath's Catholics.

ⱴas 8:00 P.M. Smashing the old church's windows, the mob broke down its doors. Some rang the bell while others went up to the belfry, from which they waved an American flag. It was not long before flames crackled and smoke mingled with the approaching darkness. Firemen arrived quickly— but too late to halt the fire's progress. The church was burned to the ground.

As the embers still smouldered, the mob poured back down South Hill to the business district. They tried to break into the Sagadahock House to grab a suspected Catholic from inside, but were deterred when the mayor, fresh from a lecture on rocks, now confronted people intent upon throwing rather than examining them.

The frenzied Nativists simply roamed through the town, looking for Catholic homes, which they pelted with sticks and rocks. About midnight, they discharged a cannon, which they had somehow procured, in front of the federal building. The rioting continued until around 2:30 A.M.

The next evening, Friday, when outbreaks continued, Mayor Bailey read the riot act but could not deter an attack on a Catholic dwelling place Saturday night. Sunday night was rainy and there was no rioting. When Monday dawned, the rain had ended—and so had the outbreaks. By this time 100 extra police were on duty. They supplemented the town's smartly uniformed (complete with tall fur hats) volunteer militia, the Bath City Grays. The City Grays had been under arms since the first night of rioting.

But they had not been called upon to act. City officials failed to directly challenge the rioters. Apparently, they felt it better to let matters run their course than to stimulate potentially worse violence. The only official who tried, on his own initiative, was an alderman, Oliver Moses, who acted to restrain the mob. At one point, the rioters tied a rope about a small Bowery Street house Moses was renting to a Catholic family, intending to pull it downhill into the Kennebec River. Moses arrived on the scene and coolly walked through the mob and cut the rope with an axe. Such acts of courage worried the alderman's friends, who maintained an armed guard at the Moses home.

Even more damning than the inaction of city officials when the riot took place was their failure to identify and prosecute rioters. The burning of the South Hill Church occurred when it was still daylight, and several members of the police and fire departments were present. Yet no arrest was made until Monday—and then of only one man, Ira Mason, who was bound over to the state supreme court, where he was acquitted of any wrongdoing. Obviously, the mob leaders were identifiable, but nothing was done.

Meanwhile, trouble had been brewing further Downeast, in Ellsworth. It went back to October of 1853. That was when John Bapst, a Jesuit priest who had recently moved to the town, challenged the Ellsworth School Committee. At issue was whether Catholic students had to read from the King James Bible, the reading of which was traditional. Bapst requested that Catholics either be allowed to read their own Bible—the Douay version—or be excused from participating in the Bible reading. Bapst maintained he was simply acting in accordance with the desires of bishops of the church, who warned against the dangers of laity being exposed to a "corrupt" translation of the Bible.

Bapst did not even suggest that the King James Bible be eliminated, nor did he ask special funds for a parochial school. (None existed at this time.)

But to the overwhelming Protestant majority in the Maine port on the Union River, a bustling center of commerce which had attracted a minority of Catholic workmen, Bapst was attacking *the* Bible and trying to undermine the public school system. According to the school committee, when the teachers allowed Catholic children to remain silent during the reading, they fooled around and disrupted reading of the Protestant Bible. On top of this, some persons unknown broke into the school and destroyed several Bibles.

This got people into a dither. When Bapst tried to explain that he was only acting on orders of his superiors, he only convinced the school committee—and many Ellsworth Protestants—that he was indeed part of a Catholic conspiracy to take their Bible out of the classroom. The school committee was set in its opinion: read the King James Bible or withdraw from school.

Bapst, a Swiss immigrant who spoke broken English, did not help the situation when he circulated a petition which about a hundred Ellsworth Catholics signed. It was simply a renewal of his original request but the language was intemperate. Reference to the King James Bible as "the counterfeit word of God" was guaranteed to upset Protestants, who accepted it as the word of God. Bapst, in his earlier work at Skowhegan, Waterville, and with the Indians at Old Town, had won the respect of Protestants for his moderation. But, in Ellsworth, he acted in a manner which undermined his cause. The school committee's intolerance may have provoked an intolerant response.

More than just the priest's rhetoric inflamed Nativism. When a promising young lady, Miss Mary Agnes Tincker, influenced by lectures given by Bapst, converted to Catholicism, she established a parochial school for students who left the public school. Her action and the conversion of other young ladies worried nervous Protestants.

Then there was the Donahoe case. Bapst encouraged Lawrence Donahoe, whose daughters had withdrawn from the public school, to seek financial compensation from the committee for the cost of his child's private instructor. This case went to the state supreme court, and while it did not directly deal with the Bible usage issue, it was intended as a "test" case. And it was clearly instigated by Father Bapst. It kept the pot boiling. In December, 1853, the school committee blamed John Bapst for the whole affair. "All was undisturbed harmony on this subject," it said, "until the Reverend Mr. Bapst, a Catholic priest, of the order of Jesuits, come among us. *He is a foreigner by birth, by education, and allegiance.**

The local newspaper, the *Ellsworth Herald*, contributed to the tense atmosphere that pervaded the town. Its editor, William H. Chaney, born in Chesterville, was a wild character nicknamed "Ugly Bill." He knocked about in the merchant marine, Navy, and the West for a dozen years. He became a self-taught, unorthodox frontier lawyer and writer of mawkish poetry. It was typical of Chaney that the first thing he did upon his return to Maine was to look up a man who had once beaten him up. He returned the favor. After a brief stint as a schoolteacher in Ellsworth, he took over management of the financially ailing *Herald*. A rival newspaper said Chaney's conduct was

*Italics mine.

characterized by "the ignoble sentiment, the licentious illustration, the vulgar trick, the blackguard joke, and the horse-laugh." For a while Chaney professed indifference to "The Catholic Bible Question." But on December 30, 1853, the *Herald* editorialized that the issue was part of a conspiracy hatched by Rome. From that point on, the *Herald* became deeply involved in the controversy, promising to "Never Cease To Do Battle against papal interference."

The pugnacious Chaney seemed to revel in his image of a tough, no-holds-barred fighter for the little people against sundry conspiracies. His diatribes in print may not have contributed to the public peace, but circulation went up. Chaney not only editorialized against Bapst, who unwisely responded with letters that simply fueled the fire; he also organized and addressed rallies, promoted a Protestant League to influence town elections, and supported a vigilante group called the "Cast-Iron Band." He probably gave this group of thugs its name. He ranted at Protestants who sympathized with the Catholic position as "Jack Catholics." Whether or not Chaney participated in acts of violence directed at Catholic property, he certainly did nothing to discourage such activity.

In early June of 1854, Bapst's residence was attacked. The former Catholic chapel was destroyed. Fearing for his priest's safety, Archbishop John Fitzpatrick of Boston transferred him to Bangor's St. Michael's Church.

On July 8, with the Donahoe case set to go before the supreme court later in the month, a town meeting was held. It did not condemn the atmosphere of violence that developed. It resolved to expend up to $6,000 from the town treasury to cover the school committee's legal costs. Then George Maddox, a rabid Nativist whose heroes were Jesus Christ and John Brown, rose to offer additional resolutions:

> RESOLVED, That . . . the Superintending School committee did nothing more than their duty . . . against the interference of the papists, and are entitled to our cordial and hearty support.

> RESOLVED, That the insulting prosecution that is now pending . . . would not have taken place, had it not been for . . . some of the office seekers and demagogues of this town. . . .

> Whereas we have good reason to believe that we are indebted to one John Bapst, S.J., Catholic Priest, for the luxury of the lawsuit now enjoyed by the school committee, therefore

> RESOLVED, That should the said Bapst show himself again in Ellsworth, that we manifest our gratitude for his kindly interference with our free schools, and attempts to banish the Bible therefrom, by procuring for him and trying on an entire suit of new clothes, such as cannot be found at the shop of any taylor, and that when thus apparelled, we present him with a free ticket to leave Ellsworth upon the first *railroad operation* that may go into effect.

Shouts and applause followed Maddox's reading of this resolution. It was later claimed that William Chaney wrote the last resolution, which sounds like his sort of humor. The meeting adopted it unanimously. The resolution was signed by W. A. Chaney, town clerk.

On July 15—a few days after the Bath riots—an attempt to burn the new Catholic Church in Ellsworth failed. On July 22 the Donahoe case was heard in Bangor. The school board was skillfully defended by Boston attorney Richard H. Dana. Avoiding a direct argument on the constitutionality of using the Bible in the classroom, Dana simply argued it was a textbook which the school committee had every right to maintain in the curriculum. They were liable for no damages in the execution of their public duty. The court would later rule in favor of the school board.

In Ellsworth, however, matters were not handled so smoothly. On the evening of October 14 word spread that Father Bapst was back in town. Why he came back is unclear. A quickly assembled mob found Bapst at the home of a former parishioner, Richard Kent. They broke into Kent's house and dragged the priest away. Bapst was stripped, tarred and feathered, and carried on a rough plank for miles in the rain. About midnight he was abandoned, unconscious, on the outskirts of Ellsworth. His wallet was stolen and his gold watch broken.

This outrage provoked condemnation in most of the Maine and national press. Prominent Bangor citizens gave Bapst $500, a new gold watch, and a letter stating "we are unwilling to see any man proscribed for worshipping God according to the dictates of his own conscience." Bapst, who managed to offer Mass the day after the attack, concluded "God knows from evil how to draw all sorts of good for his children." While he certainly recognized some of his assailants, Bapst never gave a full account of the episode.

Ellsworth did not appear repentent. At a public meeting on October 24, Chaney entertained the crowd with another anti-Catholic harangue. A resolution was then approved blaming Bapst for the whole affair.

A week later Maine Attorney General George Evans—a former U.S. Senator—presented charges against a number of men, including George Maddox, to a Hancock County grand jury in Ellsworth. The jury voted against indictment of any of the accused. Disgusted, Evans refused to take lodging overnight in Ellsworth and left immediately.

This was not the end of Nativist activity in the state. In December riots between Irish Catholics and "native" Americans broke out in Portland. The situation remained so bad that Father John O'Donnell asked for police protection for St. Dominic's Church in October, 1855. In November of that year, a mob prevented the laying of a cornerstone in Bath for a new church to replace the one burned 16 months earlier. And in April, 1856, arson demolished the Catholic church in Ellsworth and a Catholic's (luckily) unoccupied home. Gradually, the Nativist surge receded, but the scars would remain.

John Bapst, viewed by Catholics as a sort of living martyr, became the first rector of Boston College. And William Chaney was elected a delegate to state and national American Party conventions, reorganized his paper as the *Ellsworth American*, sold it, and went to Massachusetts—where he switched allegiance to the Democrats. In a poem he condemned Ellsworth:

> May fire and brimstone never fail
> to fall in showers in Ellsworth, Maine;

May all the leading fiends assail
The thieving town of Ellsworth, Maine. . . .

May want and woe each joy curtail
That e'er was found in Ellsworth, Maine;

May no coffin want a nail
That wraps a rogue in Ellsworth, Maine.

This particular rogue renounced any belief in Christianity and became an astrologer.

23 •

The Fastest Ship Afloat

In the brief age of clippers, the *Red Jacket* was the fastest ship afloat. Built at "Deacon" George Thomas's yard in Rockland, she was launched on November 2, 1853. It was not long before the big, handsome black-hulled clipper established a record passage from New York to Liverpool, England. Here is an account of the voyage.

On January 11, 1854, the *Red Jacket*, uncoppered and manned by an indifferent crew, set sail in "rainy, unpleasant weather." Two hundred and sixty feet in length, the clipper had a delicate beauty reflected in her gracefully arched stem and curved bow, in the lifesize figure head of the Seneca chief she was named for, and in her extensive gilt ornamentation. But all this masked uncommon strength. She was captained by an experienced mariner from Cape Cod, Asa Eldridge.

According to Eldridge's log, the *Red Jacket* made just 103 nautical miles her first day out. Rain mixed with snow the next day, and hail rattled on the clipper's three decks. She made 150 miles.

On January 13 and 14, rain, snow, and hail continue to pelt the *Red Jacket*, but she made 265 miles one day and 232 the next. On the 15th, the weather moderated to rain—the best weather of the voyage—and the ship's mileage dropped to 210 miles. Snow and hail resumed on January 16 and continued through January 18—on the first two days the *Red Jacket* made a total of 225 miles, but on the third the wind shifted and she made 300 miles. From this time on the seas were so heavy and the wind so fierce that Captain Eldridge had to keep his ship dead before it. As a result, he ran farther off course than he intended.

He also ran faster than any wooden sailing ship ever had. Pounded on January 19 by what Eldridge described in his log as "terrific gale and high sea," the Rockland-built ship traveled 417 miles. The no-longer indifferent crew "spliced the main brace" to celebrate this day's work.

The following day's weather was equally violent, and the Red Jacket logged 364 miles. On January 21, with "fresh gales & high sea" it made 342 miles. "Snow, strong wind, heavy squalls," were the order of the day on January 22, as the clipper cut away another 300 miles.

January 23, 1854: "Snow, strong wind, squally, dirty weather," Captain Eldridge recorded in his log. On this day he would make 360 miles and reach Liverpool. Shortly after noon he picked up a pilot off Point Lynas. In two and a half hours the *Red Jacket* proceeded a short way. The weather was so bad that no tug was in sight. The pilot refused to take the ship up the Mersey River.

Asa Eldridge was not deterred. He took the clipper up the Mersey "with every stitch of canvas drawing in the brisk northwest wind, fairly flying toward her pier." Then, to the admiration of onlookers, he brought the *Red Jacket* about, her yards thrown back, and came up alongside the pier head. It was a neat flourish few ships could execute so smoothly.

No doubt about it, she was one hell of a sharp ship. The Liverpool *Journal* wrote:

> The Red Jacket in general appearance of hull, spars, rigging, and deck arrangements is very much after the style of the celebrated *Sovereign of the Seas*; but she appears to have rather more "spring" forward and she certainly has more outside ornament in the shape of a full-length figurehead, and an elaborate design in gilt work on her stern extending also down each side of the rudder.

And she was fast. From New York to Liverpool, dock to dock, took her 13 days, one hour and 25 minutes. On her maiden voyage she established a record for sail which still stands.

In February of 1854, Donald McKay's new clipper, aptly named the *Lightning*, almost equalled *Red Jacket's* record run and, on one day, surpassed her with 436 nautical miles (a claim subsequently challenged). But almost was not quite enough.

Immediately chartered by the White Star Line for a round-trip voyage to Melbourne, Australia, the *Red Jacket* established another record—19 days from the meridian of the Cape to Melbourne—which has never been surpassed. Or even equalled.

The Maine-built ship was purchased by a British firm. Long a favorite of the traveling public, she was considered the handsomest vessel in the British merchant marine. She was sold later into the timber trade between London and Quebec and ended her days as a coal hulk at Cape Verde. Captain Eldridge, who made one immortal run with the *Red Jacket*, later perished at sea. Despite all her years of service and great fame, no photograph of this great ship has yet been discovered, but a beautiful print was made by Currier & Ives.

The 19th century was the heyday of shipbuilding in Maine. Thousands of ships of many designs slipped down the ways. Almost every coastal town went down to the sea in ships. Even little Warren, up the St. George River, built a couple hundred vessels, including two clippers. But the most famous of them all—a work of beauty and graceful power—was built in Rockland, near where a general store and some fish processing buildings now stand.

There is no monument or marker.

24 •

The Cold-Water Mayor in Hot Water

I n June of 1855, Neal Dow, mayor of Portland and America's "Napoleon of Temperance," found himself in the odd position of defending $1,600 worth of liquor from a mob intent upon destroying it. His carelessness in getting into such a fix was matched by his callousness in getting out of it.

The diminutive but pugnacious Dow was the prime mover behind enactment of Maine's 1846 Prohibitory Law. In April, 1851, he managed to be elected mayor of Portland, and immediately set about drafting a revision of the existing law, entitled "An Act for the Suppression of Drinking Houses and Tippling Shops." That May, Dow successfully lobbied the legislature to enact his bill, which was designed to make the prosecution of liquor dealers easier. The "cold-water mayor" was relentless in his efforts to root out Demon Rum. The seaport had long had a rather boozey reputation, which Dow intended to change. His crusade gained national attention.

He also gained considerable local opposition, not the least of which was his equally reform-minded cousin, John Neal. Neal once joked that his chief objection to the mayor "amounted to this, and this only; that he was too much like myself." Certainly the two combative former Quakers proved to be well-matched adversaries. In 1852 the Democrats ran an old political warhorse, former Governor Albion Parris, against Dow. Beaten by 500 votes, Dow grumbled that he had been done in by money from the "rum sellers in Boston" and the wholesale importation of Irish voters.

Undeterred, Dow took to the lecture circuit, promoting the adoption of laws similar to the "Maine Law" in other states. In Maine, he was stung by cousin John Neal's charge that there was "more intemperance and more drinking" in Portland than ever in recent times. Neal himself had been irritated by an article Dow published in a prohibition publication, a thinly veiled description of Neal's State Street neighborhood, presenting its well-heeled denizens as closet drunks. (In fact, his own law allowed the purchase of foreign liquor in "original packages," which meant upscale Portlanders could still drink in their mansions.) Even more galling to Neal was an anonymous article, which he correctly suspected Dow of writing, which made pointed innuendo about the reason why Neal and other gentlemen posted bond for one Margaret Landrigan, better known as "Kitty Kentuck," for allegedly dealing in rum. "Kitty has some remains of beauty left, and shows that she was once very handsome; her friends were truly in need," said the piece, republished in Portland newspapers. In fact, according to Neal, the fair Kitty was "a short, thick, red-faced Irish woman, about fifty years of age, living in a wretched shanty, just under the droppings of a graveyard. . . . " Dow waspishly replied to his cousin's remonstrances, "I shall not quarrel with Mr. Neal on her account. I am not accustomed to do battle in the cause off such personages, and leave the field entirely to him . . . "

Dow, an abolitionist who disliked Irish immigrants, aligned himself with Free Soilers (antislavery forerunners of Republicans) and Know-Nothings to regain the office of mayor in 1855. He won by a mere 47 votes. Neal Dow thus became mayor of a very divided city—in which Neal Dow was the major issue. He was in no mood to conciliate, and his adversaries were eager to bring him down. He gave them their opportunity by an act of incredible carelessness.

The prohibition legislation he had drafted and the legislature had dutifully enacted allowed towns to appoint bonded agents to sell liquor for "medicinal and mechanical purposes." On May 3, the new mayor chaired a committee to establish a liquor agency store in City Hall. Dow promptly ordered $1,600 worth of liquor—too promptly. He did not wait for the aldermen to make the appropriation or appoint an agent. This meant that when the booze arrived, it was billed to Neal Dow. This created a snag—the "Maine Law" specifically stated that liquor could only be legally sold to an agent. The aldermen had not appointed one. When they did, Dow would have to transfer his title to the agent. Such a sale, by the letter of Dow's own law, might be interpreted as illegal.

Dow was blind to the potential for trouble, but Alderman Joseph Ring, an opponent of the mayor, was not. Ring commented on May 31 that Dow had apparently made a good speculation on the liquor. The mayor replied, in a flip way, "I don't know but I shall." Dow, who had inherited his father's tannery and invested widely, was known to pursue the dollar almost as ardently as he waged war on Demon Rum. Ring knew Dow did not really buy the booze to turn a profit, but he leaked their conversation to the anti-Dow press. The *Eastern Argus's* editor demanded that the city marshal seize Dow's liquor and pour it into the street. According to the Maine law, the value of spilled liquor, once seized, could not be legally recovered. "Let the lash which Neal Dow has prepared for the other backs be applied to his own when he deserves it."

Royal Williams, a distillery owner, and two other men less than friendly to the mayor swore to Judge Henry Carter on June 2 that they believed Neal Dow was keeping liquor for illegal use. Carter, who was a friend of Dow, had no choice under the law but to issue the requested search and seizure warrant. However, he turned the warrant over to a pro-Dow deputy marshal rather than the anti-Dow constable Williams had brought along.

The deputy moved slowly—giving Dow, finally alerted to the danger, time to cover his legal posterior. A hastily convened meeting of the aldermen approved the city agent's bond, thus establishing a liquor agency. Dow also got the reluctant aldermen to purchase the liquor invoice. Judge Carter hurried over from the police court to lobby the majority to accept the booze from the city.

Meanwhile, a crowd gathered outside City Hall, waiting for the deputy to seize the liquor and arrest Mayor Dow. However, it is not until 5:30 in the afternoon that the deputy walked across Congress Street and seized the $1,600 cache. Even then, he refused to arrest Dow. Bystanders damned the obvious delay in the execution of justice, but, as it was the supper hour, they retired to their homes.

A few hours later a bigger, rowdier crowd assembled. Some youths hollered threats to spill "Neal Dow's liquor." It was Saturday night and the commotion attracted many spectators. Informed of the danger of mob action, Dow dispatched the city marshal and a handful of plainclothes police to "protect the public property at all hazards."

The greatly outnumbered police retreated inside the ground-floor liquor agency, from which they shouted out orders to disperse. Sheriff Seward M. Baker ventured out and read the riot act. His words were drowned out by a crescendo of catcalls and the noise of shattering glass as rocks hurled at the store's glass entrance found their mark.

Dow called for support from two of the city's militia companies. At 9:00 P.M., 24 of Captain Green's Light Guards arrived. Like the police, the guards lacked uniforms. An hour later, Dow led the guards into Congress Street to confront the noisy crowd. When he commanded the crowd to disband, Dow received a barrage of profanity and rocks. Several militiamen were hit. The excited mayor commanded the militia to fire. He had not asked the approval of the sheriff or aldermen present in issuing this order, as required by law.

"Must I fire," Greene asked Dow, "For it's hard to shoot our own citizens?"

Dow backed down and led the Guards to Middle Street, opposite City Hall, where they met Captain Charles E. Roberts with 30 Rifle Guards. Dismissing Greene's company, the mayor told the new militiamen there would be no more hesitation in dealing with the emboldened crowd. "I want every man of you to mark your man," he said. "We'll see whether mob law shall rule here, or whether your chief magistrate shall!"

There was a hitch: Roberts's men had no ammunition. They followed the little mayor back to City Hall to procure cartridges in the armory. While thus engaged, Dow heard gunfire in the street below. The police, apparently threatened, had fired their pistols.

Instead of risking another outdoor confrontation, Dow quickly led the Rifle Guards into the darkened liquor store. Through the door they could see some diehards still throwing rocks. Most of the mob had melted away. Dow, nevertheless, screamed an order to fire.

Three volleys were discharged into Congress Street. The mayor took a few militiamen into the cellar, where he planned to fire through window gratings—but there were no rioters in sight. Bayonets fixed, the militiamen were sent out to remove any remnants of the mob.

It was now almost midnight. The exultant Mayor and his men refreshed themselves in the liquor store with crackers, cheese, and, of course, cold water. A doctor interrupted the little party to inform the mayor that one of the crowd lay dead. Dow asked "if the body was Irish."

No, the doctor replied, the corpse was "American."

In addition to the dead man, sailor John Robbins, seven men were wounded. In the ensuing controversy, it was never established whether the casualties resulted from police or militia gunfire. An inquest conducted by the city coroner determined Robbins was part of a rioting mob, but anti-Dowites portrayed him as a martyr. Militia ordered out by Governor Anson P. Morrill—it emerged that Dow did not have the authority to mobilize militia—guarded the mayor's June 5 trial on the charges initially brought by the distiller Royal Williams. Nathan Clifford, a former attorney-general of the United States, prosecuted Dow for breaking Maine law. Senator William Pitt Fessenden defended the mayor. Not surprisingly, Judge Carter ruled that the aldermen's acceptance of the liquor made Dow's purchase legal. To the cheers of his supporters, the mayor was acquitted. A week later, he weathered the critical report of a second inquest by the Cumberland County Coroner.

But Dow's conduct in the bizarre battle to protect the booze was politically devastating. He chose not to run for reelection in 1856. But that was not enough for his cousin. John Neal thought the mayor should have been hanged.

25 •

Mississippi's Silver-Tongued Orator from Maine

S eargent Smith Prentiss was the the most famous Mississippian of his day. He was the idol of the South. Many, including the fabled Webster, considered him America's greatest orator. And he was a Maine native.

Prentiss was born in Portland in 1808, the son of a sea captain. He always retained a special affection for Casco Bay, which he called "fairest dimple on ocean's cheek," and Portland, "the brightest jewel in the diadem that adorns ocean's brow." But the War of 1812 ruined his father's business, and the family moved to rural Gorham, where Prentiss grew up on a farm on the old Standish road. A childhood fever resulted in the permanent lameness of his right leg, but there was nothing wrong with the boy's retentive mind. It was said that by the age of ten, he knew every book and chapter of the Bible. The voracious young reader absorbed Shakespeare, Scott, Milton, and other writers. In appearance he came to resemble Lord Byron; it was a comparison he seems to have consciously cultivated. After attending district schools and Gorham Academy, Prentiss graduated from Bowdoin at 18. He was considered something of a prodigy.

Quick-witted and ambitious, he traveled west to seek his fortune. For awhile he was in Cincinnati, but, as he told a friend, "This place is too cheap to thrive in. Phew! I can never make a living where apples are two bits a peck." He later confided, "I was haunted, too, continually by the ghosts of slaughtered swine!" Basically, the frontier city was too tame for Seargent S. Prentiss. He headed south to Natchez, Mississippi.

He arrived at the Mansion House Hotel in that river town with five dollars in his pocket. After registering, he bellied up to the bar and ordered a bottle of wine and a box of cigars. When friends later twitted Prentiss about his recklessness in expending his last few cents in this manner, he replied:

> You don't understand human nature: that five dollars *established my credit* and I never had any trouble with my landlord afterwards; besides this, I thought to myself, 'Well, now the last of my little pile is gone, and I feel for the first time that I am thrown upon my own resources. I can make my own way in the world, and I will.'

Not long after this grand entrance, Prentiss became the tutor of the Shields family at "Rokeby," outside Natchez. He made a lasting impression upon a neighbor, a retired sea captain. As Prentiss departed, the old salt remarked to his son "Do you see that lame brat riding off there?"

"I see a gentleman on horseback, Father," the son replied, "but can't discover his lameness at this distance."

"Well," Captain Magruder said, "I've just engaged him as your teacher, and he's the smartest man that ever entered this house. If he's not at the head of the bar in Mississippi in ten years, I shall be more deceived than I ever was in man."

The captain was not deceived. Although Prentiss thought of returning to Maine, he got his law license in Mississippi, where the process was a year quicker. Beginning his practice in Natchez, Prentiss moved to Vicksburg, where he gained a great reputation. In 1836, he entered the Mississippi legislature's lower house. He was considered the epitome of the Southern gentleman, celebrated for his wit. An example which shows how thoroughly Southern the Portland-born Prentiss had become, goes like this. A representative, worked up on the subject of a possible slave insurrection, concluded, "The fact is, Mr. Speaker, I warn you, sir, we are in imminent danger. . . . we may wake in the morning and find ourselves dead!"

Prentiss later poked fun of this statement in a mock session: "Mr. Speaker, I move to amend the last syllable, of the last word, of the last line, of the last speech, by adding there unto the word *drunk*."

Another member shouted, "I second it."

"Mr. Speaker, sir, this is necessary for the sense; for, for the life of me, I can't see how a dead man can wake up after he has been kilt."

Prentiss also accepted the Southern Code of Honor, becoming involved, in 1833, in two duels with the same man. Prentiss slightly wounded his adversary, General Foote, in the first encounter. When rumors were subsequently spread that Prentiss's cane gave him an advantage as a "rest," he challenged Foote to another shootout. Apparently some lads climbed up in a tree near the scene of the duel to get a better view. Prentiss called up, "Boys, you had better come down. General Foote shoots wild, you know, and you may get hit up there." Again, Prentiss wounded Foote. He never fought another duel. The Maine man personally objected to the practice but abided by the customs of his adopted state, in which if a man "does not fight, life will be rendered valueless to him. . . . "

In 1837 Seargent Prentiss was elected to Congress. This set the stage for the establishment of his national reputation as an orator. In a special election for a special session of Congress in the summer, two Democratic representatives had been elected from Mississippi. Now, in the regular fall elections, Prentiss and another Whig prevailed. The issue of who truly represented Mississippi—the two Democrats or the two Whigs—ended up before the national House of Representatives in early 1838. The issue attracted great attention due to the highly partisan struggle in Washington, D.C., between the two parties.

Although praise of Prentiss's oratory preceded him, Whigs such as Congressmen Henry Wise of Virginia were worried when, once in Washington, Prentiss plunged into a round of carousing.

"This Mississippi wonder will cease, if he does not take heed!" he fretted, but Prentiss's colleague told Wise, "Let him alone! Never do you mind! Wait and hear him!"

To his sister Abigail in Maine, Prentiss imparted a different image, writing that he was all alone with a pile of books, papers, and documents preparing for his big speech. He said "every moment or two my thoughts wander away to Portland, and leave the rights of the people of the State of Mississippi to take care of themselves. I feel but little interest in the matter, except that my pride is somewhat involved."

That was not the way he sounded when the day came and Seargent Prentiss began to address Congress. As he continued, the galleries became crowded. Senators, hearing of his power, drifted into the House chamber. He spoke for three hours on three days in succession. Men who had been his boyhood political idols—John Quincy Adams, Henry Clay, Daniel Webster—listened raptly. When he was finally done, Webster remarked, "Nobody could equal it!"

As Prentiss's brother later wrote, "The speaker himself was evidently surprised to observe the magical power he was wielding." Prentiss spoke extemporaneously and was later unable to fully reconstruct what he said. "I suppose you will wonder what I could talk about so long," he wrote to Abigail. "That's more than I can tell you," he confessed. The stenographers were so mesmerized by Prentiss's delivery that they, too, failed to capture his words.

The conclusion of the skeletal printed version of the Mississippian's oration at least gives an idea of Prentiss's fervor. Speaking for Mississippi, he said:

> . . . if you are determined to impose upon her a representation not of her choice and against her will, go on and complete her degradation. Send her a proconsul for a governor, and make a task master to rule over her. Let her no longer sit with you, a young and fair member of this proud sisterhood, but strip off the robes of equality and make of her a hand maid and a servant. . . .

This heavy-breathing rhetoric thrilled the young ladies who crowded the galleries to suffocation. Prentiss, extremely self-conscious around women because of his lameness, sought the company of prostitutes, and would marry late in life. The imagery of womanhood violated pervaded Prentiss's oration:

> Sir, you may think it an easy and a trifling matter to deprive Mississippi of her elective franchise, for she is young, and may not . . . have the power to resist; but I am much mistaken in the character of her chivalrous citizens if you do not find that she not only understands her rights, but has both the will and the power to vindicate them. You may yet find to your sorrow that you have grasped a scorpion where you only thought to crush a worm. . . .

In the light of later events, when Mississippi stood at the head of the secession movement and provided the Confederacy with its president, such words would assume a prophetic note.

> . . . You sit here twenty-five sovereign states in judgment of the most sacred right of a sister state—that which is to a state what chastity is to a woman or honor to a man. . . . But if your determination is taken, if the blow must fall, if the Constitution must bleed, I have but one request on her behalf to make: When you decide that she cannot choose her own representation, at the same moment blot from the star spangled banner of this Union the bright star that glitters to the name of Mississippi, but leave the stripe behind, a fit emblem of her degradation.

With this speech Prentiss won acclaim as one of the nation's greatest orators. So compelling was his delivery that even a slight lisp was overcome. "True eloquence . . . does not consist in speech," Daniel Webster once wrote. "It must exist in the man, in the subject, and in the occasion."

Prentiss was asked how he was able to call forth such beautiful images. He described himself, when speaking and excited, like a small boy chasing one butterfly after another in a meadow, each more alluring than the other. "It's so with me; every fancy starts a new one, till in the pursuit my whole mind is filled with beautiful butterflies."

Debate on the disputed Mississippi election consumed six weeks. "I am heartily sick of the whole matter," Prentiss wrote to his sister. In the end, both Democrats and Whigs were rejected. The speaker of the house, James Polk, a Democrat, broke a tie vote on the Whig contenders.

The matter was left up to another vote in Mississippi.

It was one of the most colorful elections in Mississippi history. For awhile a traveling menagerie, or circus, followed Prentiss about his district, taking advantage of the crowds he attracted. At one stop circus and politician joined forces, Prentiss speaking from atop a hyena's cage. Sticking his cane through the holes in his impromptu rostrum, he made the animal yell. "Listen, fellow citizens! Hark, how the very beasts of the forest utter their condemnation of this great . . . outrage upon your dearest and most cherished rights!" Prentiss thundered. Soon he was playing to the excited lion's roars, and identifying various beasts as a convention of his opponents. When the baboon made a face upon being when compared to a well-known politician, the orator said, "Ha, my fine fellow, I see I have unintentionally wounded your feelings by the comparison, and I humbly beg your pardon." This performance became part of Mississippi folklore.

On another occasion, the Democratic candidate for governor shared a platform with Prentiss, and brought up the subject of the Whig's fondness for liquor. Prentiss, in a facetious response, deflected the thrust:

> Now I will admit, fellow citizens, that sometimes, when in the enjoyment of social communion with gentlemen, I am made merry with . . . the rich wines of glorious France. It is then that I enjoy the romance of life. Imagination, stimulated with the juice of the grape gave to the world the Song of Solomon, and the Psalms of that old poet of the Lord—glorious old David. . . . Now, I have only been drunk once. Over in Simpson County I was compelled to sleep in the same bed with this distinguished nominee . . . and in the morning I found myself drunk of corn-whiskey. I had lain too close to this soaked mass of Democracy, and was drunk from absorption.

Prentiss won the election and served for about a year in Congress. A great orator, he was an indifferent statesman. His major interests were booze, loose women, and gambling. He once explained his reckless side to his friend Henry Wise: "I delight to climb great heights on the perpendicular sides of rocks, whence the staid fathers of comely daughters will expect me certainly to fall. I sport in shocking their apprehensions, to show them that . . . I am sure-footed at least. . . . "

In 1839 his brief elective career ended when he lost a Senate bid. He quickly reestablished his preeminence as a trial lawyer. Still a great "draw" for his oratory, he toured the country for the Whigs in 1840. That August he gave a speech in his native Portland which drew a huge crowd, including his mother and sister. However, the Democratic *Eastern Argus* was not impressed and made allusions to Prentiss's less-than-puritanical lifestyle. In his speech, defending the institution of credit, Prentiss had said, "the system may be abused, and so may eating and drinking—but who is he who will rise up and say, eat not and drink not for fear of surfeit?" The *Argus* responded "Not the orator, we suspect! No, not he!" At another point, warning against "false prophets," Prentiss said, "They have the goblet before your eyes, but the contents are poisonous." The *Argus* asked, "But is Mr. Prentiss the man to talk of goblets and poisonous liquids therein?" Even the speaker's salute to female beauty and character brought a telling retort: "This reckless fulminator resides, we believe, in Vicksburg, and is somewhat popular there; does he wish to save the tottering virtue of Portland females, by introducing here the customs and habits which characterize the dens of Vicksburg?"

Indeed, Prentiss's love of alcohol was a major vice; he recognized it was killing him, but he could not shake it off. In 1842 he finally married and had children. But, in debt as a result of a business failure and feeling the effects of his life on the edge, he did not live to see his family grow up. According to one biographer, Prentiss said he made two great mistakes in his life— forsaking Maine for the South, and not marrying when he first took up law. In a northern climate and with restraining home influences, Prentiss speculated that he might not have "wooed the Scorpion which is stinging me to death."

The scorpion probably was a major factor in stimulating the free flow of his oratory.

Seargent Prentiss was a Northerner who adapted to the Southern lifestyle to excess. Was it to compensate for his crippled condition, about which he was morbidly sensitive? Was it in reaction to New England puritanism? Whatever the reasons, he never went so far politically as to favor secession. Prentiss always was pro-Union. "It is said against me," he once said, "that I have Northern feelings. Well, so I have, and Southern and Eastern and Western. . . . I do most fervently pray that my eyes may not witness a division of this Republic!" Prentiss, in an address at New Orleans in 1846, cried "the Union cannot be dissolved; its fortunes are too brilliant to be marred; its destinies too powerful to be resisted."

Yet, in an address several years later in the same city, to which he had moved from Mississippi, Prentiss noted "that if such a calamity as secession came he could only cast his lot with the land of his wife and children."

He never had to make that painful decision. Seargent Prentiss died in 1850, aged 42.

George Prentiss, a noted clergyman, wrote a biography that tended to glorify his brother, omitting reference to his vices. J.F.H. Claiborne, Seargent Prentiss's Democratic opponent in the famous contested election, charged that George Prentiss presented his brother "as a semi-saint and somewhat of a puritan to please New England tastes, when we all knew he was the farthest possible removed from saintliness and puritanism." Yet Claiborne also noted of the adversary with whom he had become reconciled: "He was endowed with more genius than any man we ever met with. . . . "

In the 19th century, in Maine as well as in Mississippi, Prentiss's memory endured. During the Civil War, a federal force raided Mississippi and came to the gates of "Rokeby." Pointing to the house, the colonel, a native of Portland, said, "Soldiers, in that house young Prentiss taught his first school in Mississippi; let nothing about it be disturbed."

He wheeled his men about and left.

• 26

The Republic
of Muscongus

E ast of Pemaquid, less than a mile from the mainland in Muscongus Bay,
lies Loud's Island. For a long time it was known as Muscongus Island. The
famous chief Samoset lived here. Although settled since the mid-17th century,
the island was omitted from the geodetic survey of the State of Maine's coast.
It was an error that, while not rectified, did not bother anyone for generations.
Inhabitants considered themselves members of the nearby mainland town of
Bristol. So did Bristol authorities. The tax collector rowed over annually,
chalking the tax of each property owner on his house. As soon as the money
was paid up, the marks were rubbed off. It was all pretty simple and
neighborly. Until 1860. That is when Loud's Island undertook secession.

Most folk in Bristol voted Republican—but not on Loud's Island. Everybody
there was a Democrat. Thus, when the polls closed and the votes were tallied,
the Bristol authorities were shocked to learn the town had narrowly voted for
Stephen Douglas rather than Abraham Lincoln. To rectify this situation, the
town fathers, recalling that Loud's Island was not on the map, threw all its
votes out. Bristol's vote was now Republican.

This did not sit well with the folks on the island, who in true New England
fashion, held a meeting about the outrage. They decided if their votes were
not accepted, then they would not pay taxes. When the Bristol tax collector
showed up, they immediately erased his chalk marks and told him in no
uncertain terms they did not intend to pay: "No votes, no taxes."

The islanders also gave Bristol notice that they had seceded. They were
willing to support the United States—"but not the Town of Bristol." They
would govern themselves. In this manner, the Republic of Muscongus was
born.

Bristol ignored the Republic. When, in 1863, the names of nine men from
Loud's Island were drawn in the town's draft for Civil War soldiers, recruiting
officers rowed over to collect the men.

They did not get them. Every man and boy in the Republic of Muscongus
met them at the waterfront—armed. The recruiters were told in plain
language to head back to the mainland without any draftees. This they wisely
did.

However, one officer was foolhardy enough to return to the island and try
his luck. The first name on the list of draftees was Carter, and the major
proceeded to his house. Mr. Carter was off hauling lobsters, but Mrs. Carter
was home busily paring potatoes. When the officer made known his mission,

she quickly bombarded him with potatoes, peeled and unpeeled. He beat a quick retreat. "Almighty thunder!" he later exclaimed, "If I had a regiment of women like her, I'd take Richmond inside of three days!"

The Muscongus folk wanted to make it clear that they had no grudge against the United States. Just Bristol. So they held another meeting and each of the drafted men paid $300 to buy a mainland substitute, as was the legal custom then. The community also raised $900, which was given to the government to "help lick the rebels."

The Southern states seceded from the Union; Loud's Island—the independent Republic of Muscongus—simply seceded from Bristol, Maine.

And managed just fine, thank you.

27 •

Fix Bayonets!: The Day Maine Won the Civil War

S hortly after four o'clock on the afternoon of July 2, 1863, day two at
— Gettysburg, a brigade of Union troops scrambled up the rocky incline of a hill called Little Round Top. "I place you here!" shouted Colonel Strong Vincent to Colonel Joshua Chamberlain, commander of the 20th Maine Volunteer Regiment. "This is the left of the Union line. You understand! You are to hold this ground at all cost."

Chamberlain, until a year before a professor of foreign languages at Bowdoin College, understood. Lee was throwing Longstreet's Corps against the southern end of the Union Army. If the rebel onslaught took lightly defended Little Round Top, ignored by the Union command until literally the last moment, the Union Army's left flank would be turned. The Confederates would be in a position to win the battle and, possibly, the war.

It was as simple as that.

Chamberlain's 28 officers and 358 men stood to the left of the Michigan, New York, and Pennsylvania regiments strung out in a blue line among the boulders and scrub oak trees that dotted Little Round Top's western and southern slopes, just beneath the hill's barren crest. The 20th Maine was supposed to anchor the Union Army's left flank, yet its own flank was exposed. To provide some protection, Chamberlain dispatched B Company under Captain Walter G. Morrill to establish a skirmish line in the valley below him and at the eastern base of another, bigger hill known as Round Top. This meant the Colonel had 308 men remaining on Little Round Top.

Now, as the rebel artillery barrage ended, Chamberlain looked down to see masses of grey-clad troops "all rolling toward us in tumultuous waves." The shock of battle spread along the Union line, with the 20th Maine attacked frontally by the 4th Alabama and most of the 47th Alabama regiments. As Chamberlain confronted this threat, a more ominous movement was detected coming from Round Top. The 15th Alabama had driven off a small force of Union sharpshooters and was advancing toward Chamberlain's rear. To meet this assault, Chamberlain pulled back his own left wing until it was at almost right angles with his other wing.

The maneuver stretched Chamberlain's line dangerously, but it prevented the Alabamians from turning his flank. Instead, their rush up the hill was halted by a volley of musketry. Momentarily falling back, the much larger Confederate force regrouped and struck again and again. At least five times, the 20th Maine's line was penetrated. "At times I saw around me more of the enemy than my own men," Chamberlain said.

At one agonizing moment, when the smoke lifted, Chamberlain saw that his center was actually defended by only Color-Sergeant Andrè Tozier, holding the flag in one hand and his musket in the other. It was a rather romantic sight—and chilling in its implications. The gap was quickly filled, but a third of the 20th Maine lay dead or wounded. Blood spattered the rocks. Every tree was riddled with bullets.

A brief lull was followed by a renewed assault by the 15th and 47th Alabama troops. This time, Chamberlain noted, there were no rebel yells. The Confederates advanced up Little Round Top quietly, grimly. The Maine boys were running out of ammunition and desperately rummaged through the cartridge boxes of fallen comrades or rebels. Men began to seize their hot musket barrels and prepare to use the butts as clubs.

The critical moment had arrived.

Chamberlain ordered Captain Ellis Spear to wheel the bent left flank forward until it was even with the right. And he gave another order: "Fix bayonets!"

Then: "Charge bayonets, charge!"

As Private Theodore Gerrish recalled, "Every man understood in a moment that the movement was our only salvation, but there is a limit to human endurance, and I do not dishonor those brave men when I write that for a brief moment the order was not obeyed, and the little line seemed to quail under the fearful fire that was being poured upon it."

Lieutenant Holman S. Melcher, waving his sword, and shouting "Come on! Come on! Come on, boys!" broke the pause. With a loud shout the 20th Maine moved down the slope toward the advancing rebels, about 30 yards away.

The "right wheel forward" was executed perfectly. Stunned, the Confederates stopped in their tracks. Sweeping down the south face of Little Round Top in a wide arc, bayonets glinting in the late afternoon sun, the 20th Maine collided with the first line of Confederates. The Confederate line wavered and disintegrated. An officer fired point-blank at Chamberlain's face. His revolver misfired and he handed it, with a shrug, to the Maine colonel along with his sword. Chamberlain kept the pistol and continued down the hill. Many other Alabama soldiers simply dropped their weapons and surrendered.

The rebels tried to reform a second line at the base of Little Round Top. Suddenly, from behind a nearby stone wall, about 60 bluecoats arose. They fired a volley which further disconcerted the Confederates. It was B Company and some of the Union sharpshooters previously driven from Round Top.

The battle-hardened Alabamians panicked. Colonel Oates of the 15th Alabama later recalled "we ran like a herd of wild cattle." And as Chamberlain described it, the 20th Maine "swinging like a great gate on its hinges . . . swept the front clean of assailants." It was only with difficulty that he brought his 200 men to a halt. By 6:30 in the early evening, they had captured 368 prisoners and saved the day.

But the 20th Maine's work was not quite done. They were ordered to secure Round Top before the disorganized rebels could haul artillery to its summit. Until this possibility was foreclosed, a threat still remained to the Union left. At nine o'clock, as darkness descended, the Mainers led by Chamberlain, limping from a wound in his foot, headed up Round Top. They were still without fresh ammunition. Within a half hour, the Mainers brushed aside minimal rebel opposition.

Reinforced, Chamberlain's men spent an anxious night anticipating a Confederate counterattack. It never came. After some dawn skirmishing at the foot of the rocky hill, the 20th Maine was out of action on day three at Gettysburg.

It had done heroic work on day two. The Confederacy's hopes died that day on the bloody ledges of Little Round Top. Mainers were familier with rocky terrain. On July 2, 1863, they proved it.

28 •

Lincoln's Life-Insurance Policy

In Washington in the autumn of 1862, somebody tried to shoot Abraham Lincoln as he rode to the Soldiers' Home. A bullet perforated his stovepipe hat. If the assassin's aim had been an inch surer, Hannibal Hamlin would have become the 17th president of the United States. It was the closest the "Old Carthaginian" from Maine came to the presidency.

Lincoln downplayed the attempt. "Do you really think," he asked a friend, that "the Richmond people would like to have Hannibal Hamlin here any better than myself? In that one alternative, I have an insurance on my life worth half the prairie land in Illinois."

Vice President Hamlin was friendly with Republican radicals, who favored an aggressive policy. Emancipate the slaves, arm them, develop a more rigorous reconstruction program—this was the radical agenda. Hamlin was for it, but Lincoln proceeded slowly, too slowly for many radicals. Their leaders went to Hannibal Hamlin in the winter of 1863 and offered to back him for the 1864 Republican presidential nomination.

Hamlin would have nothing to do with their offer. He told them "they must not approach him on the subject of the presidency, since Lincoln was his friend and he was Lincoln's friend."

Lincoln and Hamlin had not met until after the 1860 election. Both were homespun-looking types with dark complexions. Southern extremists called Lincoln an "ape" and Hamlin a "mulatto." Both were strong men, noted wrestlers in their youth. And both were politicians who came to the Republican party from other parties. Lincoln was a former Whig, whose only national experience before 1861 was one term as a congressman. Hamlin, long a leader of Maine Democrats, had served for many years in Congress before switching to the Republicans in the mid-1850s. Both were shrewd figures whose countrified appearance led opponents to underestimate their abilities.

Yet there was a certain distance between them. Lincoln seldom confided in Hamlin. One of the few times he did was when he gave his vice president an advance peek at the Emancipation Proclamation. But the decision was Lincoln's. Like others in his office, Hamlin had no real power and Lincoln, like other presidents, was not about to share any.

Yet despite his apparent frustration, Hamlin desired renomination in 1864. It would be a vindication of his performance.

The Republican Convention at Baltimore in June dropped Hamlin and replaced him on the ticket with Andrew Johnson of Tennessee, a Democrat who had supported the Union. Exactly what maneuvers led to the Mainer's displacement are not fully clear. He failed to get the solid support of New England, and fellow radical Charles Sumner apparently played a key role in denying him renomination. Sumner's motives were a bit complicated. Although he liked Hamlin, he intensely disliked Senator William Pitt Fessenden from Maine. He hoped that Hamlin, out of his "fifth wheel" job, would contest Fessenden's reelection to the Senate and beat him. If this was Sumner's thinking, he would soon rue it.

During all this, the President kept his cards close to his chest. Some later accounts said he had favored Johnson, believing he could attract Democratic voters in the election. Others recall Lincoln registering disappointment when he learned of Johnson's nomination. Whatever Lincoln felt, he did not lift a finger to save Hannibal Hamlin.

After the convention, Hamlin insisted upon serving with Company A of the Maine Coast Guards, a militia outfit he had enlisted in as a private at the beginning of the war. Nobody, certainly not Captain Llewellyn Morse, expected the vice president to perform garrison duty at Kittery's Fort McClary. But Hamlin wanted to get out of Washington and do something. For a few days he took guard duty, but during most of his three months at the fort he was its cook. He did a lot of fishing and cooked some mean chowders.

At the inauguration ceremonies in March, 1865, the new vice president was drunk. Hamlin tried to cut short Johnson's rambling speech by tugging at his coattails. Lincoln was grimly embarrassed. Although a teetotaler who had gotten liquor banned from the Senate restaurant—one of his few accomplishments as vice president—Hamlin later said Johnson had been sick and had tried to steady himself with whiskey. He hardly approved, but he was careful to say nothing derogatory about his successor.

He had plenty to say about others, however, as he left Washington. "Ex-Vice-President Hannibal Hamlin departed for his home in Maine this morning," the *New York Herald* reported, "thoroughly disgusted with everything and almost everybody in public life, excepting the president. He complains that almost every one with whom he has had anything to do has played him false."

On April 14, 1865, Abraham Lincoln was assassinated. Andrew Johnson became the 17th president of the U.S.

Lincoln's "life-insurance policy," who had failed to gain Fessenden's seat, learned the news at Bangor. He returned to the capitol just in time for the funeral. What kind of president would Hannibal Hamlin have made? Possibly a much better one than Johnson. Hamlin would not have vetoed the Freedmen's Bureau or the 14th Amendment. Radical in sympathies but not a harsh man, he would have worked with Congress. He would not have come within one vote of impeachment and removal from office—as Johnson did.

He was later reelected to the Senate and served as ambassador to Spain. Hamlin always valued his association with Lincoln. He saw greatness in the man before many contemporaries did. Nothing bothered Hamlin more than rumors that later surfaced that Lincoln had wanted him off the ticket in 1864. When a Pennsylvania congressman claimed Lincoln had whispered to him that Johnson was his choice, Hamlin wrote the Pennsylvanian a letter, saying he was "sorry to be disabused." Then, as usual, he had second thoughts, "Pettis must have imagined he heard Lincoln say that," he told his wife. "I am sorry I wrote him. Lincoln was my friend; I am sure of it."

Perhaps Lincoln *was* Hannibal Hamlin's friend, but he allowed his insurance policy to lapse in the summer of 1864.

• 29

Joshua Fought the Battle of Bowdoin ...and Lost

A decade after Gettysburg, where he won the Congressional Medal of Honor, Joshua Chamberlain was fighting a losing campaign, and he knew it. The man who had received the surrender of the Army of Northern Virginia and was four times elected governor of Maine submitted his resignation as president of Bowdoin College. "I hoped to succeed," he wrote, " but I have not met my own expectation. A spirit seems to possess the college with which I cannot harmonize, and under which I cannot advantageously work. I owe the world some better service, and it my duty to seek it." The boards of trustees and overseers refused to accept Chamberlain's resignation. The embattled president stayed on. Was his gesture just another clever tactic? Far from the boulders of Little Round Top, amidst the stately brick buildings of the Brunswick campus, Chamberlain was about to confront an open student rebellion.

Before he was a soldier, Joshua Chamberlain was an educator. Born in Brewer in 1828, the boy was sent to military school by his father when he was 14 and, later, to Bowdoin. After graduating with honors from the liberal arts college, Chamberlain seemed to bend to his mother's desire that he become a clergyman. He went to the Bangor Theological Seminary, studied religion and foreign languages, and aspired to be a missionary. Instead, he married and accepted appointment as an instructor of religion at his Brunswick *alma mater*. He spent a few years as a professor of religion, of rhetoric, and oratory; he was appointed professor of foreign languages in 1861; and he was granted a leave of absence to study abroad in Europe in 1862. In another, more important decision, Chamberlain secured a commission as a lieutenant colonel of the 20th Maine Volunteer Regiment. At Little Round Top he won glory and, some felt, a fondness for fighting.

After Appomattox, General Chamberlain was drawn to politics, winning the governorship in 1866 by the greatest plurality then recorded. He was an independent-minded Republican, often at odds with his party's leaders. He upset many Republicans by his opposition to the impeachment of President Johnson. Prohibitionists were alienated by Chamberlain's apparent uneasiness with the Maine Law and adamant refusal to support a state constabulary to enforce it. And he created a furor by his stand on capital punishment. When he insisted upon the execution of a black convicted of rape and murder, critics claimed Chamberlain was insensitive and racist. Such issues obscured Chamberlain's progressive record. On top of everything, ugly rumors about his marriage surfaced. Certainly he was estranged from his wife, who disliked politicians and would not live in Augusta.

When the trustees of Bowdoin offered Chamberlain its presidency, he was receptive—on the condition that he be allowed to institute a number of reforms. Was the man who returned to Bowdoin in 1871 basically an educator, military man, politician, or the missionary he once dreamed of becoming? The answer was that he was all of these things, and it was an explosive mixture.

He intended to shake things up. Chamberlain felt Bowdoin had to become more relevant to the modern world. The curriculum should be revised to emphasize science and modern languages. Despite his classical background, he urged that Latin and Greek be replaced by French and German. Despite his theological training (or perhaps because of it), he favored a non-sectarian approach to religion on campus. "Let it be a new Elizabethan age," he challenged his audience at his 1872 inaugural address.

Not everybody was comfortable with Chamberlain's drive for innovation, coupled with a tendency for command rather than collegiality. Resistance mounted among students, faculty, and alumni, and in 1873 Chamberlain offered to resign.

The major confrontation came over Chamberlain's insistence upon a required military program. Military drill, the Civil War soldier felt, was "the kind of exercise particularly recommended by Plato, even in opposition to strictly athletic training as most suitable for young men." Maybe. But Bowdoin was hardly Plato's Republic and the appearance of four cannon and students dressed in uniforms patterned on those of West Point was not welcomed by many, on campus and off. Students grumbled about time consumed in drill; some members of the faculty and governing boards apparently indicated sympathy.

The catalyst for revolt came when the purchase of uniforms was made mandatory at the outset of the 1873–1874 academic year. Only $5.60 was involved, but the real issue was opposition to the very existence of a military department at Bowdoin. In November, a petition signed by nearly every member of the three upper classes was presented to the trustees and overseers. It called for abolition of the military program, and enumerated reasons:

First.	Injury to the institution from loss of students.
Second.	Abundant facilities for more popular and profitable exercises.
Third.	Expense incurred in purchasing otherwise useless equipment.
Fourth.	Loss of a large proportion of time otherwise devoted to study.
Fifth.	Its intense and growing unpopularity and other subordinate reasons.

The boards appointed a committee to chat with a committee of the students, but that was all. The petition was ignored. In appealing directly to the boards, the students were criticized for going over the heads of the president and faculty. Undergraduate resentment hardened into icy resolve in the winter months.

It did not thaw come spring. On May 19, 1874, "much shouting and profanity" accompanied dispersal of an artillery drill. Juniors were the prime offenders. Major Joseph P. Sanger, the drillmaster, rather Napoleonic in temper as well as in physical stature, threatened grave punishments for further demonstrations at the May 20 drill. No sooner had ranks broken than one junior declared, melodramatically, "Whoever does not keep his mouth shut about the drill now, must understand that he is sitting on his coffin." The class cheered and groaned.

Chamberlain convened his faculty to consider the crisis. The student spokesman was promptly dismissed and five other juniors suspended.

The juniors immediately voted to never drill again. Within hours, the sophomores and freshmen also voted against continued participation in drill. Seniors had already been exempted.

Again Chamberlain assembled the faculty. In a meeting that lasted until midnight, the professors appointed committees to meet with the rebellious students. During a feverish weekend, they worked to dissuade the young men from "the folly and wrong of their intended course of action."

The rebels stood firm. All three classes, after their own meeting in the college chapel, signed a no-drill pledge. When, after being rained out for two days, drill was held, no juniors showed up. The entire class was sent home. Most of the sophomores and freshmen were soon heading home as well. Band members and students excused from drill for physical reasons joined in sympathy with their classmates.

President Chamberlain's small college was practically deserted as he sent a letter to the departed students' parents. It was an ultimatum: if rebels did not surrender and comply with Bowdoin's drill requirement within ten days, they would be officially expelled. Furthermore, he wrote, if, upon their return, they missed any drill, they would be dismissed at the end of the school term.

The lines had been drawn.

Chamberlain experienced some anxious moments when it was rumored that Dartmouth College would accept the Bowdoin rebels. He breathed easier when assured by Asa D. Smith that his college would do no such thing. At least one flank was secured.

The student revolt at Bowdoin attracted national attention. Most Maine folk were probably not sympathetic with the rebels. "It is a rebellion against hard work," one newspaper writer fumed. "We cannot believe that these picked youth, the flower of the State, are such Miss Nancies as they appear in this affair." A wartime comrade lauded Chamberlain for undertaking "a far more important struggle for the national strength and well being" than even his Civil War service.

But praise was hardly universal. Even newspapers supporting Chamberlain's authority under challenge questioned the wisdom of the military program. One paper was caustic. Referring to the old soldier's earlier capital punishment stand, it felt that the:

> . . . craze for epaulets and gold lace has at length borne fruit. The same
> sickly longing for the exercise of autocratic power that once sent a thrill
> of disgust and horror through the state by needlessly and obstinately
> insisting on a legal homicide which was demanded neither by the laws nor
> by public sentiment, has made the halls of Bowdoin tenantless.

The rebel line wavered. Freshmen, meeting in Portland on June 5, agreed
to return to Bowdoin but also pledged to request dismissal at the conclusion
of their term if the boards did not abolish drill, or make it optional. The other
classes took the same course of action and, by June 8, all but three of the
rebels of May were back on campus.

Chamberlain had defeated the so-called "Drill Rebellion." But it was, as he
realized, a hollow victory. The students had lost the battle, but not the
campaign. That June the boards made drill optional. Despite Chamberlain's
insistence upon maintaining drill as an elective, it was only a matter of time
before it was abolished outright. Chamberlain ruefully conceded "perhaps it
is impracticable to bring such exercises into a regular college with traditions
like ours."

The episode damaged Chamberlain. A visiting committee of the boards,
investigating the affair, verbally slapped the general on the wrist, declaring:

> The President of a college must deal both with Faculty and Students face
> to face with unswerving directness of statement, and in a manner of one
> doing the duties of his station, because they are duties and not because his
> station is superior.

This little lecture on duty must have galled Chamberlain. Yet it seems
apparent that the military habit of command had overruled the educator's
responsibility to listen and reason.

The "Drill Rebellion" of 1874 was but one dramatic example of increased
opposition to his attempt to remake Bowdoin College. He was defeated on
other fronts, notably when his cherished science program was scrapped. It
had never included more than 30 percent of the student body. Lack of funds
was given as the main reason for axing the science experiment. In 1883—
much of the good he accomplished obscured by the clutter of controversy—
Chamberlain stepped down as president. He remained a lecturer for two
more years. When he ended that as well, Joshua Chamberlain had taught
nearly every course the college had to offer.

And he had learned something under Bowdoin's pines. Academia could
be tougher terrain than the contested hills of Pennsylvania.

• 30

Isaac Maxim
and Sons

I saac Maxim, a jack-of-all-trades who lived on the margin of Maine's wildlands, was a good-natured, philosophical man who knew his share of disappointments. He fully expected to meet Jesus Christ in Sangerville, Maine, in 1843. He did not. Isaac always wanted to shoot a bear, but, although the woods were full of the "critters," he never got one. Of a tinkering bent, Maxim hoped to invent a machine that would fly or a gun that fired many shots in rapid succession. He never succeeded here, either, but his son Hiram became one of America's most famous inventive geniuses. He invented the machine gun. Another son, Hudson, was also an inventor who specialized in explosives. Isaac's boys changed the nature of warfare. Like their eccentric father, they were Maine-grown characters, with pronounced opinions on just about everything.

Isaac was not content with the Congregational faith of his parents and, as his son Hudson observed, "Maine never has been a place where a person had to go long without a religion suited to his taste." His father became attracted to Adventist Millerism. The Millerites decided Jesus Christ would make an appearance in Sangerville, Maine, at midnight on the tenth day of the seventh month of 1843. Like other Adventists, Isaac confessed his sins, washed thoroughly, and put on white raiment the day before Christ's announced arrival. Then he stationed himself out in the front yard and waited for the Lord. His wife Harriet was not quite as expectant, requesting, "When you see Christ a-comin' call me, and I'll come out and ketch hold of your coat-tails and go up with you."

Christ didn't show. Isaac shed his white clothes—and belief in Adventism—and went to bed. (The next day the citizens of Sangerville, led by their first selectmen, rode the Adventist minister, decked out in tar and feathers, out of town on a rail.)

Isaac, who read Voltaire and Tom Paine as well as the Bible, gained a reputation for being a free thinker or, as some saw it, an infidel. He got up in church one Sunday and said:

> You folks, while you're advisin' God in your prayers to do so many things, why don't you put this flea in His ear? . . . tell Him to kill off the devil. If He's all-powerful, He easily can dispense with the devil and just clean him out. If God is all-powerful and lets the devil live, then the devil is simply His agent. If the devil is acting in accordance with God's will, then God is

responsible, and the devil's acts are God's acts; and if God isn't responsible, then where are we going to land?

"It was the greatest ambition of my father's life to kill a bear," Hiram recalled, "but he never succeeded." Hiram's grandfather—for whom he was named—bagged an average of four bears a year. The bounty and skin of the big animals yielded five dollars, a goodly sum for hardscrabble settlers of the Piscataquis River valley in Maine's north woods.

The farm in Sangerville, where Hiram was born in 1840, was in the midst of forest, and there were plenty of black bears about. One of Hiram's most vivid memories of his childhood was of a bear chasing some of the family's sheep. His mother's screams deterred the animal. It stopped, took one look at the agitated humans, and disappeared into a swamp before Isaac could get his gun. "There, Harriet," he reproved her, "if you had not screamed I could have killed that bear."

When Hiram was about six, his father sold the farm in Sangerville and moved to nearby French's Mills, where he turned wood with a couple of lathes. The boy became interested in a jam downriver where sawmill debris formed a dam. His mother was dead set against the boy's desire to see this jam, warning that "the bears in the swamp might attack you." One fine Sunday, Hiram got his father to accompany him—and, sure enough, they encountered a bear. A pole in the water started to move. Hiram spied a big bear on the other end. Isaac said, "Let us go back to the house and get the gun as quick as possible; perhaps we may kill him." Typically, he didn't have his gun when he needed it.

> It was very slow work getting through the underbrush, and when we got out and into the clearing we saw a man coming out of our house with our gun. We then learned that the bear that we had dislodged had passed very near the little schoolhouse where Sunday school was in session, and the instant the bear was seen every man ran for a gun. Soon all the men and boys in the neighborhood were on the track of the bear; but they didn't get him; they seldom did at that time. The next day it was found that dogs were not quite so numerous as they had been.

Father Isaac was always on the move. Hudson Maxim reckoned that by the time he was ten the family had moved 11 times. Yet all the homes were within a 30-mile radius along the Piscataquis River. Isaac Maxim was about "as poor as Job's turkey," and, lacking a cradle, all the Maxim children were rocked in great wooden bowls. Isaac was an expert at turning wood, and he always was able to come up with a bowl—nicely rounded on the bottom—for each child.

The Maxims were poor, dirt poor. Young Hiram, the eldest of eight children, was described as "a poor little bareheaded, barefooted boy." Hudson, always more colorful in recalling the family's poverty, wrote that he did not possess a pair of real shoes until he was 13. "In winter I sometimes tied old bags around my feet when I was going out in the barn," he recalled. "If the weather was very cold I had to stay in the house." Mother Harriet Maxim was a hardworking soul who never complained much and possessed considerable wit. It was a close-knit if rather undisciplined family (" . . . we children didn't have much more looking after than little pigs. We just ran wild. . . ."). Late

September and early August were "fly-time," but the bugs were just an accepted part of farm life. "When we gathered round the table to eat, the flies gathered there, too, but we could eat faster'n they could."

Isaac was a real Yankee tinkerer. He tried to build a flying machine and talked about inventing a gun able to fire many shots rapidly. When Hiram—who, inheriting his father's inventiveness, made an automatic mousetrap, a tricycle, and a composition blackboard—was about 14, he collaborated with Isaac in making drawings and a model of a machine gun. These were sent to a Bangor gunsmith, but the gun got nowhere. The idea was, for the time, dropped, but it stuck in young Hiram's brain.

Hiram was a persistent sort. When the family was living at French's Mills, he became obsessed with cutting down a big fir in neighbor Lucien French's pasture. For two weeks he hacked away at it with a butcher's knife for eight or nine hours a day. Finally

> . . . I heard a crackling noise at the point of the knife, and, looking up, I saw the big tree toppling over. This was the proudest moment of my long and eventful life; nothing since has equalled it.
>
> Shortly after I saw Mr. Lucien French approaching at a gallop. I expected he would pat me on the back and tell me what a wonderful boy I was. Instead of that he was extremely indignant and scolded me for having cut down a tree that afforded shade to his cattle, but when he saw that I had done it with a knife he commenced to laugh. . . .

That Hiram initially expected praise for his feat was in keeping with the special attention the eldest of the Maxim children got at home. "I think my father and mother took a somewhat greater pride in him than they did in the rest of us," Hudson Maxim later wrote. "They thought he was the great King Bee of the world, and used to hold him up to us as a model." Hiram developed a habit of poking fun at others and puffing himself up quite early in life. Once, when he was plaguing one of his siblings, Mrs. Maxim threw one of the potatoes she was peeling at him. "It didn't quite break his nose, but it put a little bit of a kink in it that remained for life." Another time, holding forth about his speaking ability to his father, Hiram exclaimed, "Father, do you know that I often am surprised at my own eloquence?" "Well, Hiram, did ye ever surprise anybody else?" Isaac asked.

Isaac Maxim moved to Orneville, where he operated a gristmill. When Hiram was 14, he worked for one Daniel Sweat, a carriage-maker in East Corinth; later he worked for another carriage-maker, Daniel Flynt, in Abbott, where he specialized in the decorative painting of dashboards. He also helped at his father's new gristmill. Like most mills, it attracted mice. Hiram perfected a better mousetrap. "Many years later I went into a shop to purchase a mousetrap," Hiram recalled. "On being shown the one which the dealer recommended as the very best, I was surprised to see the very thing which I had invented when a boy." The boy then went into the wood-turning business for Ed Fifield of Dexter. "Everything was all right at Fifield's shop except the pay." Some Englishmen, who owned woolen mills in town, encouraged boxing by locals. Hiram considered becoming a boxer. But an Englishman informed him, "Your eyes are altogether too large and prominent" and, moreover, his head was too big (Hudson knew that). A town doctor added, "Don't think of it; it is altogether beneath you; never give it a second thought." The Civil War had just begun and the same Dr. Springall told Hiram he was far too promising a lad to go to war.

"It has often been said that Maine is the best state in the Union to emigrate from," Hiram Maxim wrote, "and I had long wished to get out of it, and go to some place where I could get more for my work. . . . " And so, in 1861, he did. Two of his brothers fought in the war; one was killed and the other came back a different man. Meanwhile, Hiram was beginning a career that would make him one of America's most noted inventors—abroad.

"The State of Maine develops a type of character whereby the man who can grub thrift from its stingy soil needs only to remove to the kinder atmosphere and conditions of other states and countries to find success easy," Hudson Maxim wrote. This was the case, first for Hiram and, later, his younger brother.

After traveling about Canada and the northern United States, employed painting carriages, making cabinets, and as a mechanic (and parttime bartender and boxer), Maxim patented the first of over three hundred inventions. In 1878 he became interested in electric lighting. Edison beat him to the patent for an incandescent light by a matter of days. In 1881 he exhibited an electric machine at the Paris Exposition. Soon, hailed by newspapers as "the greatest electrician in the world," he set up a factory in England. Although he was expected to make electrical appliances, Maxim had never forgotten the machine gun his father had tried to invent. An Englishman told him, "Don't do it. Thousands of men for many years have been working on guns . . . they are all failures. . . . You don't stand a ghost of a chance in competition with regular gunmakers—stick to electricity."

Hiram informed him, "I am a totally different mechanic from any you have ever seen before—a different breed."

In 1883 Hiram Maxim invented a gun that could fire 660 rounds per minute. It was the first truly efficient weapon of its kind. The Maxim Gun was an international sensation. Important people such as Edward, the prince of Wales, tried firing the amazing gun. Maxim formed the Maxim Gun Company in 1884. In 1888 he merged with the Nordenfeldt Company, and, in 1896, his firm was absorbed by Vickers. Maxim was its director until his retirement in 1911. He became a British subject in 1900 and was knighted by Queen Victoria in 1901.

Hiram experimented with a flying machine, figuring "if a domestic goose can fly, so can a man." His contraption actually lifted off the ground, but it was too heavy and Maxim lacked the time to develop an adequate motor. Another Maxim project was to develop a substitute for coffee. He had a wide range. As Hiram confessed, he had always been a "chronic inventor."

For a while he worked with his younger brother, also an inventive genius. Hudson Maxim was named after his father, but disliked being called "Isaac" or "Ike," and took the name Hudson when he was 18. He established himself first in printing and publishing; in 1881, he produced a best-selling book on penmanship. Then he went to work with a brother, inventing a smokeless powder which Hiram, in England, refused to buy. DuPont, however, was glad to buy his patents. In 1894, while testing an explosive compound, Hudson was less alert than usual due to loss of sleep from a toothache. The result was that he blew off his left hand. About six weeks later, equipped with an artificial hand, Hudson Maxim was threatened by a drunk bully at an elevated railroad station:

> I had the habit of fighting at the drop of a hat, and I struck out with my right hand, and knocked him endwise. My other hand fell off, and so did my hat. But I picked them up and went home greatly encouraged. I felt that I could get along in the world after all. . . .

It was inevitable that Hiram and Hudson, both rambunctious types, would fall out. As Hudson recalled:

> Hiram was exceedingly jealous of his own fame, and couldn't tolerate a rival. He wanted me to attack Edison in the newspapers in an attempt to show that Edison had cribbed some of his inventions. He seemed to have a sort of mental twist about other inventors stealing his inventions. He told me one time that if the telescope hadn't been invented he would have invented it; and I think he never felt kindly toward Galileo for having got ahead of him. My own inventions irritated him to the last degree.

Of course, Hudson Maxim was, if anything, more opinionated than his very opinionated brother. Like Hiram, he was of the self-made-man school that detested socialism: "Socialism would defeat Nature's first law—the survival of the fittest—by robbing the fit of the advantage of being fit." Like Father Isaac he questioned religion, noting that "barbarous superstition and horribly cruel laws and practices are embodied in the Bible as sacred scripture, and have done infinite harm." He knew of no scientific proof for the existence of heaven or hell, but noted, "In this world, however, if a man marries the wrong woman he strikes hell, red hot. His wife will worry the gizzard out of him." The divorced Maxim apparently spoke from experience.

Hudson had a number of dislikes, which he was not bashful about sharing with the world. He absolutely hated the use of tobacco. "I look on the increased use of tobacco in the form of cigarettes as perhaps the greatest single menace to the integrity of the race." Women's perfume nauseated him. "The women don't know that many of their headaches are caused by perfumes they use," he wrote, "and that the powders and paints they put on to beautify their complexions tend to tan and embalm the skin." He claimed to *try* to tone down his swearing—"until my hand was blown off, and that was such a calamity I lost patience and cut loose." He was unimpressed with the wordiness of poets like Shakespeare and Milton: "I've cut out all the guff and whang-doodle, and my version is more scientific."

While personally pugnacious, Hudson had a low opinion of war. A lone highwayman holding up a stagecoach is considered a criminal, he noted. "But if we take a million highwaymen, arm them to the teeth, and hold up a nation instead of a stagecoach, we are engaged in the honorable profession of war"—an interesting opinion coming from a highly paid consultant to E.I. du Pont de Nemours & Company! In an about-face, Hudson blasted pacifism in the 1915 best-seller *Defenseless America*. With typical modesty, he claimed "no other thing did so much to get the United States into" World War I (which he figured was an honorable war after all). Consistency was not a hobgoblin of Hudson Maxim's mind.

Hudson blamed Hiram for their feud and, since he outlived him, he got the last word, noting "Hiram kept up his attacks to the end of his days and died a-shouting."

Hiram was proud of the acclaim he received for inventing the machine gun. But he appears to have had some mixed feelings. "It is astonishing to note how quickly this invention put me on the very pinnacle of fame," he observed. "Had it been anything else but a killing machine, very little would have been said of it." Plagued by bronchitis and frustrated by prescribed treatments, Maxim invented a special inhaler. He was criticized by friends in the gun business for "prostituting my talents on quack nostrums." Hiram made a point of recording this episode in his memoirs. It showed that "it is a very creditable thing to invent a killing machine, and nothing less than a disgrace to invent an apparatus to prevent human suffering."

Yet, for all their inventions, the sons of Isaac Maxim are most remembered for their contributions to killing. Rough and ready Yankees with native genius, these men from back-country Maine changed the face of warfare. Hiram, who died in 1916, lived to see his weapon's impact on the killing fields of Europe. Did he and Father Isaac ever visualize such carnage? Isaac's greatest ambition was, after all, to kill a bear.

Hiram's son, Hiram Spencer Maxim, also became an inventor. He invented the Maxim Silencer. He vividly remembered boyhood visits to Wayne, Maine, where his grandfather spent his last years. He always remembered a station along the way where a cage of bears was kept. Returning to Maine almost a half-century later, he watched for the same station. "In due time we came to it, and I remembered it distinctly. The bears were gone, and the cage, but the grass plots were there and the track arrangement and the general layout were just as I remembered them. If I am not mistaken the place was Lewiston."

31 •

The Tattooed Man

O n the evening of August 17, 1884, somebody entered an Augusta cemetery and chiseled from the tombstone of James G. Blaine's firstborn child the date of the boy's birth. The deed was perhaps the lowest incident in a squalid presidential campaign.

An Indianapolis newspaper had charged that the Republican candidate and his wife had engaged in premarital sex and Blaine married Harriet Stanwood "at the muzzle of a shotgun." Stanwood Blaine was born three months after this supposedly forced union. The tale was juicy stuff in Victorian-era America. The candidate, at his summer home at Bar Harbor, hotly denied the *Indianapolis Sentinel* story on August 14 and filed a libel suit against the paper. He also claimed that there had been *two* marriage ceremonies, one previously unrecorded. This story did not convince doubting Democrats. Then came the midnight desecration of the child's tomb.

Blaine, the most prominent Republican leader of his time attracted controversy. A handsome, charismatic figure, Blaine as a young man reversed the usual pattern and migrated eastward from Pennsylvania to Maine. In Augusta, with the aid of his wife's family, he became editor of the *Kennebec Journal*. Journalism proved a springboard to politics. An early Republican backer of Lincoln, Blaine rose to the speakership of the state legislature. By the mid-1860s, he was elected to Congress. Within a few years he was the speaker of the U.S. House of Representatives. "Blaine of Maine" was ambitious and clever. While speaker, he was known as a friend of various special interests. Without any visible source of big income, he lived well. Some said he was in financier Jay Gould's pocket; Blaine never explained where his money came from. He may not have been more corrupt than his peers, but neither did he rise about the rather low ethical standards of contemporary Gilded Age politics. Perhaps if Jim Blaine had not been so flashy and controversial, his character would not have received so much scrutiny.

In 1875, Democrats were in control of Congress for the first time since the Civil War. Blaine rekindled memories of the conflict with an impassioned—and coldly calculated—attack on the granting of amnesty to Jefferson Davis. Blaine held Davis responsible for the mistreatment of Union prisoners of war at Andersonville. There was not "a civilized government" on earth that would not have tried Davis "and shot him within thirty days," Blaine charged. He did not propose execution, but he was opposed to full political rights being restored to the former Confederate leader. This provoked, as Blaine intended, a hot response from Southern Democrats. It made it easier for Republicans to associate Democrats with the late rebellion, distracted attention from Grant administration scandals, and helped propel James G. Blaine to the front of the pack seeking his party's 1876 presidential nomination. Blaine was so much a politician's politician that, after his Davis speech, one of his Southern opponents, upon seeing him walk by, muttered, "Now there's Blaine. Damn him! But I do love him."

But in 1876 rumors about shady dealings with the Little Rock and Fort Smith Railroad surfaced. Incriminating evidence was supposedly contained in letters possessed by one James Mulligan. In an act of sheer bravado, Blaine went to Mulligan's hotel and managed to get him to hand over the letters. Then he rose in the House of Representatives and, waving the packet in his hand, thundered, "Thank God Almighty, I am not afraid to show them." He proceeded to "invite the confidence of 44 million of my countrymen while I read those letters from this desk." After reading from them—selectively—Blaine turned the tables on his Democratic opponents by accusing them of suppressing evidence that would clear him. The result was a sensation.

At the 1876 convention, Robert Ingersoll nominated Blaine for the presidency in a classic speech:

> Like an armed warrior, like a plumed Knight, James G. Blaine marched down the halls of the American Congress and threw his shining lance full and fair against the brazen forehead of every traitor to his country and every maligner of his fair reputation. For the Republican party to desert that gallant man now is as though an army should desert their general upon the field of battle. . . .

But the Plumed Knight's armor was badly tarnished, and he lost the nomination to the colorless but safe Rutherford B. Hayes of Ohio. In 1880, Blaine again fell short and supported his friend James Garfield for the nomination. Once elected, Garfield named Blaine his secretary of state. Unlike most public men of his time, Blaine had a real interest in foreign affairs. He was preparing to do great things when Garfield was assassinated. The assassin's bullet whizzed by Blaine's ear as he was accompanying the president to a train in the Washington railroad station. Railroads were always bad luck for the Plumed Knight. Out of a job, he set about writing the first volume of his memoirs—and campaigning for the 1884 presidential nomination.

This time Blaine was successful on the fourth ballot. But he carried too much political baggage. Reform-minded Republicans deserted the ticket. Although few in numbers, these "Mugwumps" kept up a drumbeat of criticism of Blaine's past. And for many voters the image of the Plumed Knight was overshadowed by cartoonist Bernard Gilliam's "Tattooed Man." It portrayed the naked candidate with the names of various scandals tattooed to him. "If caricature decided the election," the London *Pall Mall Budget* observed, "Blaine's chances would be hopeless."

Thomas Nast, who had first used the "Tattooed Man" motif in 1876, was particularly nasty with a series of cartoons that reworded Blaine's best-selling book, *Twenty Years of Congress*, into "Twenty Years of Sleight of Hand," "Twenty Years of Masquerading," and, on election day, "Are Twenty Years of Blaine Enough?"

The Democrats nominated Governor Grover Cleveland of New York. Dull and unimaginative, "Grover the Good" was associated with no scandal when his party gave him the nod in June, 1884. His greatest virtue was that he was not James G. Blaine. For the first five weeks of the campaign, he was clearly the front runner.

Then came the bombshell of July 21. The Buffalo *Evening Telegraph* published "A Terrible Tale; A Dark Chapter in a Public Man's History." It revealed that the bachelor Cleveland had fathered an illegitimate child by one Maria Halpin. Cleveland admitted the story was true.

Suddenly, the Halpin affair brought Cleveland's chances into doubt. "It was like the shadow of a great rock in a weary land," Charles Edward Russell noted. "Better 'The Tattooed Man' than a sexual sinner."

Desperate to strike back, some Democrats latched on to the rumor of Blaine's premarital indiscretion. And then, in September, the *Boston Journal* published yet more letters obtained from James Mulligan, who had apparently bided his time to again wound Blaine. One letter, to Boston railroad lawyer Warren Fisher, appeared particularly incriminating. It ended "Kind regards to Mrs. Fisher. Burn this letter!" Now Democrats chanted at their rallies:

> Burn this letter!
> Burn this letter!
> Burn, burn, oh, burn this letter!
>
> Blaine! Blaine!
> The Continental liar
> From the State of Maine!
> Burn this letter!

With no issues really discussed, the campaign of 1884 degenerated into a vicious personality contest. In a tight race, Blaine broke with tradition. While Cleveland stayed at his governor's desk, the Republican candidate campaigned vigorously throughout the Midwest and Northeast, where his potential electoral victory lay. He made over four hundred speeches. Blaine was a brilliant extemporaneous speaker, who needed little preparation to establish intimate rapport. He seemed to be making headway, but the toll of the campaign was showing in its final days. Blaine was tired, irritable, and constantly barraged to go here and there by his managers. New York loomed very important and against his judgment they urged him to travel again to that state.

And it was in New York, on October 19, that Blaine blew his chance for victory. By his own account:

> I was engaged in my room with the committee and other visitors when I was summoned to the lobby of the hotel to meet the clergymen. I had prepared no speech; in fact, had not thought up a reply. When their spokesman, Reverence Doctor Burchard, began to address me, my only hope was that he would continue long enough for me to prepare an appropriate response. I had a very definite idea of what he would say and so paid little attention to his speech. In the evening the reporters began rushing in and wanted my opinion of Doctor Burchard's statement that the main issue of the campaign was 'Rum, Romanism, and Rebellion.' If I had heard him utter these words, I would have answered at once, and that would have been effective, but I am still in doubt as to what to say about it now. The situation is very difficult, and almost anything I say is likely to bitterly offend one side or the other. . . .

It was a monumental lapse. The notable bigot Reverend Samuel Burchard referred to the Democratic Party's antecedents as "Rum, Romanism, and Rebellion." It was a slur on Irish Catholics, whose votes Blaine—with a Catholic mother and a record of standing up to the British abroad—hoped to win. Hardly any press covered Blaine's meeting with the ministers at the Fifth

Avenue Hotel, but one reporter who did immediately realized the impact of Burchard's words. So did the Democrats, who quickly reprinted the statement and associated it with the G.O.P. candidate.

Chauncey M. Depew remembered riding through the streets of New Haven shortly afterward with Blaine and being barraged by thousands of Democratic "Rum, Romanism, and Rebellion" leaflets. "They so filled the air that it seemed a shower, and littered the streets." Blaine finally got around to disavowing the statement, and Reverend Burchard claimed he was misinterpreted. But it was too late.

On the evening of the vote, Blaine returned to his Augusta home. Neighbors and friends gathered in the drawing room as the vote seesawed throughout the night. A special telegraph was set up in the library, and for a while the candidate listened as it clattered out his fate. It was clear that the vote in New York would be close. A heavy rain upstate threatened to lower the vote there, while the Burchard affair had done its damage with New York City's Irish voters. Blaine reckoned that if he carried that state by a thousand votes or less, "They will surely count me out." "I'm going to bed," he told his private secretary, Tom Sherman. "Don't disturb me unless something decisive comes in." Mrs. Blaine recalled that night several weeks later:

> It is all a horror to me. I was absolutely certain of the election. . . . Then the fluctuations were so trying to the nerves . . . the click-click of the telegraph, the shouting through the telephone in response to its never-to-be-satisfied demand, and the unceasing murmur of men's voices, coming up through the night to my room, will never go out of my memory—while over and above all, the perspiration and chills, into which the conflicting reports constantly threw the physical part of one, body and soul alike rebelling against the restraints of nature, made an experience not be voluntarily recalled.

Cleveland swept the South. Blaine carried the West and most of the North, except Indiana, Connecticut, New Jersey—and New York.

He lost Indiana 49.8 percent to 48.5 percent, Connecticut 49 percent to 48 percent, and New Jersey 49 percent to 47.3 percent. New York went to Cleveland 48.3 percent to 48.2 percent—a margin of 1,140 votes. In the electoral college, Cleveland edged Blaine 219 to 182. A switch of less than 600 votes in New York would have elected Blaine.

The Plumed Knight—at least publicly—took the results well. Despite charges of vote fraud in New York and elsewhere, he refused to consider a recount. He calculated that the loss of New Jersey and Connecticut were "easily preventable accidents," and in New York the weather and Dr. Burchard had done him in. He wrote a friend, "As the Lord sent upon us an ass in the shape of a preacher, and a rainstorm to lessen our vote in New York, I am disposed to feel resigned to the dispensation of defeat which flowed from these agencies. In missing a great honor I escaped a great and oppressive responsibility."

Blaine's daughter Harriet remembered how "white-faced and quiet" Blaine's friends at Augusta were and how even her resolute mother broke down. But her father remained serene, even cheerful. The man who could overreact to a small cold took his greatest defeat philosophically.

Blaine had ability and even some vision. He might have been a good president. But he was too hungry and too clever. In the end, it wasn't Cleveland or even Reverend Burchard who beat him. The Plumed Knight lost to the Tattooed Man.

• 32

The Long-Haired Student Agitator

W hen Arthur Sewall returned from the 1896 Democratic Convention, the people of Bath gave him a rousing reception. Crowds escorted his carriage home from the railroad depot, church bells clanged, the streets were bedecked with flags, congratulatory speeches were read. The occasion? The famous shipbuilder, whose highest elective office had been city alderman, had just been nominated for vice president of the United States. Ironically, the Maine delegation had dropped Sewall from the Democratic National Committee when, breaking with his fellow delegates, he supported the "free silver" advocates led by William Jennings Bryan. But Bryan won the party's nomination after his impassioned "Cross of Gold" speech—and, 36 hours after he was dropped from his national committee post, Sewall was made Bryan's running mate. All that was forgotten on July 11, as Bath received her most famous citizen.

For a small town on the Kennebec, Bath had already enjoyed plenty of excitement. In 1889 President Benjamin Harrison dropped by, gave a speech in the rain, and walked the keel of Sewall's *Rappahannock*, which was about to become the largest wooden ship afloat. In 1890 a naval squadron including the new armored cruiser *Baltimore* and the old, famous steam frigate *Kearsarge*, made an appearance enroute to Bar Harbor. But these events—and Sewall's homecoming—were soon to be topped by the arrival, on September 26, of William Jennings Bryan in town. That drew "undoubtedly the largest crowd which ever assembled in Bath."

On the face of it, the supposedly radical Bryan and the genteel Sewall were a political odd couple. The shipbuilder did not appear to have a radical bone in his body. In his trade, he avoided innovation and continued building bigger and bigger wooden vessels well into the era of steel. His politics were similarly conservative. Unlike most Democrats, he favored a high tariff and was an ardent imperialist, eager for the acquisition of far-flung islands. He was a very wealthy man, engaged in banking and railroading as well as in shipbuilding. He seemed the direct opposite of the sweating orator from Nebraska's plains who championed the red-necked debtor class. Yet he was opposed to the gold standard. The combination of Sewall's business reputation and his agreement on this key issue made him appear the perfect man to balance the ticket. (This was taking ticket-balancing a bit too far for Populists, who endorsed the Democratic presidential candidate and pointedly nominated their own vice presidential candidate.)

Despite Sewall's nomination, Maine remained rock-ribbed Republican; but that did not prevent tens of thousands of the curious from converging upon Bath to hear Bryan's fabled eloquence. Railroads and steamboats brought them from all over the state. Local authorities were understandably nervous about what to expect. They were especially determined not to let any disturbance provoked by opponents of Bryan mar the town's big day. That was a tall order; more than most politicians the Nebraskan was a controversial man. Yet it was not the ordinary folk that worried authorities.

It was those smart-aleck college kids. The rude reception Bryan was accorded by Yale students at New Haven, Connecticut, was fresh in the authorities' minds. They were aware of rumors that students from Bowdoin planned to disrupt Bryan's speech in Bath.

On the evening of Mr. Bryan's appearance, just before the Democratic candidate clambered up on a chair to speak to the crowd jamming Post Office Square, a group of 150 Bowdoin boys alighted from a train. The college boys immediately began singing their "war song," "Phi Chi," and some pro-McKinley songs. They also started cheering loudly—too loudly for the waiting officials.

A Marshal Kittredge intervened. One of the students tried to explain that his fellow students meant no harm. A slender lad with a patrician head, he was the secretary of Bowdoin's Republican Club. He was also a member of the Delta Kappa Epsilon fraternity, editor of the *Bowdoin Orient*, and manager of the college's baseball team. Young Percy was furthermore—although the authorities did not know it—the son of Portland's Republican mayor, a very wealthy and influential man. Evidently unimpressed with the boy's story and even less by his appearance, Kittredge arrested him and lodged him in the Bath jail as a precautionary measure.

Exactly what Bryan said that evening is not recorded—probably it was the same basic stump speech that worked so well for him elsewhere. There was no disturbance. But there was a sequel to the story, growing out of Marshal Kittredge's arrest of Percy Baxter.

The young man was shortly released. He promptly sued the Bath authorities for improper arrest, demanding $10,000 in damages. The case was tried in Portland. Mayor James Phinney Baxter paid his son's court costs. Newspaper coverage was considerable and not always sympathetic. One reporter wrote that Baxter's boy "looked very much like a very ordinary student of the common long-haired variety. So it came to pass that his sacred person was violated by the touch of the marshal's hand." While it could not be demonstrated that the students intended any serious disruption that September evening, the jury was sympathetic with Kittredge; he had had a great responsibility to prevent any incident that might cause a nasty scene.

Therefore, the jury found in favor of the plaintiff—and directed the Bath marshal to award him damages of one cent!

Percival Proctor Baxter felt vindicated by the verdict. He would later become governor of Maine, a Republican of course, but considered by some conservatives a "socialist" for his opposition to entrenched corporate power. Baxter's desire to conserve Maine's natural heritage led him in later years to buy up and sell to the state Mount Katahdin and the surrounding timberland. Baxter State Park is the legacy of the "long-haired" student leader.

• 33

The Spanish Are Coming!— Aren't They?

I n April 1898, two months after the sinking of the *Maine,* Congress declared war on Spain. The public, stimulated by sensational press coverage, blamed the Spanish for the battleship's destruction, although no hard evidence ever was found. The war fever that swept the United States was accompanied by a shudder of fear along the Eastern seaboard. The Spanish Atlantic Squadron, commanded by Admiral Pascual Cervera y Topete, steamed out of the Cape Verde Islands on April 28. Its destination was unknown; along the American coast, including Maine, there was concern about when and where Cervera would show up.

Maine's governor, Llewellyn Powers, an Aroostook County lawyer, noted "there was considerable anxiety in some of the towns and cities along the coast, fearing that they might be attacked by gunboats or cruisers of the Spanish navy. . . . I was convinced . . . that the only real and effective defense for our coast towns was to establish batteries and mines, and to obtain from the United States, cruisers to sail along our shores. . . . " Two cruisers actually were dispatched, briefly, to Maine waters, making calls as far Downeast as Eastport. The city fathers of Portland were so insistent in their demand for protection that the Navy Department sent a warship to stand guard in Portland harbor. It is doubtful how much good this Civil War-vintage ship could have done if confronted by the more modern Spanish warships. Just to make sure, the three channels of Portland harbor were mined.

Submerged mines were also placed across the entrances of the Kennebec and Penobscot Rivers in early May.

Despite the mining, residents of Bangor remained nervous. They petitioned Congress for more protection. In the spring of 1898, the idea of a Spanish squadron bombarding Bangor did not seem farfetched. In April, Frederick T. Jane, the British naval expert who compiled the authoritative *Jane's Fighting Ships*, wrote that Spain's best strategy would be to make naval raids along the U.S. coast. The Spanish, he believed, had the ability to make Americans "rue the day that the meddling finger of Uncle Sam was thrust into the hornet's nest of Cuba." And Jane did not foresee the poor gunnery and command confusion which would characterize U.S. naval operations. The capacity of battleships to rain carnage upon coastal cities had already been demonstrated 1878 War of the Pacific. The Yankee coast was not immune to similar treatment. And Maine's experience of enemy warships was a long one.

In late May, Cervera was sighted in the Caribbean. The ease with which the Spanish ships eluded the U.S. Navy and slipped into Santiago harbor was not reassuring.

The War Department, responding to the clamor from Downeast, decided to reactivate Fort Knox. Built in the mid-19th century in response to Aroostook War-era concerns about the British, the huge fort overlooked the Narrows just below Bucksport, in the town of Prospect. It was constructed from granite quarried nearby. By the Civil War it bristled with over a hundred cannon, many of the gigantic, smooth-bore Rodman variety. When the fort fired a salvo in 1865 to salute a vessel carrying the remains of Maine's last veteran of the Revolution, windows were shattered in Bucksport. But the bastion had never defended the entrance of the Penobscot from hostile vessels. Indeed, during the previous decade the fort had been manned by only one soldier, Sergeant Leopold Hegyi, an immigrant from Hungary who had joined the U.S. Army in 1867. An accomplished horseman, Sergeant Hegyi had instructed members of the U.S. Cavalry in the West, including soldiers who rode with Custer. But the old horse soldier's chief activity in his Maine post was walking down the steep hill from Fort Knox to a grocery store, where he would chat with locals and sip a beer. Then he trudged back up the hill. In June of 1899 Sergeant Hegyi's solitary command was relieved by Colonel Charles Burdett, with six companies of the Connecticut Volunteer Infantry.

When the Colonel got his orders to "take station at Fort Knox, near Bucksport, Maine," he had to make inquiry as to where Bucksport was. Trainloads of troops began arriving at the usually sleepy fort. Soldiers kept arriving throughout the month, some by steamer, until 409 personnel were encamped in a clearing in the nearby birch woods. For some unknown reason, the Connecticut troops did not utilize the spacious fort—except in stormy weather. One of the rooms in the fort was renovated and made into a reading room for the men. The thunder of cannon reverberated again in Bucksport during daily gunnery practice.

Fort Knox contained an electric battery with wires running to the mines laid in the Narrows below. From deep in the bowels of the fort, the "buoyant torpedoes" could be detonated. Naval patrol boats cruised about the minefield to prevent any unsuspecting fishing vessel from hitting one of the weapons, which would also trigger an explosion.

The major enemy the garrison encountered was boredom. In late June, the government ordered the Connecticut troops to participate in Bangor's Fourth of July celebration. After taking a steamer up the river to the clearly less nervous Bangor, the command put on another such performance at Bucksport.

The Spanish were not coming. On July 1, Cervera had attempted to break out of Santiago. Although it took some 9,433 rounds to score 122 visible hits on the four Spanish ships, the Americans sank them all and fished the admiral out of the water in wet underclothes. Maine and the Eastern seaboard could breathe easier. The closest the Spanish got to Maine was Portsmouth, New Hampshire, where many of the captured Spanish sailors were interned until the "Splendid Little War" ended.

Two weeks after the sinking of Cervera's squadron, word came from Washington that Fort Knox was to be evacuated. The troops cheered the news and burned down temporary shelters made from brush and saplings. They almost succeeded in burning their tents in the process. At sunset on July 14, Sergeant Leopold Hegyi resumed his solitary command of the big fort. Two years later he died. Most of Fort Knox's cannon were given away to towns and cities throughout Maine. Purchased by the state in 1923, Fort Knox became a park. The assistant secretary of war at the time of sale described Fort Knox, which cost almost $1 million to construct, as "an old brick and granite fortification and a few outbuildings. Value $1.00."*

The real attack on the Maine coast, of course, did not come from the Spanish, but from increasing numbers of super-rich summer people who "colonized" prime tracts of real estate starting in the 1870s. One of these was the mighty J.P. Morgan, who had allowed the U.S. Navy to use his yacht, the *Corsair*, during the Spanish-American War. The *Corsair* was bigger than many of the ships in either country's navy.

---

*Maine purchased Fort Knox from the federal government for $2,121.

Vacationland

(Twentieth Century)

The Return of the Native

O n the afternoon of August 17, 1911, Merrill Hall at the State Normal School in Farmington, Maine, was crowded with nearly 1,800 simple country folk. At three o'clock Hiram Norton, dressed up in his Sunday best (and only) suit, escorted the famous opera star Madame Lillian Nordica to a stage decorated with ferns and goldenglow. The great singer was dressed to the hilt in a white satin dress, bedecked with pearls, emeralds, and diamonds. Madame Nordica aimed to give the folks a real concert. She had performed before hundreds of other audiences across the United States and Europe, but this audience was hers in a special way.

Madame Nordica was born Lillian Norton in 1857, the fifth daughter of Edwin and Amanda Norton, who lived in an area of Farmington called Norton's Woods. Her father was a gentle man who played the fiddle and sang in the church choir. He did not particularly like farming. His wife Amanda also was musical, but of a sterner temper. She was determined that one of the Norton girls would become a great singer. Amanda pinned her hopes on Wilhelmina, her fourth daughter. Lillian was initially ignored, although it is not clear why. "My mother has told me that, with my head on her breast, I followed her in the singing of a scale before I could speak," she later wrote.

Then, in November, 1868, a month after a disastrous flood submerged half of Farmington, typhoid fever claimed Wilhelmina Norton. After her sister's death, Lillian became the focus of her parents' ambitions. She was equal to the task. "God didn't give me my chin for nothing," she would say. Like her mother, Lillian had a most determined chin.

When she was 14, Lillian was placed under the supervision of Professor John O'Neill at Boston's New England Conservatory of Music. "I do not think that one of the original class which began with him when I did was with me in the end," Nordica wrote. "He was severe, and many cannot stand four years of faultfinding." O'Neill molded Lillian, with her fine, clear soprano voice, for an operatic career.

Against his advice, however—with her mother as a constant chaperon— she embarked on a tour of the country as a soloist in Patrick Gilmore's Band in the fall of 1876. O'Neill was beside himself: "After all my training, my advice, that you should come to this. A whole lifetime of ambition and years of the hardest study consumed—to fit you to go on the road with a brass band. Pah!" But Lillian gained experience before audiences and made some money. As she headed onstage before Madison Square Garden's great hall on opening night, Gilmore whispered in her ear, "Now, little girl, don't be afraid. Sing right out." She did.

In April, 1877, before going abroad, she sang at the Farmington Methodist Church. That was appropriate. Lillian's grandfather was the well-known hellfire Methodist revivalist Camp-Meeting John Allen. Camp-Meeting John was a colorful character. When some poor soul in the gallery scoffed at one of his performances, he shouted, "Come down out of that, you ill-begotten, slab-sided, God-forsaken stakepole of Hell. Come down and give your soul to God!" Lillian left Farmington when she was seven, but Camp-Meeting John spent the rest of his very long life there. He must have had some doubts about her travels in the wide, licentious world. (In 1883, he seemed reassured, saying "Lilly is a singer, not an actress.")

She went to Europe with Gilmore, then resumed her study of opera under the able guidance of Antonio Sangiovanni at the Milan Conservatory. He helped arrange her debut—and gave her a name Italians could pronounce. As Lillian Nordica, she made one of her first operatic appearances in Verdi's *La Traviata* in Brescia on the evening of April 26, 1879. "I have had a grand success and no mistake," she excitedly wrote her father back in Boston. "Such yelling and shouting you never heard." Nordica took nine curtain calls that night. She was on her way. As Amanda Norton observed, "She is probably the only girl from Farmington who will arrive at what she is today, in our generation."

But it was not all smooth sailing. As Nordica later said, " I have not leaped into success; it has been a long, painful, and often discouraging struggle." Early critics were harsh. When Lillian sang at the Paris Grand Opera in 1882, *Music and Drama*'s critic wrote that Nordica was wasting her money pursuing an operatic career. "I am sure the money would have bought her a good farm with a nice homestead in some Western state," he sneered, "where she could have sung on the Sabbath at the Baptist Conventicle." Another critic conceded that the young singer received enthusiastic applause, "but this was on account of her face and figure, her laughing eyes and handsome head of hair more than on account of her voice. . . . "

Nordica persevered. Amanda, perhaps the ultimate "stage mother," continued to push and shield her daughter. "Her devotion to me and to my career meant the sacrifice of home ties, and the very giving up of her life that we might enjoy the privilege of study and travel together." Edwin Norton died while mother and daughter were in Europe; in 1891 Amanda, died in London. "Once she put her hand to the plow, she never turned back."

After many years of operatic performances and concert tours, Nordica, always a favorite with the public, scored a critical breakthrough in 1894 at Bayreuth, Germany. Her role of Elsa in Wagner's *Lohengrin* was a smash. Wagner required great technical ability and stamina. Nordica later wrote that Wagnerian operas "are not for babes." Nordica was strong, and that was helpful. "The strength to carry out the physical part alone of the *Brunnhildes*; the courage in climbing to the top of the wings—the weight of the shield, helmet, spear, and cuirass, until one's shoulders ache, to say nothing of one's lungs—so much is demanded that I wonder that so many accomplish it," she observed in *Hints to Singers*. "And yet if one little slip occurs the house titters. Such trifles one must not mind, but thrust them aside, and go straight ahead."

From 1894 to 1909 Lillian Nordica was recognized as one the world's greatest singers. Despite all the acclaim and riches she won, she never forgot, or turned her backed on, her humble origins. Beside talent, she possessed much common sense in her dealings with rivals, management, and the press. As one biographer noted, "She was not the first America prima donna, but she was in some ways the most identifiably American." Lillian Nordica was the "Yankee Diva."

The one area where Nordica's common sense deserted her was in picking husbands. Married three times, she was disappointed each time. Her first mate was the wealthy, talented Frederick Gower, who was also, apparently, insanely jealous of her fame. After she instituted divorce proceedings, Gower took off in a balloon over the English Channel and disappeared. It was not clear if he accidentally drowned or was a romantic suicide. Nor was it altogether clear that he was dead. For years Nordica was terrorized by rumors that Fred Gower had been seen here or there. Her second husband was the Hungarian opera singer, Zoltan Dome. Zoltan fancied other ladies. Nordica suspected her operatic rivals and divorced him. Her last husband was the very rich George W. Young. Nordica wrote her sisters that he had "duped, betrayed, deceived, and abused" her. She died before she could divorce him. With such experience, it is hardly surprising that Lillian became a leading voice for women's suffrage.

Lillian Nordica, a beautiful girl at the outset of her career, became more buxom as she matured. She explained that the "great amount of oxygen" singers use "tends to expand and develop the body." Nordica added: "With progress in one's career, and [when] one has a reputation to sustain, the nervous strain becomes increased, and one evidently needs one's nerves covered with fat to shield them. . . . "

When Lillian Nordica returned for the last time to Farmington in 1911, her greatest days were behind her, she was middleaged, overweight, and, as usual, unhappily married. But all this was secondary to the occasion. The farmhouse by Norton's Woods had been refurbished and made to look as it had when Nordica was a girl. "It all comes back with a rush," she murmured upon seeing it.

At the auditorium in town, she sang operatic arias and popular numbers. Nordica ended the concert singing "Home, Sweet Home," her eyes fixed upon the open windows, gazing in the direction of the house on a hill two miles away. The effect was electric. Lillian Norton had come home. In a long career, this was her most dramatic appearance.

Several years later, on a concert tour of the Pacific, Nordica was shipwrecked and died of pneumonia. A young violinist from Lewiston, Francis Holding, whom she had selected to accompany her, played her favorite selections as she slipped away, so far from her native Downeast. He returned to tell the press of Nordica's typical courage. Within a year he was dead, his own promise unfulfilled.

35 •

The *William P. Frye* and Sisters

T he *William P. Frye* was a huge windjammer, one of a fleet of steel ships that the Sewalls of Bath, long-established builders of wooden vessels, launched at the turn of the century. She was destined to become the first American ship sunk in World War I. As one writer put it, "Maine offered the first American sacrifice to Prussian militarism on the high seas."

Named for a Maine Senator who, like Arthur Sewall, was an expansionist, the *William P. Frye* was the last of five steel ships the Sewall firm built for its own use. Her sister ships were the *Dirigo*, the *Erskine M. Phelps*, the *Arthur Sewall*, and the *Edward Sewall*. The *Dirigo* was launched in 1894; the *Frye* hit the water in 1901. Thus old Arthur Sewall, who died in 1900, lived to see the transition from wood to steel. The last vessel built by the Sewalls was the steel schooner Kineo in 1903. Between 1823 and 1903 three generations of the Sewall family constructed 105 vessels of a total of 131,000 tons. Most of these ships became part of one of the world's biggest and most famous family-owned fleets.

The four-masted *William P. Frye* was the biggest windjammer ever built. She was 332.2 feet long and weighed 3,374 tons. She was slightly larger than three steel ships—the *Astral*, the *Acme*, and the *Atlas*—that the Sewalls built for the Standard Oil Company in the early 1900s. Indeed, the *Frye* was bigger than the Sewall's *Roanoke*, the largest wooden square-rigger ever built by Americans. In the history of American sailing ships, only Donald McKay's *Great Republic* rivaled the *Frye* in size.

Built for work rather than speed, the Frye nevertheless made respectable time on the perilous Cape Horn route. In 1911 she navigated the passage from Kahaliu, in the Hawaiian Islands, to Philadelphia in 124 days—despite a severe buffeting by heavy winds and snow off "Cape Stiff," with a sea filled with menacing icebergs thrown in for good measure.

The *Frye* was active in the sugar trade with the Hawaiian Islands. It was a rough voyage, particularly under her first captain, Arthur Sewall's second cousin Joe. Joe Sewall was a competent mariner but a notorious martinet. Consequently, crews were hard to come by and the *Frye* sometimes was manned by Oriental sailors. After 1909, the great ship was captained by H.A. Nickerson and, finally, Captain Kiehne.

The *Frye* had better luck than her sister ship, the *Arthur Sewall*, which was lost at sea in 1907. Nobody knew her fate, although there were rumors of a mutiny or possibly a collision with the bark *Adolph Obrig*, also lost without a trace.

The *Edward Sewall* also had a number of close scrapes. In 1910, while she was hauling coal to Hawaii, her giant steel foremast started to settle into the deck. A fire had penetrated the base of the mast. The resourceful captain, with the appropriate name of Quick, cooled the superheated mast by boring a hole in it and pouring in water. He also had canvas tied about its head to end a wicked draft which fed the fire. Captain Quick made Honolulu, his hold filled with smoldering coal, and finally pulled and fixed the mast.

The *Edward Sewall* endured until 1936, when it was sold to the Japanese for scrap metal. It was the magnificent *William P. Frye* that met a violent end.

The trouble developed in early 1915 when the *Frye* was bound from Seattle to Queenstown with a $300,000 cargo of wheat. In the South Atlantic—that old Confederate hunting ground—the *Frye* encountered the *Prinz Eitel Friedrich*. The *Prinz Eitel* was a German liner which had been converted into a commerce raider at the outset of World War I. Crossing the Pacific from China, she eluded the British and, off the South American coast, joined forces with the cruiser *Karlsruhe* and another commerce raider, the *Kronprinz Wilhelm*. Together, the three ships sank about forty vessels.

One was the *William P. Frye*. After a "not particularly eventful" passage around Cape Horn, the *Frye* was stopped on January 27, 1915, off the coast of Brazil, by the *Prinz Eitel*. Over a megaphone boomed the broken English command: "Better you stop!"

The German boarding party conferred with Captain Kiehne, ate supper, and put the crew to work shoveling wheat into the sea. The Germans did not want to sink the Yankee ship, but were determined that her grain should never reach the British. But there were over five thousand tons of wheat and the task proved a slower, more laborious task than they had anticipated.

Captain Thierickens changed his mind. After her crew was removed in the early morning hours of January 28, dynamite charges were set off on the *William P. Frye*. The proud ship shuddered, her white sails collapsed, and she sank, within half an hour.

"I cried when the ship was sunk," the Captain's wife recalled, "for it was virtually my home and I spent many, many pleasant days on her. And, would you believe it, there were tears in the eyes of Captain Thierickens . . . as we stood on the deck and watched the *Frye* go down."

Later, the German captain told a reporter, "It was the saddest thing I ever witnessed. But I considered it in the line of my duty. It could not be helped."

It was Kaiser Wilhelm's birthday.

The sinking of the *William P. Frye*, the first American merchant vessel sunk by the Germans, caused a diplomatic furor. There would be more such sinkings before, in April of 1917, the United States declared war on Germany. Long before that, in the spring of 1915, the *Prinz Eitel*, badly in need of provisions and repairs, put into Hampton Roads, Virginia. The commerce raider was promptly interned. When she next put to sea it was as the U.S. destroyer *De Kalb*.

On May 31, 1917, the *Frye*'s sister ship, the *Dirigo* was shelled by a German submarine off the English coast. Mate John Ray of Eastport jumped into one of the boats put away—and missed, drowning. The Germans then boarded the *Dirigo*, set bombs as they had on the *Frye*, and sank her.

The war was good for business at Bath shipyards. But the day of the great windjammers was coming to a close. When the *William P. Frye* went down, it was more than a wartime incident. The event signaled the end of the glorious days of sail.

36 •

Dirty Linen

I n his home state of Maine, William R. Pattangall, a small-town lawyer, newspaper editor, and politician, was a leader of the Democratic Party. More than that, he was celebrated for his biting wit, reflected in "The Meddybemps Letters" and "Maine's Hall of Fame," which he wrote for the *Machias Union* and the *Waterville Sentinel* in the early 20th century. Portraying one Republican leader, Pattangall noted, "Oklahoma had nothing on Maine when it sent a blind man to Congress. We had a dumb representative at Washington before Oklahoma was invented for . . . Standard Oil to exploit."

At nine o'clock on the sticky, hot evening of June 28, 1924, the delegate from Maine addressed the tense Democratic National Convention at Madison Square Garden. Pattangall followed Senator Robert L. Owen of Oklahoma (not the blind senator). Owen had just spoken in opposition to a minority plank Pattangall had presented; it condemned "any effort on the part of the Ku Klux Klan . . . to interfere with the religious liberty or political freedom of any citizen, or to limit the civic rights of any citizen or body of citizens because of religion, birthplace, or racial origin."

This was an explosive issue because, in 1924, the Ku Klux Klan was a power in state and national politics. It had demonstrated strength not only in the South, but in some Northern states, including Maine. While most of its adherents, in Maine as elsewhere, were rural Protestants, the KKK also was visible in cities such as Portland. Its brand of "Americanism" in Maine was directed against Catholics in particular. It was common gossip that key Republican politicians such as Ralph Owen Brewster were Klan sympathizers—or worse. To the usually humorous Pattangall, a non-Catholic, the Klan was no laughing matter.

When he had introduced the minority plank, a catch in his throat prevented Pattangall from reading the entire resolution. Amidst pandemonium on the floor and in the galleries, the convention clerk completed it. A few hours later, however, Pattangall had clearly found his voice.

Noting that a spirit of intolerance had "crept into the life of the United States," he called upon the convention to condemn it by name. Then:

> I have in my pocket a card issued by this organization, whose methods, not whose membership, I condemn, with questions written on it: "Are you a Protestant?" "Are you white?" "Are you native born?" Well, I am reasonably white [Laughter], I am native born; my ancestors have lived in the State I live in for 200 years [Applause]. I am a Protestant [Loud applause]. I am a Knight Templar Mason. So I am eligible to that order if I want to join it. It can not discriminate against me according to race or color or birthplace. But when I find that it does send out a questionnaire like the one I have in my pocket I wonder if its leaders, when questionnaires were being prepared in 1917 to send to the youth of America [Loud applause]—I wonder, I wonder if when Senator Owen patriotically voted for a draft law as a member of the United States Senate, he or anybody else suggested that we should only draft to defend our country the boys who were "white," "Protestant" and "native born" [Loud Applause].

> In your training camp, in your ships that ran across the water, on the battlefields of France, Catholic, Jew, Protestant, Negro, and naturalized citizen fought side by side to maintain the institutions that mean so much to me.... [As for those who maintain] that a man who was born of Jewish parents or of Catholic parents, or who was born in Canada and came here to make his home, or who is colored, can not be eligible to serve his country in civil life but shall serve it in military life if we need him, I will condemn them everywhere I meet them on the face of God's green earth [Loud cheers and applause].

Pattangall was the second to address the convention in the time allotted to the Klan issue. There were seven more speakers; the last was the Grand Old Man of the Party, William Jennings Bryan. Bryan spoke against the minority plank. He claimed, "We can exterminate Ku Kluxism better by recognizing their honesty and teaching them that they are wrong." Bryan, like other party leaders, was afraid that a specific condemnation of the Klan would divide the Democratic Party and ruin its chances against the G.O.P.

At 11:35 P.M. the roll call began. It continued for two wild hours, punctuated by many verbal and physical fights. A thousand extra policemen were called in to maintain order. Confusion was rampant. Nearly every state was divided. William Pattangall's wife, also a Maine delegate, voted *against* the minority report her husband sponsored.

Senator David Walsh of Massachusetts, the convention chairman who had spoken for the anti-Klan plank, announced the tally: by one vote, the Democrats had declined to condemn the activities of the Ku Klux Klan. New York delegate Franklin D. Roosevelt shouted for an immediate adjournment. Walsh, also wanting to terminate the scene, ignored the chorus of "nays" from the floor, and declared the session ended. But the damage was done. The extended debate—carried on radio to the nation—had openly divided the Democratic Party.

After a record-setting, benumbing 103 ballots, the Democrats nominated for president a West Virginian who never uttered a word about the Klan. He was badly beaten by the Republicans' Silent Cal Coolidge. It was one of those years.

Pattangall, who must have had some interesting words with Mrs. Pattangall, returned to Maine and ran for Governor against Ralph Owen Brewster. Brewster was supported by the Klan. He won.

Although he later became a Republican and was awarded a judgeship, Pattangall never changed his mind about the Klan. When he walked away from the podium that hot evening in 1924, he was heard to mutter, "I hate bigotry."

Postscript: In 1987 and 1988, the modern Klan made two forays into Maine—in a field outside strike-torn Rumford and in the parking lot of the Maine Mall in South Portland. The handful of white-robed men attracted much press and a handful of curious onlookers in Rumford. In Portland they were driven out of the shopping mall parking lot by anti-Klan demonstrators.

The day when dirty linen was common in Maine is over. William Pattangall would be pleased.

37 •

White Bird, Lone Eagle

O n May 8, 1927 *L'Oiseau Blanc*—the *White Bird*—took off from Paris's Le Bourget airfield. It flew into the morning mists, beyond view of a large crowd restrained by troops with bayonets. The white 450-horsepower biplane was piloted by World War I aces Captain Charles Nungesser and Captain Francois Coli. Nungesser was a legendary figure who had shot down 45 German aircraft (and one British plane by mistake); the one-eyed Coli, who wore a jaunty black eyepatch, was wounded five times and commanded several air squadrons when the Armistice was signed. Their destination was New York City, where they expected to arrive 40 hours after take-off—the first men to fly nonstop across the Atlantic.

Five hours after leaving Le Bourget, the *White Bird* was sighted off the Irish coast, heading out over a turbulent sea against a strong headwind. It was never seen again.

By the foggy afternoon of May 9, there were reports from Newfoundland to Maine that an airplane had been heard. In the 1920s, a flying machine was still an unusual competitor to the seagulls.

Seventeen-year-old Fred Dennison, fishing with his father east of Machias, Maine, heard a loud noise in the air "like an old-fashioned cream separator."

A while later, the solitary woodsman Anson Berry, who hunted and fished around Round Lake, mentioned to another Machias resident that he had heard a plane, too. "He said it was sputtering and he heard a big crash," recalled Albert Mattatall, 60 years later. Berry, not a sociable type, only emerged from the woods once a week. A contemporary observed, "There might have been more people looking in the area if they liked him better."

The story that the *White Bird* might have gone down in the forests beyond Machias has remained part of local folklore. There have been more recent reports, by hunters, of the wreckage of an airplane engine, but subsequent searches have yet to locate it. Perhaps Nungesser and Coli *did* make it across the Atlantic.

Maine's other transatlantic flying connection is better known. There is, of course, no question that shortly after the *White Bird* flight Charles Lindbergh, alone, in the much lighter *Spirit of St. Louis*, flew from a Long Island airfield to Le Bourget. He won fame and a $25,000 prize.

Lindbergh was drawn to the Maine coast by the presence, in her millionaire father's North Haven summer "cottage," of Anne Morrow, whom he courted and, in 1929, married. In the years that followed, the Lindberghs continued to spend summers in Maine. In 1931, they flew from the Maine island on a trip that took them across Canada's northern wilderness, Alaska, and Siberia to Japan and China, an adventure Anne Morrow Lindbergh described in *North to the Orient*. Back on North Haven, their firstborn, Charles Augustus, spent his "one, happy summer." The abduction and murder of the child in the spring of 1932 shocked coastal Mainers with a special poignance.

But in September the Lindberghs were back. As the *Rockland Courier Gazette* of September 15 observed, "When the Lindbergh plane passed over Rockland at 6 P.M. . . . it was flying so high that it could easily have been mistaken for a seagull. Landing conditions on the island were reported as unfavorable that night, but Col. Lindbergh has a way of conquering such obstacles."

Still something of the daredevil pilot, the Lone Eagle was not content to spend his time sailing or on the golf links. He often took friends on flights over the islands. When a reporter asked islander Floyd Duncan, "Did he do any stunts when you were in the plane?" Duncan exclaimed, "Not on your life!" The *Courier Gazette* noted, "Floyd would probably be willing to paddle a canoe across the bay in a nor'easter and not turn a hair, but riding upside down, 2,000 feet in the air, is quite another matter, even when the pilot is the only man who has ever flown alone from New York to Paris." When Duncan stepped out of Lindbergh's plane, a bit wobbly, "Mrs. Lindbergh took his place, and then there was some stunting."

If the *White Bird* is ever located, the remains of Nungesser and Coli will be flown back to Paris—starting at their planned destination, New York.

38 •

Islands in the Bay

T ucked into the middle of the front page of the February 23, 1932, edition of the *Rockland Courier Gazette* was a story entitled, "Why Edna! How Can You?" It concerned Edna St. Vincent Millay, born in the Knox County seaport almost exactly 40 years earlier. It seemed that the famous poet and her husband, Dutch-born businessman Eugene Jan Boissevain, had set sail for Spain aboard a freighter. "I like Spaniards, I like their poetry, and that's all," Millay was quoted. "This trip is an impulse from which I may never return, but it's a lot more fun than doing the biggest of things conventionally." She added that she had equipped herself with plenty of pencils and old letters "so she could scribble down ideas when they wake her up at night."

It was typical. Barely five feet tall, birdlike, with sometimes-green eyes and sometimes-red hair—like Edna, they were always changing—the poet who wrote about burning the candle at both ends was an incurable romantic. She was also very much a Mainer. In 1951 Vincent Sheean wrote, "It was odd that anybody like Edna . . . should have come from Rockland, which, although a fine town and a good port in the old days or even now, is hardly what you would pick as a cradle for poets."

That Edna St. Vincent was born in the same city that launched the *Red Jacket* is hardly surprising unless, like Sheean, you are not from Maine. Her glory days were just as brief, but equally memorable. And for a while, she was the fastest poet afloat.

Her parents separated when Edna was about eight; Cora Millay and her three daughters moved to Camden in 1904. With her mother scrimping by as a practical nurse and her father a school superintendent in other towns, the little red-haired eldest daughter was encouraged to pursue her musical and literary ambitions. Her hands were too small for a piano; Edna submitted her first poem, "Forest Trees," to *St. Nicholas Magazine* in the summer of 1906. Her last contribution to that children's magazine was published in 1910, a year after she graduated from Camden High School. At the end of her teenage years, "Vincent" Millay was at home, without clear prospects.

She was not necessarily unhappy. In a letter to her absent mother in July, 1911, she described a boating excursion with friends: "We started at 8 A.M. and didn't get home until 11 P.M., we went all around in and out through the islands to Pulpit Harbor where we landed on a little uninhabited island. I felt like Robinson Crusoe. Fun? Believe me, kid!" Later that summer, in another letter to Cora Millay, the daughter exuberantly wrote, "Mother, I can swim lots better than I could last year. . . . We've been in lots of times. I swam a real long swim a few days ago down on the shore below the lime-kiln. . . . I am going down in a few minutes to measure the distance. . . . " She also enjoyed climbing one of the Camden Hills, Mount Battie, which overlooked a panorama of woods, Lake Megunticook, and an island-dotted shoreline. When Cora Millay urged Edna to submit a poem to a contest for a projected book of contemporary poetry, she sent a poem entitled "Renaissance." It began:

> All I could see from where I stood
> Was three long mountains and a wood;
> I turned and looked another way,
> and saw three islands in a bay.
> So with my eyes I traced a line
> Of the horizon, thin and fine,
> Straight around till I was come
> Back to where I started from;
> And all I saw from where I stood
> Was three long mountains and a wood.

Ferdinand Earle, editor of *The Lyric Year* was so impressed with the poem by "E. Vincent Millay, Esq." that he wrote her, indicating she would surely win first prize. He was wrong. In fact, the other judges disagreed and Millay received no prize. She was, however, published in *The Lyric Year*, winning immediate praise from other poets, including some who assumed "it takes a brawny male of forty-five" to end a poem as cleanly as "E. Vincent" did. Informed of their opinion, she responded, "I simply will not be a 'brawny male.' Not that I have an aversion to brawny males; *au contraire, au contraire*. But I cling to my femininity!" She also responded sharply to suggestions that she had gotten the vision in "Renascence" (the title was anglicized by the editors) from reading another poet: "I'll slap your face. I never get anything from a book. I see things with my own eyes, just as if they were the first eyes that ever saw, and then I set about to tell, as best I can, just what I see."

In the summer of 1912, while she was working at a local hotel, the Whitehall Inn, Millay's reading of "Renascence" caught the special attention of Caroline Dow. The well-connected New Yorker helped "Vincent" enroll at Vassar and meet prominent artists and writers. She was on her way. Success was hardly instantaneous. Dreams of the stage unrealized and with little income from her poems, she wrote pulp fiction under the pseudonym "Nancy Boyd." The critical year was 1923. Always frail, she managed to survive a serious operation, married the wealthy importer Eugene Jan Boissevain, and won the Pulitzer Prize for *Ballad of the Harp-Weaver*. The 1920s and early 1930s were her most creative period. Edna St. Vincent Millay found herself one of America's most popular poets. And controversial: she marched with protestors against the execution of Sacco and Vanzetti. It was all very heady, but could she last the night?

The coast of Maine still exerted an attraction for her. The summer following her freighter voyage to Spain, she visited a friend at Bailey Island. One morning she spied a rocky island on the horizon. "That's the most beautiful island I've ever seen," she said. "I want that island." In 1933 she got it.

Ragged Island was called Rugged Island when the Reverend Elijah Kellogg owned it in the 19th century. Kellogg used the 50-acre island as the setting for many of his popular boys' stories. Edna and Eugene made the minister's house their own hideaway, returning to it every year. In a letter to a friend in March of 1935, the poet wrote that she and Eugene were heading northward from the Caribbean to their New York country estate, "Steepletop":

> . . . to pick up the car; and then on to Ragged Island, where we shall be entirely alone in our little house and entirely alone on the island, to gather driftwood, and haul our lobster-traps, and make fish-chowders, and sail, and read, and sit on the rocks, all through the month of April. As Eugene would say just here, "Yes, it's a hard life."

In the late 1930s, Millay turned from her personalized lyrics to consideration of economic and social issues. Critical acclaim withered, as did her health. In the following years she experienced a failure of creativity, and, in 1944, a nervous breakdown. In the years of decline and depression, she increasingly longed for the solitude of her Maine island:

> Oh, to be there, under the silent spruces,
> Where the wide, quiet evening darkens without haste,
> Over a sea with death acquainted, yet forever chaste.

On the remote island on the northern fringe of Casco Bay, Edna was, however briefly, revitalized in the presence of the restless sea. Visiting her in the summer of 1945, Sheean was struck by the transformation: "She was glowing with health and spirits; her red hair was blown free and her green eyes were shining." And she still felt free in the water, swimming naked for hours, impervious to the coldness.

In 1949 Eugene died. A year later, alone and far from her beloved island, Edna St. Vincent Millay succumbed to a heart attack.

> I should be happy!—that was happy
> All day long on the coast of Maine;
> I have a need to hold and handle
> Shells and anchors and ships again!

She had traveled around the world, in luxury liners and freighters, but she never quite left the point she started from.

• 39

The Battle of
the Bridge

O n April 21, 1937—"Red Wednesday"—a thousand striking shoe workers attempted to cross the North Bridge from Lewiston to Auburn. A phalanx of police, special deputies, and state troopers blocked their progress across the dirty Androscoggin River. The result was the "Battle of the Bridge." The biggest strike in Maine history turned violent.

Events in the Twin City area had been building toward an explosion. Lewiston and Auburn were company towns. A walkout at the huge Cushman-Hollis shoe factory in 1932 had been quickly quashed. A strike by textile workers in 1934 took a bit longer to crush, but it collapsed in the face of united opposition by owners, state and local authorities, and the clergy. The state police, modeled on the union-busting "Black Hussars" of the Pennsylvania Constabulary, were called in, along with units of the National Guard. Local manufacturers had a tradition of refusing to recognize collective bargaining. But the passage of the federal Wagner Act and creation of the militant CIO combined to confront owners with their greatest challenge. The law supported the right of workers to unionize; the CIO, fresh from victories in the auto, steel, and rubber industries, sent representatives of the United Shoe Workers of America to Lewiston-Auburn.

Powers Hapgood, a key lieutenant of John L. Lewis, was informed by the president of the manufacturers' association that "not now, nor on the Fourth of July, will I or any of the manufacturers do business with you." Most of the CIO operatives were from Boston; the owners, aided by the press, continually portrayed them as "outside agitators." Local workers lacked the experience of militant unionism required to confront the business leaders successfully. As a consequence, non-Mainers *did* predominate at the forefront of the developing struggle. On the evening of March 24, 1937, three thousand workers crammed into Lewiston's City Hall Auditorium to hear CIO speakers. Anti-union hecklers were there, and the meeting became raucous; CIO leader William J. Mackesy, fearing a riot, rushed through a roaring voice vote favoring a strike for better pay, improved working conditions, a 40-hour week, and, above all, union recognition in Lewiston-Auburn shoe factories.

The manufacturers responded, as usual, by enlisting local authorities to suppress the strike. Enter the two "Dirty Harrys" of this tale. On March 29, Auburn Police Chief Harry Rowe declared no picketing would be allowed within 500 feet of any mill (most of the shoe factories were located in Auburn, while most workers lived in Lewiston). Rowe's police were augmented by 56 state troopers. When strikers contested the picketing restriction, nine CIO organizers were arrested for "conspiracy to intimidate" nonstriking laborers. By April 1, about three-quarters of the normal work force in 19 factories had left their benches. The owners began replacing them with scabs; they also filed for an injunction. Their petition was considered by Supreme Court Justice Harry Manser of Auburn. Manser acted as if he had never heard of the Wagner Act. After Patriot's Day, the judge abruptly ended the injunction hearings and issued his ruling. He declared the strike illegal on the grounds that no strike could be called until a certifiable majority of the workers involved were organized. In fact, the federal law said that a strike that *attempted* to win majority support was legal. Ignoring federal law, Harry Manser granted the injunction. Anybody who picketed, interfered with access of "loyal workers" to the mills, or even spoke publicly in favor of the strike was liable to contempt-of-court charges.

Manser's decision was announced on Tuesday morning, April 20. In the afternoon an exasperated Bill Mackesy defied the injunction in a speech to strikers at Lewiston's City Hall. While disavowing a violent response, Mackesy said "the responsibility for what will happen in the future" rested with Judge Manser. He encouraged the crowd to visit "your friends in Auburn." Five hundred marchers crossed the North Bridge to Auburn, passing a billboard proclaiming "WORLD'S HIGHEST STANDARD OF LIVING: There's no way like the American Way," and headed for the Cushman-Hollis factory. They sang "Hail, Hail the Gang's All Here" as Chief Harry Rowe's little army formed a line in front of the public library on Court Street. A scuffle ensued; police clubs swung and the marchers were turned back. Some strikers, who eluded police by driving to the scene ahead of the crowd on foot, got as far as the railroad tracks next to the factory. There they tangled with police. One officer, Hartwell B. Grant, was hit by a stone and with fists. "It was," the *Lewiston Daily Sun* reported, "the first open combat between police and strikers."

It was only a prelude.

At another tumultuous meeting on Wednesday at Lewiston City Hall, Powers Hapgood told the crowd that he had just received John L. Lewis's personal assurance that the Maine strike would receive the total support of the CIO. Hapgood and other speakers pilloried Judge Manser and assured workers that their strike was lawful; one CIO orator said, "I say to you brazenly and openly that that injunction means nothing to the United Shoe Workers of America. If that be treason, then I am here to take the consequences."

"Are we going back to the factories?" Mackesy, a thin and middle-aged but dynamic figure, asked the audience.

"No!" it roared.

"Are you going back when our union is recognized?"

"Yes!"

Mackesy, who had earlier warned women strikers "to throw nothing more serious than powder puffs," again suggested, "Pay your friends in Auburn a friendly visit."

A crowd of about a thousand marched toward the North Bridge to do just that. Their objective was the Cushman-Hollis factory, still operated by strikebreakers and non-union workers, a special target of the strikers' attention. This time, state and Auburn police were massed at the bridge to stop them. The strikers surged forward, cramming onto the sidewalk, which was protected by a windbreak erected in the winter. They were packed so tightly that the bridge's iron rail seemed in danger of breaking. A number of strikers and spectators crawled up onto the windbreak and shouted insults at the police below. The windbreak, which shuddered from their weight, also shielded the crowd from the view of regular traffic. The dangerous situation became ugly when an officer clubbed a woman striker. The *Sun* reported the blow "appeared" to be aimed at a male striker. The crowd did not see it that way. It shouted "Get him." and pressed forward.

As police fought to restrain the sidewalk strikers, Special Deputy Ed Gagne, normally a janitor at the County Building, tried to halt some strikers marching across the auto ramp. Gagne was knocked down. Hundreds got by the police on the bridge, many again by automobile, and "The Battle of the Bridge" was followed by a series of running clashes on the Auburn side of the Androscoggin. About five hundred strikers and police became engaged in a free-for-all that surged back and forth between the public library and the Cushman-Hollis factory, where the afternoon shift was ending.

Chief Rowe was in the thick of the melee, losing his cap as he swung his club at strikers near the railroad tracks. He hit a man named William Parks a resounding whack on the head. As Parks, blood streaming from his head, staggered to the sidewalk, the crowd was momentarily stunned, then set upon the police.

State Police Lieutenant George Fowler proved to be in the wrong place at the wrong time. He wrestled with a woman, attempting to make an arrest, which aroused the ire of a group of strikers. Fowler was felled by a rock. Other officers pulled one Arthur Nadeau off the stricken Fowler, and rushed the trooper to the hospital. It was some time before he regained consciousness.

Meanwhile, the police lobbed tear gas bombs into the crowds, the first time tear gas was used in a Maine labor dispute. The strikers dispersed, but the gray clouds caused the eyes of police as well as those of their targets to stream. One girl spectator was gassed and ran blindly down the tracks until she collapsed. Some bombs landed among the automobiles of passing by, forcing drivers and passengers to abandon their cars.

The confused confrontation, with swinging clubs and swirling smoke, lasted for an hour and a half. That evening some four hundred National Guardsmen, dispatched by Governor Barrows upon the request of Augusta's mayor, arrived. In a prepared statement, the governor said, "When there is open defiance to the orders of our court and our officers of the law, there is little difference from anarchy. We shall not tolerate this situation for a moment."

The day after what anti-CIO newspapers dubbed "Red Wednesday," the guardsmen—supplemented by 40 deputies with tear gas and a submachine gun—stood ready to repel another attempt by strikers to cross the polluted river. None came.

The CIO protested, calling police action "outrageous." If the police had allowed the strikers to march peaceably by the factories, Hapgood said, "this thing would never have happened." In a fiery speech to workers the following Sunday, Hapgood's wife said that the strikers' special commissary would close "only at the point of a bayonet. If they close [it] our blood will be on their hands." But such rhetoric and Mary Donovan Hapgood's Socialist politics only turned conservative Maine opinion more against the strike. In reporting the events of "Red Wednesday," The *Sun* observed, "Many strange faces were noticed all day. . . . " The predominantly rural jury members who found defendants guilty in separate conspiracy and contempt trials probably viewed them as troublemakers "from away." Ethnic and religious divisions were also clearly a factor: most strikers were Catholic French-Canadians. Protestant Yankees—and the Catholic clergy—opposed the strike. Thus, in the end, it did not matter that the National Labor Relations Board ordered union elections. The owners simply refused to bend to federal law. As hard-pressed workers, too poor to sustain more than three months out of work, returned to their jobs (if they had not been replaced), the CIO had to accept defeat.

The "Battle of the Bridge" was the most dramatic example of militant unionism in Maine. In a hostile environment, such unionism was doomed. Miraculously, nobody was killed. But the labor movement was badly wounded.

40 •

Shootout at a Sporting-Goods Store

A t 8:25 A.M., October 12, 1937, Grace Hardy was sitting in a car parked in front of Dakin's Sporting Goods Store in Bangor, writing a letter. She barely noticed another automobile pull up behind her. Five minutes later, as a store clerk finished sweeping the pavement, a big black Buick sedan with out-of-state plates parked nearby. Miss Hardy did not see the first man get out of the Buick and enter the sporting goods store, but she saw two other men step out onto Central Street. At that moment, the man in the car behind her yelled, "Look out!" She dropped to the floorboards as gunfire erupted. Across the street, barber Harry Johnson heard the first shot and, looking out his shop window, remarked to a customer, "Look, a man just committed suicide." As more shots—many more—rang out, the alarmed customer cried, "Look out Harry, some of those bullets may come this way!" A few minutes later a Vermont customs agent, just arrived in Bangor on business, asked a policeman, "What kind of town is this? Just a ways down the street, the road is full of bodies."

Downtown Bangor had become a shooting gallery.

The chain of events that culminated in carnage had begun about two weeks earlier when the sleek black car with Ohio license plates had first parked outside Dakin's. A dapper young man stepped out and entered the store, where he examined a number of guns before purchasing two Colt .45 automatics, three extra clips, and a box of ammunition. Although he was clean-shaven and courteous, there was something about the stranger that did not sit right with proprietor, Everett S. "Shep" Hurd. His suspicion deepened when he observed the shifty-eyed men waiting in the big sedan outside. After the stranger left, Hurd contacted Bangor Police Chief Thomas Crowley. Crowley, equally suspicious, contacted the FBI in Washington.

About a week later, the same shiny Buick was back. The same neatly dressed man bought another .45 automatic and an extra clip. He threw one gun he had examined back, saying "It isn't any good." Then he asked Hurd if he could obtain some more clips. The store manager said he was not sure, but would try.

Leaning closer to the counter, the stranger said, "I'd like for you to get me a tommy gun."

"We aren't allowed to handle those," the store manager replied.

"Well," the stranger said, "I'll be back next Monday or Tuesday. Just see what you can do."

The stranger was accompanied by another tough-looking man. Hurd was so nervous when his mysterious customers left that he did not dare check the black sedan's license plates. From photographs sent to the Bangor police by the FBI, Hurd identified his gun-hungry visitors as James Dalhover, a member of the infamous Brady Gang, and Brady himself.

The Brady Gang had been the subject of a year-long national manhunt. It was responsible for at least three murders—an Ohio grocery store clerk, an Indianapolis police sergeant, and an Indiana state trooper had been gunned down as the gang pulled off a string of robberies across the Midwest. Its leader, Al Brady, 26, described in *Official Detective Magazine* as a "weak-chinned former Sunday School teacher," had reputedly vowed, "Someday I'll make John Dillinger look like a piker." Big words for the five-foot seven-inch Brady, who recruited a band of even shorter men dubbed "Midget Dillingers." But J. Edgar Hoover took Brady seriously, making him Public Enemy Number One. The other pint-sized killers included former Kentucky moonshiner and convict James Dalhover, 30, who acted as Brady's "front-man," Clarence Lee Shaffer, Jr., 20, "whose apple-red cheeks and wavy hair belied the fact that he was a merciless killer at heart." The gang specialized in holding up jewelry stores and looted a total of $100,000 in gems. After breaking out of an Indiana jail, the trio headed east. In August, 1937, they escaped a police raid on their Baltimore hideout in a running gun battle.

Now they were in Maine.

"It was a bad move," Dalhover would later admit. "After we ran from

Baltimore, the other two voted to go to Maine. I didn't want to go, but we had decided on the two to one vote, so I went along, although my hunch against the move sure turned [out to be] right." Brady apparently had the bright idea that the approach of the hunting season would make the purchase of guns and ammunition in rural Maine appear innocent, although .45 automatics and tommy guns were not usual deerhunting weapons, even in Maine.

As the *Bangor Daily News* commented, "Brady and his gang were supposed to be masters of crime. . . . But in their tragic adventure here they acted, from first to last, with almost incredible stupidity."

"In fact," the newspaper observed, "they all but engaged a press agent to let Bangor know they had arrived." A waitress in an Exchange Street restaurant served Brady several times before the fateful Columbus Day Shootout. He only ordered orange juice and always flipped her a dime. The gang acted as if it were on vacation. A young woman would later report seeing the trio on a motorboat on Camden's Lake Megunticook, and there were similar stories up and down the coast. Perhaps only half were true, yet the image of a supremely reckless Al Brady emerges.

Meanwhile, the FBI was busy. Beginning with four agents who flew into the small airport on Saturday, October 9, a small army of G-men converged on Bangor. Led by agent Myron Gurnea—"tall, dark, quiet, and decisive"—the federal crime-fighters organized a deadly trap for the Brady Gang. Local police, including state troopers, were assigned minor, supporting roles in the operation. This caused some ruffled feathers, but Gurnea couldn't have cared less.

On Monday, October 11, Hurd received a call inquiring if Dakin's would be open on Columbus Day. Hurd told the unidentified caller, whom everybody assumed was one of Brady's men, that his store would indeed be open for business.

Right on target, at precisely 8:30 Tuesday morning, the black Buick made its third—and final—stop outside Dakin's. Plenty of stolen license plates, along with an arsenal of weapons were stashed in the back seat, but the telltale Ohio license plates had not been changed.

The gangsters had driven into a trap. Federal agents were stationed in nearby cars, in a machine-gun nest in a second-floor window across Central Street, and behind the store's counters, poised to spring. Several Indiana troopers were in the wings with Maine policemen.

A signal was arranged. Agent Walter Walsh, disguised as a clerk at a counter next to "Shep" Hurd would pull a string connected to a piece of cardboard hanging in the store window. When the cardboard fell, the G-men would move in.

The regular clerks played their parts to perfection. Everything appeared to be dull business as usual when Dalhover, in a chipper mood, approached Hurd's counter. It was as if he were greeting an old friend.

"Now if you have the stuff I ordered. . . . "

Before he could finish the sentence Dalhover faced the business end of Agent Walsh's revolver. As other armed men materialized, the gangster surrendered without a fight.

Walsh pulled the string. The cardboard fell. Brady and Shaffer had gotten out of the sedan. They were outside, exposed, and in a split second they realized something was very wrong. An agent yelled at Miss Hardy to duck. The "Midget Dillingers" grabbed their pistols.

A burst of gunfire punctured the sleepy early morning quiet. The staccato of machine-gun fire mixed with the popping of handguns. Bullets riddled Dakin's storefront. Two slugs fired by the gangsters shattered a plate glass window in a tailor shop across the street. A bullet slammed into a model house hanging in front of a real estate office. Other bullets hit the doors of a restaurant and a barber shop. A hail of lead was flying up and down, as well as across, Central Street.

The only concession the G-men made to the safety of innocent passersby was, at the last moment, to shut off automobile access to the street by blocking its entrances with cars. Pedestrians were on their own. There were quite a few, because Central Street was just off downtown Bangor's main intersection. One bullet perforated the coat and dress of a clerk headed to work at a department store. It just missed her thigh. "I didn't have time to be frightened until afterwards," she confessed. Miss Hardy, only a few feet from the targets of the massed gunfire, crouched in her car until—in only 30 seconds—it ended. Remarkably, no pedestrian was shot.

Al Brady was not so fortunate. Caught in a lethal crossfire, he fell in the street. There, as the *Bangor Daily News* gruesomely reported, he "lay grotesquely on his back, a human sieve, his flesh torn into bits."

Shaffer backed into the middle of the street, shooting blindly. Hit repeatedly, he appeared to try to run toward the Norumbega Mall. Like so many other adventurers, he never made it to Norumbega. Riddled with lead, he toppled onto the streetcar tracks.

His blood "mingled with that of Brady. It spread in an ever-widening crimson lake. For a few minutes the street seemed full of it."

Firemen brought a hose and washed away the blood. Assorted policemen and the curious stared at the corpses in the street. Somehow Shaffer's heart continued to beat for eight minutes. His face was untouched, but the rest of his body was shredded with bullet holes.

Miss Hardy emerged unscathed from her car. "Gosh," she remarked, "those G-men were awful good-looking and brave, too." Agent Walsh was wounded in the shoulder, the only lawman injured in the shootout.

Dalhover was hustled to the Penobscot County Jail. He grinned for photographers, complained that he had not been able to die fighting like his comrades, and assured a wary matron he would not bite. Dalhover's mother, informed of his capture, said, "It's too bad he wasn't killed like the rest of them,"—and fainted. He was soon flown to Indiana to face murder charges. Shaffer was shipped back to Hoosierland in a box. His Baltimore "wife" was relieved to learn of his demise. "I thought they would be caught in Maine," Minnie said, "because they often said they would go to Maine sometime. We told police. . . . " Nobody claimed Al Brady's corpse. On October 15, the man whose ambition in life was to surpass Dillinger was buried in a cheap wooden box in a far corner of Mount Hope Cemetery, in a pauper's grave. Burial expenses were taken care of with some of the $5,000 retrieved from the gangster's pockets.

"We thought Maine was a hick state, but we found it was the toughest rap we ever faced," James Dalhover admitted.

41 •

Atlantic Charter

W HAT A WEEK!" began an item in the August 14, 1941, edition of the *Rockland Courier Gazette*. "With Union Fair in the height of its usual success, and with Camden-Rockport celebrating their 150th birthday, next week is going to be a dizzy one for the residents of Knox County." The coastal newspaper also ran a short press release announcing that President Franklin D. Roosevelt and Prime Minister Winston Churchill "have met at sea and produced a platform of war aims for the U.S. and England. . . . " Details were sketchy. *Where* had the two leaders met? *What* was the nature of their agreement? In the fateful summer of 1941, with war for the second time in a generation ravaging Europe and reaching across the Atlantic with German U-boats, a gnawing uneasiness accompanied the enjoyment of blueberries and windjammers.

Then came the dramatic news that the president was coming ashore at Rockland. The city, described as "agog with excitement," scrambled to prepare for FDR's scheduled arrival at Tillson's Wharf on Saturday, August 16. Hundreds of newsmen poured into Rockland, anxious to relay the president's description of, as the *Courier* put it, "his epochal sea conference."

It was somehow fitting that, at one of the key moments of his presidency, Roosevelt was coming to Rockland. Not that Knox County was a hotbed of Democrats. In the last three elections, only one town—South Thomaston— had broken the solid G.O.P. ranks. That was in 1936, when Jim Farley quipped, "As Maine goes, so goes Vermont." In 1940, the maverick town was back in the fold; Rockland voted 1,979 to 1,471 for Wendell Willkie, and North Haven, from which the president was steaming on the *Potomac* to Rockland, voted 193 to 50 against Roosevelt.

Yet the Maine coast was very much a part of Franklin D. Roosevelt's experience. As he remarked to Rockland's mayor in 1936 during a quick transit from the railroad station to Tillson's wharf, where the presidential yacht awaited to begin a leisurely cruise Downeast to Campobello, "I began coming to Rockland 40 years ago." The young FDR became familiar with Maine as one of the summer people; the aristocratic New York family owned an estate on New Brunswick's Campobello Island, separated by a few hundred yards of water from Lubec and just across the bay from Eastport. In those days the island was accessible only by boat, although the Roosevelts often took a train as far as Eastport. Whether from a railroad car's window or the deck of a sloop, FDR saw a good deal of Maine. But he was always passing through. "I'm here to have a good time," he told reporters in 1936. "I haven't the faintest idea where I'm going or when, except to work to the eastward."

Nobody would mistake Roosevelt for a Mainer, but he enjoyed good times on the rocky shore. In 1913, then assistant secretary of the Navy, he used his political pull to have the battleship U.S.S. *North Dakota* lend its presence to Eastport's Fourth of July celebration. Attired in his summer flannels, Roosevelt received a 17-gun salute as he boarded the warship. Franklin Roosevelt relished such flourishes, but, as Lieutenant William F. Halsey, Jr., learned, FDR was not just a dilettante yachtsman. During World War I, Roosevelt asked to take the helm of Halsey's destroyer in Frenchmen's Bay and, to the young captain's surprise and relief, proved that he "knew his business" negotiating the difficult channel off Mount Desert Island.

James Roosevelt would recall that his father taught his sons to sail:

> . . . maybe because this was the one activity he loved above all others and wanted us to love. He was a superb sailor. The straits and narrows around Campobello and the nearby islands are treacherous, the tides strong and tricky, but he knew them well. While he would not tolerate our fooling around on board a boat, he delighted in demonstrating his own ability with a near-reckless handling of the ship through rocky passages, so close to the jagged reefs as to scare the wits out of us. . . .

Not all the memories of Franklin and Eleanor Roosevelt were idyllic; there was very rough sailing associated with Campobello and the Maine coast. It was in the summer of 1916 that FDR fretted about a polio epidemic that extended to Maine. Then, in August of 1921, Roosevelt was felled by the dread disease, which paralyzed his legs. A special railroad car was dispatched to Eastport and, on September 13, Roosevelt, in acute pain, was carried by stretcher from his cottage to a motor launch, which took him across the bay to an Eastport dock. In a luggage cart, he made the bumpy ascent to the waiting car. The ever-faithful Louis Howe had, by a ruse, momentarily distracted the waiting press. By the time they reached his railroad car, Roosevelt was smiling and smoking in bed, putting on a grand show. But it would be a dozen years before he would return to Campobello and its wrenching memories. In the 1920s, FDR speculated in a Rockland lobster-packing plant. The idea was to develop pounds for the lobsters, and once the price went up, sell them to restaurants and hotels. However, lobster prices dropped and Roosevelt lost $26,000 on his Maine investment—another less-than-happy association.

Now, almost exactly 20 years after he was crippled at his beloved summer retreat, Franklin D. Roosevelt was coming back to Maine. He had ended his meetings with Churchill off the coast of Newfoundland on the afternoon of

August 12, and, aboard the cruiser U.S.S. *Augusta*, set sail for Blue Hill Bay. There, accompanied by Harry Hopkins and a few cronies, the president boarded the waiting yacht *Potomac*. Incredibly, FDR had been absent from Washington for nearly two weeks, his whereabouts unknown to the press or the nation. In no hurry, the presidential party spent a day fishing. On August 15, with a brief announcement of the conference released, the yacht anchored at Pulpit Harbor, North Haven.

Meanwhile, local officials, state police, and the Secret Service bustled to prepare Rockland for the chief executive's arrival. A particularly commanding figure was Colonel Edward Starling of the Secret Service, a man who had been guarding presidents since the days of Teddy Roosevelt. He had not lost one yet, although an assassin came close against then-president-elect Franklin Roosevelt in 1932. During FDR's 1936 visit to Rockland, an embarrassed city alderman had "the rather thrilling experience" of being frisked by an agent. Alderman Maurice Lovejoy had been standing near the president's car with his hand in his pocket.

August 16 dawned foggy and drizzly. By afternoon, however, it had become hot and humid. Thousands of spectators, including a good number of tourists and many children, crowded along the president's parade route from the public landing to the railroad station. Curbstone flags hung limply, and, after a three-hour wait in the hot sun, only the electric sense of expectancy kept the people lining the streets from likewise wilting.

At 3:30 P.M. the *Potomac* completed the ten-mile voyage from North Haven to Rockland and eased into an old steamboat slip. The rusty slip had been oiled and tested by the Secret Service. The gangway was lowered and reporters with special clearances were allowed aboard the yacht. FDR was about to give press conference 761 of his administration. He appeared, as usual, relaxed and in good spirits, wearing a brown suit and blue shirt, his trademark cigarette in a long holder at a jaunty angle. A local reporter discerned little evidence of a man worried by the burdens of his office; according to him, FDR seemed eminently "at peace with the world. . . . "

The world was not at peace, however, and despite the smiles and good-natured repartee, Roosevelt was guarded in his comments about the Atlantic Conference. He even refused to even indicate its location—the *Courier Gazette* would state the meeting was "believed to have been near Isle au Haut." Reporters could not help noticing the anti-aircraft and submachine guns on the *Potomac*'s decks. Roosevelt claimed he had even objected to the announcement of his landing at Rockland. "However," he said, "it was foggy between North Haven and Rockland, and while it's open season out there, no submarine fired a torpedo at us as far as we could see. . . . "

Roosevelt opened with a statement of his most dramatic impression of the Atlantic Conference:

> I think the first thing in the minds of all of us was a very remarkable ser-
> vice on the quarterdeck of the Prince of Wales last Sunday morning. There
> was their own ship's complement, with three or four hundred blue jackets
> and marines from American ships, on the quarterdeck, completely
> intermingled, first one uniform and then another uniform. The service was

conducted by two chaplains, one English and one American and, as usual, the lesson was read by the captain of the British ship. They had three hymns that everybody took part in, and a little ship's altar was decked with the American flag and the British flag. . . . I think everybody there, officers and enlisted men, felt that it was one of the great historic services. I know I did.

It was an arresting picture. But what did it mean? Roosevelt and Churchill did not travel thousands of miles across a submarine-infested ocean to sing hymns together. Roosevelt, sensitive to isolationist sentiment, described the meeting as "primarily an exchange of views . . . a swapping of information." He spelled out no details about lend-lease aid to Great Britain, or possibly to the Soviet Union. Harry Hopkins, who had just been to London and Moscow, sat in a corner of the cabin but did not utter a word during the 25-minute press conference. Nor did Roosevelt choose to elaborate on the significance of the joint statement dubbed the "Atlantic Charter," except to observe that Nazi activities in occupied countries bore the need for greater examination. "The more that is discussed and looked into, the more terrible the thought becomes of having the world as a whole dominated by the kind of influences which have been at work. . . . "

The key exchange came midway through the session:

Q. Are we any closer to entering the war, actually?
A. I should say, no.
Q. May we quote directly?
A. No, you can quote indirectly.

Roosevelt was, of course, being evasive. In his own mind, he had decided that Hitler must be defeated. That would involve more than hymns sung together on a British battleship. Some historians have maintained Churchill was disappointed by the lack of a firm commitment by FDR at the Atlantic Conference. The president made sure nothing like a treaty or even a signed protocol emerged from their meetings. The "Atlantic Charter" was an unsigned mimeographed statement of shared objectives. Yet the symbolic importance of the event, which FDR chose to emphasize in his press conference, was unmistakable.

The press conference over, the Secret Service was on edge. When State Police Chief Henry Weaver bolted forward to shake FDR's hand as he stepped onto Tillson's Wharf, agents—not recognizing the local lawman—almost dunked him in Rockland Harbor.

The motorcade proceeded to the railroad station by way of what used to be called "Sea Street," a street long considered unsafe to venture upon at night. A leading seaport, Rockland used to be a tough town and no part of town was tougher than Sea Street, with its rowdy sailors and wanton women. But on the muggy afternoon of August 16, 1941, it resounded to cheers. Roosevelt bowed and waved. There was no speech. Once again, for the last time, he was just passing through.

42 •

Sixty Seconds in Lewiston

H eavyweight championship boxing matches have been fought in some pretty out-of-the-way locations, but the one between Muhammed Ali and Sonny Liston in a Lewiston hockey arena on May 25, 1965, was perhaps the most remote. It certainly was one of the most bizarre and controversial. And, to the dismay of the spectators who plunked down $100 for ringside seats, it set a record as one of the quickest heavyweight decisions ever.

"It's going to be more exciting than the last one," the brash new champion declared. Ali was referring to his victory over seven-to-one favorite Sonny Liston in Miami on February 25, 1964. The hulking Liston, who specialized in knockouts, had refused to enter the ring in the sixth round of that fight, giving the fast-talking "Louisville Lip" a technical knockout. The inevitable rematch was scheduled for Boston in November, 1964, but Ali's emergency operation for a hernia postponed the bout; a dispute over promotional background, compounded by the general ill repute of a sport in which men try to beat each other's brains in, sent promoters scurrying to find an alternative site. They settled upon Lewiston, a textile town of 40,000 with a history of minor-division boxing.

Governor John Reed and other public officials were eager to have the fight in Maine. It would be worth a million dollars in publicity.

Ali, who had become a Black Muslim and changed his name from Cassius Clay, related to a friend a dream he had had while in training for his return engagement with the menacing Sonny. "The bell rang and I jumped up and ran out and hit him with a right hand," the 23-year-old champ related. "I leaned back and moved away as he pursued me for maybe a minute. Then all of a sudden I saw him coming in and I hit him with a right hand—bam!—right on the chin and The Big Bad Bear fell on the floor. I stood over him, yelling, 'Rise and shine . . . rise and shine.' "

Liston had different expectations. Ali, he admitted, was fast, but "I'm gonna catch up to him sometime and get him. He may run but not forever." Sonny had a longer fight in mind. The match would be scored by a system under which the winner of each round got ten points and the loser nine or less. "It don't make any difference," Liston said. "All we need is a referee who can count to ten."

The referee was to be a former heavyweight champion, "Jersey Joe" Walcott. His counting ability would play an important part in the bizarre fight at Central Maine Youth Center, better known as St. Dom's hockey rink. The place, described by an Associated Press sports writer as "an overgrown Quonset hut," could only seat about six thousand. With tickets ranging from $25 to $100, it was doubtful if it would be filled to capacity. Working-class Lewiston did not appear overly excited. "Beano as usual Tuesday night, 7:30," the sign in front of a local Catholic church announced.

The Empire Theater was showing a flick called *None But the Brave*, starring Frank Sinatra. From the way the press was describing the possible threats to Ali from followers of the murdered Malcolm X, only the brave would dare go to the arena. The story was that Ali, as the most prominent Muslim in America, would be "hit" in retaliation for the renegade Malcolm X's assassination by members of the sect. All the talk about Muslims baffled Lewistonians, whose idea of a mosque was the local Kora Temple of the Masons. Ali discounted the furor. "Nobody wants to kill me," he shrugged. "If they shoot, the gun will explode in their hands, the bullets will turn. Allah will protect me."

Ali suspected that Liston was not so sure that bullets intended for Muhammed would turn away from him. Sonny, who arrived early from his Denver home, worked out at a hill resort of Poland Spring, overlooking the rolling countryside of western Maine. In its turn-of-the-century heyday, operated by the bearded Ricker clan, it was one of the premier resorts in New England. The menu included everything but liquor; Poland Spring was fabled for its pure spring water—the Rickers had made a virtual shrine of the spring—and good, clean, fun. Now Sonny Liston and a small entourage insisted that they have the Mansion House wholly to themselves. Of course the other buildings of the sprawling complex were not empty. About a thousand news, radio, and television men used Poland Spring as their base. The taciturn Liston, a man with a criminal record, was no match for Ali in the battle of the quote—"When the Bear leaves Maine, he will be in pain"—but he got off at least one lame joke: "I like it better here than in Denver. The cops walk beside me, instead of behind me."

At noontime on the appointed day, the champion, who had trained in Massachusetts, entered the ring for the pre-fight weighing-in ceremony. He was greeted by boos from a sizeable crowd of spectators. Ignoring them, he danced about, shadow boxing, as a grim Liston was weighed—incorrectly. He was reweighed and announced to pack just over 215 pounds. Ali, who came in at a relatively light 206 pounds, shouted something at Liston, who growled, "You shut your mouth. I'll take care of you tonight." The press was also in a bad mood, particularly the photographers, because too many "dignitaries," local and otherwise, insisted upon climbing into the ring. The atmosphere was still off-key that evening.

About 4,280 customers, passing up a chance to play Beano or watch Frank Sinatra at the Empire, filed into the arena. The 200-odd police present searched the building for bombs and inspected the purses of women spectators. Rumors of carloads of armed men en route from New York circulated in the fetid, smokey air as the preliminary card was rather quickly concluded. None of the featured six-rounders went the distance. Amos "Big Train" Lincoln, a Liston sparring partner, put away Abe Davis in 35 seconds flat. Clay's sparring partner, Jimmy Ellis, also prevailed easily. (Unknown to the crowd, Ellis had hurt Ali in training with a vicious jab to the ribs; the Champ had also been stung in a quarrel with his wife).

The introduction of VIPs seemed to take longer than the preliminary card, and singer Robert Goulet managed to forget the words of the national anthem. Then the main event began.

Ali hit Liston almost at once with a right and left to his head. Unfazed, Sonny began to stalk the agile Ali and seemed to have the champ partly boxed into a corner. Liston moved in.

The next moment he thudded heavily onto the canvas. Rocky Marciano, at ringside, later admitted, "I never saw the punch. I kept my eyes on Liston and didn't see what hit him."

Neither did Sonny Liston. "Where did the right hand come from?" he wondered. It was a short, fast right cross. So fast hardly *anybody* saw it. Ali later claimed that it was a "phantom punch" he had been taught by Stepin Fetchit, who had learned about it from the legendary Jack Johnson. Liston claimed he was hit on the left cheek; others claimed he was downed by a blow to the Adam's apple. Many swore he had not been hit at all. Yells of "fake" and "fix" resounded in the Lewiston arena.

Nobody was more confused than the referee. The old ex-champion appeared in a daze. Walcott looked into the crowd, trying unsuccessfully to spot the timekeeper, Francis McDonough. He hovered over Liston, and tried to steer away Ali, who screamed, "Get up off that floor, Sonny! You're supposed to be so bad!" Finally spotting McDonough, "Jersey" Joe wandered off to ringside to confer with him. He had not started the count. McDonough later claimed, "If that bum Clay had gone to a neutral corner instead of running around like a maniac, all the trouble would have been avoided."

"I didn't want to get right up," Liston later said. "The referee never started the count. I didn't know when to get up."

Liston, who had never been knocked down before, was plainly groggy. Attempting to get up, he fell back, then regained his feet. Ali immediately pounded him three more times in the head.

By this time the confused referee was informed by the timekeeper that he had counted to 12 while Liston was prostrate on the canvas. Nat Fleischer of *Ring Magazine* yelled, "The bum is out." "There is no question in my mind," McDonough said, "that Liston was knocked out." Walcott rushed back to end the already-ended fight.

Announcer Johnny Addie grabbed the microphone and cried, "The winner and still champion—Muhammed Ali. The time: one minute."

The disgruntled audience erupted in boos.

At 60 seconds, it could have been the shortest heavyweight title match in history—if it were indeed one minute. Even the time was disputed. Broadcast reruns indicated that a time of 1:45 minutes was more accurate. The befuddled Walcott called the match at 2:12 minutes.* The Maine State Boxing Commission stuck to the one minute verdict.

The champ "bounced and bounded around like a rowboat on a rough sea,"

---

*Thus Walcott ended fight based on timekeeper's count rather than his own, contrary to boxing rules.

and repeatedly screamed, "Where's Floyd Patterson? Where's the Rabbit?" Ali wanted to fight the aging Patterson next. The former champion was an onlooker who, unlike many, saw the punch. "It was a good lick," he allowed. "He really hit him. . . . "

On his way out of the chaotic scene of his triumph Ali, as usual, had the last word: "I knew I was going to knock out the Big Bear in the first round. I'm just too fast for everyone. My punches are a blur." He claimed that all the talk about an attack on him "had Sonny frozen stiff with fear," and that "Allah was with me—he told me what I was going to do. I have been saying my prayers and living righteously. This was a victory for good."

The opinion of one spectator, speaking for many, was quite different. "Why," he asked, "did thousands of people work nine months and spend so much money for a fight that lasted only 60 seconds and stunk?"

Jimmy Breslin wrote, "A fight for the heavyweight championship of the world came to an end . . . at a high school hockey rink in a dreadful little Maine backtree town. . . . The name of the place in which this atrocity took place is the St. Dominic's Youth Center, which is owned by St. Dominic's church. So, in the end, boxing gets itself a Catholic burial."

Various politicians, including U.S. Senator John Tower, called for an investigation. But boxing endured and the flap blew over.

Liston went back to Denver and oblivion. Muhammed Ali continued to be the most controversial boxer of modern times—and probably, as he often claimed, "The Greatest." Finally, like Liston in Miami, he failed to answer the bell for the 11th round of a 1980 fight against a much younger Larry Holmes. Over too many years he had absorbed too many punches. Recently asked what changes he would like to see made in boxing, the once-loquacious "Louisville Lip" haltingly replied, "They should . . . stop . . . the fights . . . sooner."

That was not a complaint in Lewiston in 1965.

Author's Note
on Sources

T he author has attempted to include only stories from Maine's past that can be substantiated. Some works were especially useful and were consulted for several chapters. These include William D. Williamson, *The History of the State of Maine*, two volumes. (Hallowell: Glazier, Masters & Co., 1832), dated but still informative about the Colonial and Revolutionary Era; Louis C. Hatch, *Maine: A History* (Somersworth, New Hampshire: New Hampshire Publishing Co., 1974, a reprint of the original three-volume 1919 edition), particularly valuable for 19th century political history; Henry S. Burrage, *Beginnings of Colonial Maine, 1602-1658* (Portland, Maine: Marks Printing House, 1914), the best volume on early 17th century Maine; and Ronald F. Banks, *Maine Becomes a State: The Movement to Separate Maine from Massachusetts, 1785-1820* (Somersworth, New Hampshire: New Hampshire Publishing Co., 1973), informative on Maine politics in the early national era. W. Storrs Lee, ed., *Maine: A Literary Chronicle* (New York: Funk & Wagnalls, 1968) was also useful.

The *Collections* of the Maine Historical Society (abbreviated *MHS Coll.*), including its monumental *Documentary History of Maine* and the more recent *Maine Historical Society Quarterly* (*MHSQ*) were virtual gold mines of information. While *Sprague's Journal of Maine History* (*SJMH*) should be approached with some caution, it was another key source. Various unpublished Ph.D. dissertations, notably at the University of Maine at Orono, were useful.

Some newspapers were valuable sources, notably the *Portland Eastern Argus* for the 19th century and the *Bangor Daily News, Rockland Courier-Gazette, Lewiston Journal, Portland Press Herald*, and *Portland Evening Express* for the 20th century.

While many local histories reflect more myth than history, several fairly solid works have been written. In this category I would include Charles E. Banks, *History of York*, two volumes (Boston: Calkins Press, 1931); Cyrus Eaton, *History of Thomaston, Rockland, and South Thomaston, Maine*, two volumes (Hallowell: Masters, Smith & Co., 1865) and *Annals of the Town of Warren* (Hallowell: Masters and Livermore, 1877); Henry W. Owen, *History of Bath* (Bath, Maine: Times Co., 1936); James W. North, *The History of Augusta* (Somersworth, New Hampshire: New England History Press, 1981 reprint); Jacob Stahl, *History of Old Broad Bay and Waldoboro*, two volumes (Portland: Bond Wheelwright, 1956); George and Henry Wheeler, *History of Brunswick Topsham, and Harpswell, Maine* (Somersworth, New Hampshire: New Hampshire Publishing Co., 1974 reprint); and William Willis, The *History of Portland* (Somersworth, New Hampshire: New Hampshire Publishing Co., 1972 reprint).

Unfortunately, much of what passes for Maine history is more romance than fact and does not reflect the solid research of modern Maine historians. There is no comprehensive work reflecting their labor, a situation which one hopes will be corrected in the near future. In the interim, collections of essays such as Ronald F. Banks's *A History of Maine* (Dubuque, Iowa: Kendall/Hunt Publishing Co., 1976) and David C. Smith's and Edward O. Schriver's *Maine: A History Through Selected Readings* (Dubuque: Kendall/Hunt, 1985) are of at least limited usefulness. A major gap is the lack of an authoritative work on Maine in the 20th century.

What follows is a selective list of suggested readings.

Bibliography

DOWNEAST DAWN OF AMERICA (1524–1692)

Banks, Charles E., "The Pirate of Pemaquid," *Maine Historical and Genealogical Recorder*, Vol. 1 (1884), 57–61.

Champlain, Samuel de, *Voyages of Samuel de Champlain,* W.L. Grant, ed. (New York: Barnes and Noble, 1907).

Clark, Andrew H., *Acadia: The Geography of Early Nova Scotia to 1760* (Madison: University of Wisconsin Press, 1968).

Dow, George F., and John H. Edmonds, *The Pirates of the New England Coast, 1630–1730* (Salem, Massachusetts: Marine Research Society, 1923).

Faulkner, Alaric and Gretchen, *The French at Pentagoet, 1635–1674: An Archaeological Portrait of the Acadian Frontier* (Augusta: Maine Historic Preservation Commission, 1987).

Godfrey, John E., "Baron De Saint Castin," *MHS Coll.*, Series 1, Vol. 7 (1876), 41–72.

Godfrey, John E., "Claude de La Tour," *MHS Coll.*, Series 1, Vol. 9 (1887), 97–113.

Gorges, Sir Ferdinando, *A Brief Narration of the...Advancement of Plantations,* reprinted in *MHS Coll.*, Series 1, Vol. 2 (1847), xiii-109.

Lescarbot, Marc, *Nova Francia: A Description of Acadia,* E. Denison Ross and Eileen Power, eds. (New York: Harper and Bros., 1928).

Libby, Charles T., ed., *Province and Court Records of Maine,* 2 Vols. (Portland: *MHS,* 1928–1931).

McLain, Jim, *A Brief Account of the Wicked Doings of Dixie Bull* (New York: Court Printers, 1980).

Morison, Samuel E., *The European Discovery of America: The Northern Voyages, 500–1600* (New York: Oxford University Press, 1971).

Morison, Samuel E., *Samuel de Champlain: Father of New France* (Boston: Little, Brown, 1972).

Preston, Richard A., *Gorges of Plymouth Fort* (Toronto: University of Toronto Press, 1953).

Reid, John G., "French Aspirations in the Kennebec-Penobscot Region," *MHSQ,* Vol. 23 (Fall 1983), 85–92.

Russell, Howard S., *Indian New England Before the Mayflower* (Hanover, New Hampshire: University Press of New England, 1980).

Sawtelle, William O., "Mount Desert: The Story of Saint Sauveur," *SJMH,* Vol. 9 (July-September 1921), 101–120.

Sawtelle, William O., "Sir Samuel Argall: The First Englishman at Mount Desert," *SJMH*, Vol. 12 (October-December 1924), 201–221.

Sprague, John F., "Baron de Saint Castin," *SJMH*, Vol. 4 (April 1917), 297–310.

Webster, John C., ed., *Acadia at the End of the Seventeenth Century: Letters, Journals and Memoirs of Joseph Robineau de Villebon, Commandant in Acadia, 1690–1700* (Saint John, New Brunswick: New Brunswick Museum, 1934).

Winthrop, John, *The Life and Letters of John Winthrop,* Robert C. Winthrop, ed., 2 vols. (Boston: Little, Brown, 1869).

THE WILD, WILD EAST (1700–1820)

Ahlin, John H., *Maine Rubicon: Downeast Settlers During the American Revolution* (Calais, Maine: Calais Advertiser Press, 1966).

Allis, Frederick S., ed., *William Bingham's Maine Lands* (Boston: Colonial Society of Massachusetts, 1954).

Callahan, North, *Henry Knox: General Washington's General* (New York: Holt, Rinehart & Co., 1958).

Cummings, E.C., ed., "The Mission of Father Rasles as Depicted by Himself" (Letters from Rale to his brother 1723–24), *MHS Coll.*, Series 2, Vol. 4 (1893), 155–169 and 265–301.

Dwight, Timothy, "The Story of General Wadsworth," reprinted in *MHSQ*, Vol. 15 (Fourth of July, 1976), 227–256.

Eckstorm, Fannie H., "The Attack of Norridgewock," *New England Quarterly* Vol. 7 (September 1934), 541–78.

Faibsiy, John D., "Penobscot, 1779: The Eye of a Hurricane," *MHSQ*, Vol. 19 (Fall 1979), 91–117.

Forbes, Esther, *Paul Revere and the World He Lived In* (Boston: Houghton Mifflin, 1942).

Goold, Nathan, "General Samuel Thompson of Brunswick and Topsham, Maine," *MHS Coll.*, Series 3, Vol. 1 (1904), 423–458.

Goold, William, "Col. William Vaughan of Matinicus and Damariscotta," *MHS Coll.*, Series 3, Vol. 8 (1881), 293–315.

Hatch, Robert M., *Thrust for Canada: The American Attempt on Quebec in 1775–1776* (Boston: Houghton Mifflin, 1979).

Kevitt, Chester B., *General Solomon Lovell and the Penobscot Expedition* (Weymouth, Massachusetts: Weymouth Historical Commission, 1976).

Leamon, James, "The Search for Security: Maine After Penobscot," *MHSQ*, Vol. 21 (Winter 1982), 119–153.

Lomask, Milton, *Aaron Burr: The Years from Princeton to Vice President, 1756–1805* (New York: Farrar, Straus, and Giroux, 1979).

Moody, Robert E., "Samuel Ely: Forerunner of Shays," *New England Quarterly*, Vol. 5 (1932), 105–134.

Morrison, Kenneth M., "Sebastien Racle and Norridgewock, 1724; The Eckstorm Conspiracy Thesis Reconsidered," *MHSQ,* Vol. 14 (Fall 1974), 76–97.

Picking, Sherwood, *Sea Fight off Monhegan* (Portland: Machigonne Press, 1941).

Rawlyk, G.A., *Yankees at Louisbourg* (Orono: University of Maine Press, 1967).

Roberts, Kenneth, ed., *March to Quebec: Journal of the Members of Arnold's Expedition* (New York: Doubleday, 1947).

Rolde, Neil, *Sir William Pepperell of Colonial New England* (Brunswick, Maine: Harpswell Press, 1982).

Shipton, Clifford K., "Peleg Wadsworth," *MHSQ*, Vol. 15 (Fourth of July, 1976), 211–226.

Smith, Marion J., *General William King: Merchant, Shipbuilder, and Maine's First Governor* (Camden: Downeast Books, 1980).

Sprague, John F., *Sebastian Rale: A Maine Tragedy of the Eighteenth Century* (Boston: Heintzemann Press, 1906).

Taylor, Alan, "The Smuggling Career of William King," *MHSQ*, Vol. 17 (Summer 1977), 19–38.

Taylor, Alan, "The Disciples of Samuel Ely: Settler Resistance Against Henry Knox on the Waldo Patent, 1785–1801," *MHSQ*, Vol. 26 (Fall 1986), 66–100.

Wadsworth, Peleg, "Letter from General Peleg Wadsworth to Massachusetts Council, August 19, 1779," *MHS Coll.*, Series 2, Vol. 5 (1894), 421–426.

Wadsworth, Peleg, "Brg. General Wadsworth's Deposition, Court of Inquiry, Penobscot Expedition," *MHS Coll.*, Series 2, Vol. 6 (1895), 291–299.

Wadsworth, Peleg, "Letter from General Peleg Wadsworth to William D. Williamson, January 1, 1828," *MHS Coll.*, Series 2, Vol. 2 (1891), 153–162.

Williamson, Joseph, "Colonel Benjamin Burton," *MHS Coll.*, Series 1, Vol. 7 (1876), 325–335.

STATE O' MAINE (Nineteenth Century)

Blaine, Harriet S., ed., *Letters of Mrs. James G. Blaine*, Vol. 2 (New York: Duffield & Co., 1908).

Byrne, Frank L., *Prophet of Prohibition* (Madison: State Historical Society of Wisconsin, 1961).

Cleaveland, Nehemiah, and Alpheus S. Packard, *History of Bowdoin College with Biographical Sketches of Its Graduates* (Boston: James R. Osgood and Co., 1882).

Cutler, Carl C., *Greyhounds of the Sea* (New York: Putnam's, 1930).

Depew, Chauncey M., *My Memories of Eighty Years* (New York: Scribner's, 1924).

Dickey, Dallas C., *Seargent S. Prentiss: Whig Orator of the Old South* (Baton Rouge: Louisiana State University Press, 1945).

Dow, Neal, *The Reminiscences of Neal Dow: Reflections of Eighty Years* (Portland: Evening Express Publishing Co., 1898).

Elwell, Edward H., "Enoch Lincoln," *MHS Coll.*, Series 2, Vol. 1 (1890), 137–157.

Gerrish, Theodore, *Army Life: A Private's Reminiscences of the Civil War* (Portland: Hoyt, Fogg, and Donham, 1882).

Hakola, John W., *Legacy of a Lifetime: The Story of Baxter State Park* (Woolwich, Maine: TBW Books, 1981).

Hamilton, Gail, *Biography of James G. Blaine* (Norwich, Connecticut: Henry Bill Publishing Co., 1895).

Hamlin, Charles E., *The Life and Times of Hannibal Hamlin* (Cambridge, Massachusetts: Riverside Press, 1899).

Hatch, Louis C., *The History of Bowdoin College* (Portland: Loring, Short and Harmon, 1927).

Hofstadter, Richard, and Michael Wallace, eds., *American Violence* (New York: Vintage Books, 1971).

Howe, Octavius T., and Frederick C. Matthews, *American Clipper Ships, 1833–1858,* Vol. 2 (Salem, Massachusetts: Marine Research Society, 1927).

Hunt, Draper, *Hannibal Hamlin of Maine: Lincoln's First Vice-President* (Syracuse, New York: Syracuse University Press, 1969).

Jones, George W., "An Historical Duel, 1838," *Maine Historical and Genealogical Recorder*, Vol. 6 (1889), 385–395.

Jones, Howard, *To the Webster-Ashburton Treaty: A Study in Anglo-American Relations* (Chapel Hill, North Carolina: University of Northern Carolina Press, 1977).

King, Horatio, "History of the Duel Between Jonathon Cilley and William J. Graves," *MHS Coll.*, Series 2, Vol. 3 (1892), 127–148 and 393–409.

Lincoln, Enoch, *The Village* (Portland: Edward Little & Co., 1816).

Looney, William H., "Seargent Smith Prentiss," *MHS Coll.*, Series 3, Vol. 2 (1906), 389–413.

Lubbock, Basil, *The Colonial Clippers* (Glasgow: Brown, Son & Ferguson, 1975).

Lucey, William L., *The Catholic Church in Maine* (Francestown, New Hampshire: Marshall Jones Co., 1957).

Maxim, Hiram P., *A Genius in the Family* (New York: Harper and Bros., 1936).

Maxim, Hiram S., *My Life* (New York: McBride, Nast and Co., 1915).

Maxim, Hudson, with Clifton Johnson, *Reminiscences and Comments* (New York: Doubleday, Page and Co., 1924).

Mitchell, Edward P., "Bowdoin of 1825," in *An Institute of Modern Literature at Bowdoin College...in Commemoration of the...Class of 1825* (Lewiston: Lewiston Journal Co., 1926).

Muzzey, David S., *James G. Blaine: A Political Idol of Other Days* (Port Washington, New York: Kennikat Press, 1934).

Neal, John, *Wandering Recollections of A Somewhat Busy Life: An Autobiography* (Boston: Roberts Brothers, 1869).

Prentiss, George Lewis, *Memoir of S.S. Prentiss,* 2 Vols. (New York: Charles Scribners, 1855).

Pullen, John J., *The Twentieth Maine* (Philadelphia: J.B. Lippincott, 1957).

Rowe, William H., *The Maritime History of Maine* (New York: Norton, 1948).

Russell, Charles E., *Blaine of Maine: His Life and Times* (New York: Cosmopolitan Book Co., 1931).

Scott, Winfield, *Memoirs*, Vol. 2 (New York: Sheldon & Co., 1864).

Schlup, Leonard, "Bryan's Partner: Arthur Sewall and the Campaign of 1896," *MHSQ,* Vol. 16 (Spring 1977), 189–211.

Seitz, Don C., *Famous American Duels* (New York: Thomas Y. Crowell Co., 1929).

Shields, Joseph D., *The Life and Times of Seargent Smith Prentiss* (Philadelphia: J.B. Lippincott & Co., 1883).

Skoglund, Nancy, "Assault on John Bapst...," in Richard Sprague, ed., *Handful of Spice...* (Orono: University of Maine Press, 1968).

Sprague, John F., "Sir Hiram Maxim," *SJMH,* Vol. 4 (April 1917), 283–295.

Sprague, John F., *The Northeast Boundary Controversy and the Aroostook War* (Dover, Maine: Observer Press, n.d.).

Staples, Arthur G., ed., *The Letters of John Fairfield* (Lewiston, Maine: Lewiston Journal Co., 1922).

Stevens, William O., *Pistols at Ten Paces: The Story of the Code of Honor in America* (Boston: Houghton Mifflin, 1940).

Verrill A. Hyatt, *Romantic and Historic Maine* (New York: Dodd, Mead, 1953).

Wallace, Willard M., *Soul of the Lion* (New York: Thomas Nelson, 1960).

Whitmore, Allan R., "Portrait of a Maine 'Know-Nothing': William H. Chaney (1821–1903), His Early Years and His Role in the Ellsworth Nativist Controversy, 1853–1854," *MHSQ,* Vol. 14 (Summer 1974), 1–57.

Wise, Barton H., *The Life of Henry A. Wise* (New York: MacMillan Co., 1899).

VACATIONLAND (Twentieth Century)

Ali, Muhammad, with Richard Durham, *The Greatest: My Own Story* (New York: Random House, 1975).

Braynard, Frank O., *Famous American Ships* (New York: Hastings House, 1956).

Brubaker, Bill, "The 'Louisville Lip' Now Speaks Slowly," *Washington Post,* February 22, 1989.

Condon, Richard H., "Bayonets at the North Bridge: The Lewiston-Auburn Shoe Strike, 1937," *MHSQ*, Vol. 21 (Fall 1981), 75–98.

Davis, Kenneth S., *The Hero: Charles A. Lindbergh and the American Dream* (New York: Doubleday & Co., 1959).

Fleischer, Nat, and Sam Andre, *A Pictorial History of Boxing* (New York: Bonanza Books, 1989).

Hennessy, Mark W., *The Sewall Ships of Steel* (Augusta: Kennebec Journal Press, 1937).

Lindbergh, Anne M., *Bring Me A Unicorn, 1922–1928* (New York: Harcourt, Brace, & Jovanovich, 1971).

Lindbergh, Anne M., *Hours of Gold, Hours of Lead, 1929–1932* (New York: Harcourt, Brace & Jovanovich, 1973).

Lubbock, Basil, *The Down Easters* (Boston: Charles Lauriat Co., 1929).

Macdougall, Allan R., ed., *Letters of Edna St. Vincent Millay* (New York: Harper & Bros., 1952).

Roosevelt, Eleanor, *Autobiography* (New York: Harper and Bros., 1962).

Roosevelt, Elliott, and James Brough, *An Untold Story: The Roosevelts of Hyde Park* (New York: G.P. Putnam's, 1973).

Roosevelt, James, *My Parents: A Differing View* (Chicago: Playboy Press, 1976).

Sheean, Vincent, *The Indigo Bunting: A Memoir of Edna St. Vincent Millay* (New York: Harper & Bros., 1951).

Staples, Arthur G., ed., *The Meddybemps Letters, Maine's Hall of Fame, and Memorial Addresses by William R. Pattangall* (Lewiston: Lewiston Journal Co., 1924).

Wald, Matthew L., "Lindbergh Rivals' Wreck Sought in Maine Woods," *New York Times*, February 22, 1987.